IF *BUCKLEY* FELL

If *Buckley* Fell

A First Amendment Blueprint for Regulating Money in Politics

◆

Edited by
E. Joshua Rosenkranz
of the Brennan Center for Justice
at NYU School of Law

Sponsored by The Century Foundation
and the Brennan Center for Justice
at NYU School of Law

1999 ◆ THE CENTURY FOUNDATION PRESS ◆ NEW YORK

The Century Foundation, formerly the Twentieth Century Fund, sponsors and supervises timely analyses of economic policy, foreign affairs, and domestic political issues. Not-for-profit and nonpartisan, it was founded in 1919 and endowed by Edward A. Filene.

LIBRARY OF CONGRESS CATALOGING-IN-PUBLICATION DATA

If Buckley fell : a First Amendment blueprint for regulating money in politics / edited by E. Joshua Rosenkranz of the Brennan Center for Justice at NYU School of Law.
    p. cm.
    Includes bibliographical references and index.
    ISBN 0-87078-439-0 (alk. paper)
    1. Campaign funds—Law and legislation—United States.
2. Freedom of speech—United States. 3. Law reform—United States.
I. Rosenkranz, E. Joshua. II. Brennan Center for Justice.
III. Century Foundation.
KF4920.I39 1999
342.73'078—dc21   99-41195
                                            CIP

Cover Design Claude Goodwin

ABOUT THE BRENNAN CENTER FOR JUSTICE AT NEW YORK UNIVERSITY SCHOOL OF LAW

The Brennan Center for Justice at New York University School of Law unites thinkers and advocates in pursuit of a vision of inclusive and effective democracy. Its mission is to develop and implement an innovative, nonpartisan agenda of scholarship, public education, and legal action that promotes equality and human dignity, while safeguarding fundamental freedoms.

One of the primary areas of focus of the Center's Democracy Program is campaign finance reform. The Brennan Center has been a leading force in framing the debate on the free speech implications of campaign finance regulation. In addition to publishing extensively on the law and policy of campaign finance, the Brennan Center counsels legislators, reformers, and officials at the state and federal levels on legal and constitutional issues surrounding campaign finance reform. The Center is either counsel or co-counsel in litigation regarding campaign finance reform measures at the state and federal level, including cases in California, Arkansas, Maine, Missouri, North Carolina, Arizona, and Wisconsin. The Center has also filed numerous amicus briefs in the Supreme Court and lower courts on issues relating to democracy, and campaign financing in particular.

CONTENTS

ACKNOWLEDGMENTS

This book was a joint venture between the Brennan Center for Justice at New York University School of Law and The Century Foundation. Many of the authors' ideas developed in the course of a series of conferences and colloquia that the two organizations sponsored to bring some of the nation's leading constitutional scholars together with the nation's leading legal and political science experts on campaign financing.

Many people had a hand in bringing this book to life. I am very grateful to my colleagues at the Brennan Center for their enthusiastic participation in this project. Marcy Schuck organized the conferences with her customary flawlessness. The staff of the Brennan Center's Democracy Program were a constant source of good ideas, sound advice, and brilliant analysis. Dessaline Lambright patiently and expertly typed in many rounds of editorial changes.

The Century Foundation's research fellow, Andrew L. Shapiro, now a First Amendment Fellow at the Brennan Center, was a wonderful partner. The project would not be the same without his early encouragement and ideas.

We are all grateful to the numerous experts who informed, challenged, and influenced the ideas of the contributing authors. They were Anthony Corrado, Nicole A. Gordon, Richard L. Hasen, Ruth Jones, Jonathan S. Krasno, Thomas E. Mann, Ellen Miller, Daniel R. Ortiz, Jamin B. Raskin, Roy A. Schotland, and Donald J. Simon.

The Open Society Institute provided financial support for the conferences that led to this book. Other foundations, which have generously supported the Brennan Center's campaign finance work, also deserve credit for supporting this book: the Florence & John Schumann Foundation, the Carnegie Corporation of New York, the Ford Foundation, the Joyce Foundation, the Deer Creek Foundation, the Arca Foundation, and the Stewart R. Mott Charitable Trust.

Finally, as always, Sydney—my wife, my inspiration, and my best friend—provided the moral support without which this project would never have happened.

EJR

INTRODUCTION

E. Joshua Rosenkranz

"Disastrous."[1] "Misguided."[2] "Tragically" so.[3] "Ludicrous."[4] "Wrong headed (not to say bone-headed)."[5] "Illogical."[6] "One of the Court's less impressive monuments."[7] A "really terrible decision."[8] A "mistake."[9] A "sort of 20th-Century stepchild to Dred Scott."[10] These are the epithets that scholars and commentators have hurled at a single Supreme Court opinion, *Buckley v. Valeo,*[11] the landmark 1976 decision best known for prohibiting campaign spending caps. The case may not be as famous as *Roe v. Wade* nor as morally reprehensible as Dred Scott or *Plessy v. Ferguson,*[12] but among those who care deeply about the health of our democracy, the case is every bit as controversial. And for those who are desperately troubled about the flood of money into politics, the decision looms as large. The case has been vilified as "an untenable distortion of the First Amendment and the democratic process"[13] that "has torn the fabric of democracy—public trust—into a thousand pieces"[14] and left us "stuck with a warped system."[15] It has been derided as a "hodgepodge of almost loony distinctions"[16] displaying "a certain naïveté about how the political game is played in America,"[17] and leaving us with "the worst of all possible democratic worlds."[18]

1

Buckley arose out of Congress's comprehensive 1974 reforms, which were passed in the wake of Watergate. Congress had imposed contribution limits (caps on the amounts that can be given directly to a candidate) and spending ceilings (limits on the amounts candidates or others can spend in support of campaigns). In *Buckley,* the Supreme Court upheld the former—but struck the latter as a violation of the First Amendment. This schizophrenic result, perhaps more than any other aspect of the case, has brought scorn from a wide spectrum of critics, and may spell the ultimate demise of the case.

How in the world could the Supreme Court have upheld contribution limits, yet struck spending limits as categorically impermissible? The Court began with the unobjectionable observation that money is the fuel for speech, and, as a result, limits on the flow of money toward any message call into play First Amendment concerns. That is not to say that any regulation of the money flow is impermissible, but only that government must be sensitive to the free speech implications of the regulation. Next, as it does in so many areas of constitutional doctrine, the Court balanced the importance of the speech right being infringed against the weightiness of the government's reasons for the infringement. For both sides of the balance— the speech value and the government justification—the Supreme Court concluded that contributions and spending were different.

As to the speech value of these two activities: A contribution, the Court held, has little speech value. It is a mere "signal" of support whose message does not depend very much on the size of the contribution. Spending, the Court believed, has greater speech value. It is much more akin to direct speech, because every dollar spent will actually increase "the number of issues discussed, the depth of their exploration, and the size of the audience reached." Or so the Court thought.

As to the reasons for regulating: The Court concluded that contributions are more corrupting than spending. The Court easily saw that a candidate could be corrupted by large contributions, for large contributions could give rise to tacit political debts. In contrast, the Court could not see how candidates could be corrupted either by their own campaigns' unlimited spending or by the extravagant spending of others outside their campaigns. The Court rejected the notion that a candidate might give special consideration to a supporter who independently spends $1 million on television ads advocating the candidate's election rather than writing a much smaller check directly to the campaign. Nor did the Court recognize any danger that the endless money chase might corrupt a candidate's agenda or priorities, or that the more desperate a candidate was to raise money, the more corrupting any particular contribution could be.

Why all this talk of corruption? *Buckley* held that preventing corruption (or guarding against the appearance of corruption) is the only rationale that will justify any restrictions on campaign finance. Specifically, the Court rejected any notion that the government might limit the flow of money into elections in the name of equality. The Court famously opined that "the concept that government may restrict the speech of some elements of our society in order to enhance the relative voice of others is wholly foreign to the First Amendment."

The Court's distinction between contributions and spending means the government cannot limit how much of the family fortune a Steve Forbes can sink in his own campaign. It means no end to the money chase that consumes candidates. And it means no lid on the funds a nominally independent player, like the AFL-CIO or a wealthy benefactor, may spend on television ads promoting a candidate. On the other hand, and equally critically, the Court held that contributions made directly to a candidate may be limited—but only to a point. A contribution can be limited only if it is (or would appear to be) corrupt, defined narrowly to mean that it might engender a return favor.

Buckley, then, leaves us in the worst of all possible worlds. A world where candidates are constantly clamoring for, and willing to compromise for, the next dollar. A world where candidates spend more time raising money than attending to government business or constituent needs. A world where monied interests are entitled to drown out everyone else's speech. A world where the wealthy—or their friends—have a special claim to public office. A world where a politician's cash constituency claims more of his attention and allegiance than his voting constituency. A world where superb candidates do not run, whether because they are sick to their stomachs about the money chase or because they are dismissed as not viable without mega-wealth or a Midas touch. A world in which every reform worth adopting is weakened from the start by constitutionally mandated loopholes.

I used to say *Buckley* leaves us with a world where reformers are basically playing baseball with a huge oak tree in the middle of the field—and whenever you hit the tree, it's an automatic out.[19] Not anymore. The way the lower courts have contorted the case, it behaves more like one of those apple trees in the *Wizard of Oz* that wave their branches wildly and can snatch balls right out of midair. *Buckley* does not just ban spending limits anymore. As interpreted by the lower courts, it threatens virtually any measure that a legislature or a group of citizen initiative drafters might devise to wrestle back control of their elections. Want to set a contribution limit? Don't set it too low, or a court might strike it as inconsistent with the anticorruption rationale.[20] How about trying to level the playing field a bit by banning war chests, leftover campaign funds that politicians roll over to the next election? There is a good chance a court will block the step because a candidate cannot be corrupted by campaign funds already raised.[21] How about trying to shorten the fundraising season, so that contributors cannot curry favor by making contributions the day after an election, when no one knows how the next, distant election will shape up? Courts have been striking these provisions on the ground that an early contribution is no more corrupting than a later one. Interested in limiting out-of-state contributions? Some court is bound to balk on the ground that the corrupting impact of a contribution does not depend on whether the donor will be represented by the candidate.[22] And just try to regulate corporations that shamelessly skirt campaign finance rules by funneling mountains of money secretly into campaign attack ads that are thinly veiled as issue ads. Lower courts have been striking such regulatory fixes with a vengeance.[23]

All this in the name of free speech. Each new expansive interpretation of the First Amendment diminishes the ability of creative lawmakers to address one of the most vexing problems plaguing our democracy. The result is an ironic minuet in which courts—the branch of our government that is least likely to understand politics and is least accountable to the public—overrule the judgments of the public's representatives who intimately understand how elections work. And at the same time, the courts lend a fig leaf to self-interested politicians who reflexively resist any change in the rules of the game that brought them to power. Politicians who have never encountered a First Amendment violation they didn't like suddenly align themselves with the American Civil Liberties Union to claim that any impinge-ment on the free flow of money into politics is unconstitutional.

Consider, for example, arguments (all citing *Buckley*) that this alliance has advanced against some popular reform ideas.[24] One lead-ing proposal was to offer free or half-price air time to candidates who agreed voluntarily to cap their campaign spending, but the plan was attacked as a "coercive and punitive scheme, designed to compel candidates to accept spending limits . . . and to penalize those who refuse," which "violates First Amendment principles." Similar chal-lenges are being leveled against proposals to close the so-called soft-money loophole. That is the technique by which candidates bypass contribution limits by soliciting millions in contributions to their political party—primarily from corporations in huge increments of six and seven figures—knowing that the party will funnel those funds into attack ads for the candidate's benefit. To preserve a perceived advantage, politicians have insisted that the ploy, which undermines the very foundation of campaign finance regulation, is constitution-ally protected.

When a case is as controversial as *Buckley*, when a case pro-duces that much mischief and so thoroughly undermines popular will, it is only a matter of time before the Court revisits the issue. That is particularly true when a linchpin of the case—here, the dis-tinction between contributions and spending—is so thoroughly discredited by critics with polar agendas. First Amendment abso-lutists and proponents of regulation alike have ridiculed the distinc-tion. It is as if *Buckley* were rotting from both sides and the only question is which way it will fall. Will it fall to permit greater gov-ernment latitude to regulate *both* spending and contributions, or will it fall in favor of absolute First Amendment protection of both—to allow patrons, for example, to make $1 million or $10 million con-tributions directly to politicians with the power to return the favor with many times that value in public goodies?

The fissures are already evident. In a recent case, three justices, without invitation from the parties, flatly rejected *Buckley*'s distinc-tion between contributions and expenditures.[25] On one side was Justice Stevens, who declared his belief that both contributions and expenditures can be regulated. He was joined by one of the Court's newest members, Justice Ginsburg, who reached this conclusion in the very first campaign financing case she considered as a justice. On the other side was Justice Thomas, who declared that neither contributions nor expenditures can be regulated. Already, with little prompting, a third of the Court (one shy of the number needed to accept a case for Supreme Court review) is prepared to abolish *Buckley*'s distinction between contributions and expenditures.

Perhaps tellingly, none of the other justices expressed shock or dismay at the notion of overruling *Buckley*. No words of approbation escaped their lips. Not a word in defense of the basic underpinnings of *Buckley*. Not a breath about the importance of adhering to precedent. The three centrist justices who wrote the lead opinion said merely: "Overrul[ing] . . . this Court's entire campaign finance jurisprudence developed in numerous cases over the last 20 years . . . seems inconsistent with this Court's view that it is ordinarily 'inappropriate for us to reexamine' prior precedent *'without the benefit of the parties' briefing.'*" All they said was, in essence, "Not now. Not this case."

More recently, the Supreme Court heard arguments in a case that presented a frontal assault on *Buckley*. In that case, *Nixon v. Shrink Missouri Government PAC,*[26] the United States Court of Appeals for the Eighth Circuit had struck Missouri's contribution limits as unconstitutionally low. Such a holding would not ordinarily raise eyebrows. As we have seen, the lower courts are swatting low contribution limits like flies. What was startling about this holding is that Missouri's contribution limits were $1,075 for statewide races—higher than the current federal limits. The lower court's logic cast doubt on whether *any* contribution limit could pass constitutional muster. Significantly, when the Supreme Court reviewed the case, one of the issues presented to it was whether the Court should treat this case as a vehicle for reconsidering the entire structure laid by *Buckley*. The Court declined the invitation, narrowing the case to consider only the question whether Missouri's limits are too low, not whether all contribution limits are unconstitutional. Once again, though, most observers see the Court's action as nothing but a delay of the inevitable. It's not a question of whether the Court will reconsider *Buckley*, but when. And the Court's action in *Shrink Missouri* was a reiteration of its sentiment, "Not now."

The case will come. It is inevitable. There is no predicting how it will turn out, but there is little doubt that one nagging thought must be going through the justices' minds even now: It is easy enough to make the case for overruling *Buckley,* but how can we have the confidence that we will not leave in its wake a jurisprudence that is every bit as flawed? One can almost picture several justices poised on the edge of a diving board, but hesitating to jump in for fear that there is no water in the pool.

This book brings together five of the nation's leading constitutional theorists to quiet those fears. They all agreed to engage in an exercise of imagination. They all begin with the supposition that the Supreme Court has overruled *Buckley* in a way that offers greater latitude for regulation of campaign finance. Their common charge was to imagine what the First Amendment landscape could look like if the Supreme Court junked *Buckley.* Together, they sketch a compelling and coherent vision of a First Amendment that tolerates greater regulation of the flow of money into elections, without sacrificing any of the First Amendment moorings that are so critical to a free society.

The point of departure for these legal scholars is a perspective that was unavailable to the justices who decided *Buckley.* This book opens with the modern history of campaign finance regulation, as seen by Frank J. Sorauf, a dean of the political science community, who, after decades of studying campaign finance, is uniquely situated to offer a dispassionate critical assessment of the role of the Court in destabilizing our campaign finance system. In Chapter One, after an extensive review of the how the role of money in politics has changed over the past twenty-five years, Professor Sorauf concludes that *Buckley* "failed the tests of adaptation" because it was "crafted with little concern for the political realities the Congress was attempting to regulate."

Building upon that historical and factual foundation, Ronald Dworkin, one of the world's leading legal philosophers, develops a breathtakingly fresh vision of the First Amendment in Chapter Two. He observes that *Buckley* grew out of a reading of the First Amendment that views democracy as nothing but "a political arrangement designed to enforce the will of the majority." He advocates a more ambitious vision of democracy "as a partnership in collective self-government in which all citizens are given the opportunity to be active and equal partners." That vision of democracy, Professor Dworkin persuasively demonstrates, yields "a more fine-grained and

discriminating, though still rigorous, test for deciding when government should be permitted to regulate political speech in the interest of
democracy"—a test that would ultimately tolerate spending limits
and other reforms that seem to be in peril under current law.

Frederick Schauer and Richard H. Pildes strengthen Dworkin's
hand by anticipating one of the most forceful arguments against it.
The argument is that it is wrong to single out election related speech
and develop a set of exceptions to the First Amendment rules that
would ordinarily apply in other contexts. Professors Schauer and
Pildes question the very premise on which the argument is built. They
demonstrate that "the idea of a standard, normal, or off-the-rack
conception of even political speech is an egregious oversimplification." Rather, First Amendment doctrine has evolved into a variety of
different sets of rules that change from one context to the next. So
there is no reason to resist applying a different set of First Amendment
rules to elections than to other contexts simply on the ground that
exceptions to the First Amendment should be disfavored, for there is
no general First Amendment rule from which elections would be
excepted. The real question, they conclude, is not whether elections
are exceptions to the general First Amendment rules. Rather, the
important questions to answer are (1) whether the peculiar features of
elections warrant different rules for election-related speech than for
speech relating to politics generally, and (2) whether it is possible to
develop a sufficiently meaningful line to distinguish elections from
other political speech.

That is where Richard Briffault comes in. In Chapter Four,
Professor Briffault answers both those questions. He demonstrates
that the Supreme Court has already developed a significant jurisprudence that treats elections differently from other political speech, and
that the reasons for doing so apply with equal force to rules governing the funding of elections. Professor Briffault then proceeds to
address one of the thorniest issues in the constitutional doctrine governing campaign finance law—where to draw the line between election-related speech and all other political speech. *Buckley,* in a section
that has received less attention than the ruling on spending limits,
grappled with that question. The Court concluded that the special
rules for elections would apply only to speech that included certain so-
called magic words expressly advocating the election or defeat of a

candidate—words such as *vote for* or *elect*. Professor Briffault demonstrates that this line is too restrictive, and offers an alternative constitutional doctrine that defines the line in more practical terms without chilling political speech.

Burt Neuborne closes the book with a chapter that demonstrates why overruling *Buckley* would have little impact on the rest of First Amendment doctrine. The First Amendment concerns itself primarily with protecting the autonomous speaker from governmental regulation on the basis of the viewpoint embodied in the speech. Unlimited campaign spending does not fit the model of the type of activity that lies at the heart of the First Amendment, Professor Neuborne demonstrates. For one thing, unlimited campaign spending cannot be viewed as a truly voluntary act of expression, for candidates are locked in an arms race that forces them to raise and spend as much as they possibly can. Moreover, First Amendment doctrine has always tolerated content neutral limits on speech so long as the government can offer compelling reasons to justify the limitations, and when it comes to campaign spending, there are numerous compelling justifications for limits. Among them are the need to restore public faith in our democracy, the goal of enhancing political equality, and the necessity to diminish corruption. In the end, Professor Neuborne argues, overruling *Buckley* enhances the core interests of the First Amendment rather than undermining them.

Ultimately, this book provides a complete road map. It is not just a road map for how to overrule *Buckley*. It is a complete vision of what First Amendment doctrine could look like if *Buckley* fell.

1

WHAT *BUCKLEY* WROUGHT

Frank J. Sorauf

Only twenty-five years after the passage of the Federal Election Campaign Act (FECA) in 1974, Congress's attempt at reform is foundering. What earlier was change is now volatility, and we are already fully into the third era of the campaign finance regime FECA established. What appeared to be regime stability in the late 1980s has now become a wild, even manic hunt for money, and everywhere FECA's regulatory boundaries seem to be collapsing. It is a collapse mirrored in regulatory systems in almost every state.

Failed regulation usually invites a search through the ashes of history for evidence of pivotal events, legislative failure, or administrative ineffectiveness. Only rarely since the New Deal crises of the

Note: I would like to thank Joshua Rosenkranz and Jonathan Krasno for their perceptive and constructive readings of the previous draft of this chapter; Robert Biersack for his help with FEC data, especially the late-breaking totals for 1998; and Gerald Elliott and David Frisch for helping assemble data and information from a number of sources.

1930s has the search included an assessment of the weight of the Supreme Court's constitutional interpretations. In this case, however, the failures of the regulatory structures in the nation and the states— virtually all of them dating from the reforms post-Watergate—are in many ways the results of First Amendment jurisprudence.

The division of labor in this book leaves it to the legal scholars to envision a workable First Amendment jurisprudence that would permit successful regulation of the campaign finance regime. It seems to me, though, that their inquiry would benefit from a comprehensive review of what has gone wrong under FECA and how constitutional doctrine has contributed to the failure. That is the mission of this chapter.

I. Eras One and Two: 1974 to the 1990s

The Era of Adaptation: 1974 to 1984

In truth the "first" era of FECA was the one that never happened. Congress had started the crafting of FECA in 1971 with tentative attempts to contain the escalating costs of campaigns, but, emboldened in the aftermath of Watergate, Democratic majorities in Congress passed amendments to the 1971 law that effectively created a whole new regulatory structure in 1974. Then for the first time Congress adopted a commanding plan to restrict all the transactions in a campaign's finance. As the Introduction describes in greater detail, the plan limited the amounts candidates could spend—of their own resources and of funds raised from others—and all contributions to candidates. And it limited direct spending in the campaigns by parties, political action committees (PACs), and individuals. Moreover, it established a pioneering program of public funding for all aspects of the presidential campaigns, and it created a regulatory agency to oversee its reforms.

That imposing regulatory edifice never went into effect. Great chunks of it fell to the Supreme Court's assault in *Buckley v. Valeo* in 1976. For reasons that are summarized in the Introduction, all statutory limitations on spending by candidates (both by their campaign committees and by themselves) and on independent expenditures by groups and individuals ran afoul of the Court's extension of First

Amendment protections to campaign finance. As drastic as the results of that first application of the First Amendment to campaign money were, none of us, I dare say, foresaw the full effect the new embrace of the First Amendment would eventually have.

Since the Supreme Court dismantled FECA before it took effect, the first genuine era of FECA began with the elections of 1976 and lasted through those of 1984. It was a period of innovation as parties, candidates, and other players adapted to the surviving limits on contributors. The most inventive and least constrained of the innovators, the PACs, grew spectacularly. Between 1974 and 1984 the number of PACs registered with the new Federal Election Commission (FEC) increased from 608 to 4,009, and their contributions to candidates for Congress rose from $22.6 million in the 1976 cycle to $111.5 million in 1984. They accounted for 19 percent of the receipts of congressional candidates in 1976, and by 1984 their contributions totaled 27 percent. PACs even made the cover of *Time*[1] and quickly became the public's whipping boys for the excesses of campaign finance.

FECA did not create PACs. They existed in American electoral politics ever since 1943, when organized labor founded the original PAC—called, prophetically, the Political Action Committee. But before 1974, PACs operated in the shadow of the legendary "fat cats," the wealthy individuals who gave up to several million dollars to presidential candidates. Congress intended in FECA to eliminate the fat cats from federal elections, and it succeeded. But by ending their massive contributions, Congress carved out a new niche for major contributors. Moreover, in allowing a PAC to contribute five times as much as an individual donor ($5,000 versus $1,000) and in failing to limit the total amount that any one PAC could contribute to all candidates and parties combined as it did for individuals ($25,000 per year), Congress created incentives for PAC proliferation. And it did so precisely when more and more Americans were shifting their political loyalties from political parties to specific economic or social groups.[2]

Although they rode the crest of group ascendancy in American politics, PACs furnished some of their own impetus. Corporate and business groups in particular, historically more timid politically than labor unions, found in PACs a useful device for organizing their political activists—and for challenging the power of organized labor. All PACs benefitted also from organization itself; as organizations specializing in politics, they brought new levels of longevity, information, political purposefulness, and strategic sophistication to campaign finance, assets that even the wealthiest individual contributor rarely commanded.

Their newfound sophistication, however, did not save PACs from excessive political optimism. In the late 1970s they had entered electoral politics confident of the political power that accrued to the affluent contributor. Many PAC executives at first believed not only that well-placed contributions would secure access to officeholders (the legislative strategy) but also that strategic giving could affect election outcomes, even defeat unfriendly incumbents (the electoral strategy). So they mixed the strategies in the first era of FECA, only to discover that the electoral strategy was far less successful. Incumbent members of Congress were virtually invincible; reelection rates for House incumbents remained above 90 percent from 1976 into the 1990s. They had a formidable ability to raise the money they needed, and their name recognition and campaigning skills fended off even the well-financed challenger. Moreover, PACs and other contributors who sought access to members of Congress found the two strategies contradictory; by resolutely pursuing an electoral strategy that backed incumbents and challengers alike, so long as they fit a particular ideology or agenda, PACs risked losing the very access to incumbents that they sought in the legislative strategy.

In a classic case of political learning, PACs absorbed their lessons in only a few election cycles. By the mid-1980s PACs and other purposeful contributors, chastened and wiser, began to retreat to a more purely legislative strategy. In 1980 PACs as a group had given 20.8 percent of their contributions to House challengers and 38.0 percent to Senate challengers; those figures dropped to 10.5 and 20.6 by 1986. The pragmatism inherent in the legislative strategy was typified by the willingness of corporate PACs to contribute to the Democrats, however unfriendly, who controlled the House in the 1980s. By 1988, for example, they gave Democratic incumbents a larger share of their total contributions than they gave to Republican incumbents.

THE ERA OF STABILITY: 1985 TO 1990

So, FECA's second, less innovative era (1985–86 through 1989–90) slipped quietly into place. Both stability and pragmatism marked the new era. The number of PACs remained around the four thousand mark, and the sums PACs contributed to candidates failed to keep up with inflation. In fact the expenditures by all congressional candidates fell from $451.0 million in 1986 to $446.3 million in 1990. If PACs were the icons of the first era of FECA, incumbents were the icons of the second. They raised money with newfound vigor, even aggressiveness, reminding contributors that in the exchanges of campaign finance incumbent candidates often had as much leverage as contributors. They also padded their reserves (their "cash on hand"). In an era of stability and modest political goals, it was not surprising that the creatures of the status quo, the incumbents, should be its exemplars. So, only fifteen years into FECA's history, a period of testing, growth, and exuberance in campaign finance had yielded to a less exciting era of stability, incrementalism, and pragmatism. Maturity, and even middle age, had come quickly to the regime of FECA.

By this point it was evident that campaign finance under FECA had adjusted to *Buckley*. The regulatory regime that was still intact combined disclosure and limits on contributions. While no statutory limits on spending remained, the finite supply of political money and the limited will to give and raise it provided restraint. The advantages in the regime accrued to the comparatively underregulated PACs, but FECA was to blame, not *Buckley*. After the initial period of exploration and learning, PACs' growth leveled off, as did their expectations of influence. Campaign spending initially grew faster than the consumer price index, but before very long it was dampened by incumbent strength and its consequences: fewer candidates in congressional primaries and elections, weakened challengers, and what appeared to be the Democrats' entrenched majorities. Even the unlimited opportunities for independent spending attracted only a brief flurry of activity led by the National Conservative PAC (NCPAC). In truth, such spending had never been an effective political tool, and candidates soon learned how to neutralize it by running against it.

The serene political landscape of the late 1980s, however, concealed the fragility of FECA's regulatory regime post-*Buckley*. The stability was possible only in the short-term political equilibrium of the time, and it was easily undermined by the intensely competitive politics of the 1990s.

II. The Third Era: The 1990s

Competition Draws More Money

The political stability of the second era began to erode immediately in the new decade, at least in part because of its own liabilities. Stability's companion was policy deadlock and legislative gridlock. Furthermore, the stable membership of the Congress, with incumbent reelection percentages well above 90 for the House,[3] appealed far more to the incumbents than it did to many Americans. Not only did officeholders appear to take their reelection for granted, they appeared as well to be careless in their ethics. The lax financial arrangements of the "bank" of the House of Representatives came to represent those ethics. A national movement for constitutionally mandated term limits blossomed, and incumbents found themselves under attack from all directions.

Inevitably, perhaps, increasing numbers of incumbents decided not to seek reelection in the early 1990s, but the revolt against incumbency was only one of several reasons. Reapportionment and redistricting after the 1990 census left many members of the House with redrawn districts in which tens of thousands of new voters did not know them or their names. In a few instances incumbents feared that voters would be intolerant of their ethical lapses. For all of these reasons, incumbent resignations and retirements rose. In 1988, only twenty-three House incumbents had chosen not to seek reelection; in 1990, only twenty-seven. But in 1992, the number jumped to sixty-five.

Consequently, congressional elections became vastly more competitive. The number of open seat races, always among the most competitive because of the absence of an incumbent, increased significantly. There were sixty Democrats and Republicans vying for House open seats in the 1990 general elections; in 1992 there were 144. Moreover, challengers running against incumbents who chose to seek reelection often raised funds at a more competitive level than in the past, for the vulnerability of incumbents showed up in early local polls, precisely at the proper moment to impress would-be contributors. Ultimately, too, better electoral prospects encouraged the recruitment of "better" challengers, which is to say, people who were politically more experienced, had greater name recognition, or had identifiable political followings; they were, that is, more electable.

Competition in congressional elections rose in the 1990s also because the stakes in them rose. By the campaigns of 1992 Republicans sensed a chance to take over one or both houses of Congress. They succeeded in 1994, and the battle for control of the legislative branch continues into the late 1990s. Moreover, competition for the presidency increased in the 1990s after the Reagan-Bush ascendancy of the 1980s. Not only were the presidential elections of 1992 and 1996 the closest since 1976, they were also made more uncertain by the candidacies of Ross Perot. Indeed, within two election cycles, control of both the White House and the Congress changed party hands.

Not surprisingly, by 1992, these upheavals yielded a new era in the life of FECA.

◆   Receipts and expenditures rose markedly. Just to take the total expenditures in congressional campaigns, candidates as a group spent $450.9 million in 1986 and a bit less in 1990, $446.3 million. The figures for the third era are of a new magnitude: $680.2 million in 1992, $725.2 million in 1994, and $765.3 million in 1996.

◆   Some of the more flexible contributors, PACs primarily, returned to electoral strategies. Challengers raised and spent more; they accounted for only 16.1 percent of the total spent by House general election candidates in 1990, but 23.7 percent in 1996.

◆   Party spending on candidates rose, both party contributions to them and party spending on their behalf.[4] Statutory limits constrained the increases in each category, but the two major parties—national, state, and local committees—spent $23.8 million on candidates in 1990, 57 percent of that by Republicans. That total rose in 1996 to $58.8 million, 59 percent by Republicans. Total party spending of all kinds rose even more dramatically. In the 1990 campaigns, Democratic committees spent a total of $54.5 million, the Republicans $172.4 million. In the 1996 cycle, the Democrats disbursed $214.3 million, the Republicans $408.5 million.

◆   In 1996 political parties began to make independent expenditures. Although the Supreme Court decision freeing them to do so

did not come down until June 1996,[5] two of the six national
party committees contrived to spend $11.5 million in the remain-
ing months of the congressional campaigns. As if stimulated
by the new "competition" or a new comradeship, PACs almost
doubled their independent spending in the same races—from
$4.6 million in 1994 to $9.1 million in 1996.

In the 1997–98 cycle, however, the upward spiral of spending
in congressional campaigns was broken. Preliminary data (as of
November 23, 1998) indicate a decline in overall spending in all
House and Senate races from $765.3 million in 1996 to $704.1 million in 1998. (If recent experience holds, these November totals will
increase about 2 percent, or $14 million, in the reports for the end of
calendar 1998.) The explanation for 1998's declining totals is clear:
the surge of competition for congressional seats had receded by 1998.
The number of major party candidates in the House and Senate campaigns dropped from 941 in 1996 to 852 in 1998, and although there
were fifty-three House open seats and thirteen in the Senate in 1996,
there were only thirty-four and five in 1998. Yet the average spending of Democratic and Republican general election candidates for a
House seat actually rose in 1998 over 1996 (using the November
preliminary data in both cycles), from $464,210 to $472,532. The
money chase had reached a new plateau.

In brief, the 1990s were an affirmation of one of the governing
truths of campaign finance: levels of electoral competition are the
major determinants of campaign spending. In the decade of the 1990s
all players in the system—all contributors and all spenders—were
more active, more energized than they had been in the far quieter era
of the late 1980s. Driven by the fears and opportunities of competition, candidates raised money with a renewed zeal, and, aided by a
prospering economy, politically opportunistic contributors answered
their summons.

The transformation described to this point happened within the
boundaries set by FECA—at least within the boundaries that remained
after *Buckley*. That is to say, I have dealt only with hard money rev-
enues and expenditures: money raised and spent under the limits of
FECA. But that is only part of the story. The third era was marked as
well by what went on outside the regime of FECA—by the explosion
of its regulatory boundaries, the opening of broad new avenues of

expenditure, and the rise of the political party as master of these new extramural aspects of campaign finance.

Before reviewing how that happened, we should realize that the regulatory boundaries set in FECA were by no means natural or inevitable. FECA's restrictions extended initially to all categories of contributors to candidates (individuals, PACs, and party committees), to the candidate and the campaign committee, and to direct spending on the candidate's behalf by the candidate, the parties, and all independent spenders. In other words, Congress specified the unit of regulation as the candidate's campaign and all the actors and all the transactions that funded it. If not "natural," those boundaries at least reflected the realities of the candidate-centered campaign in the 1970s.

For whatever reason, during the first and second eras the boundaries largely held; everyone knew who the players were, what their options were, and what limits applied to them. They also knew that everyone paid with hard money and that all transactions had to be reported to the FEC. While the Court's decision in *Buckley* altered the instruments of regulation, it did not directly alter the shape or parameters of the regulated universe. Not until the 1990s did the boundaries of FECA's regime collapse. The twin explosives were soft money and issue advocacy.

THE BOUNDARIES COLLAPSE: ISSUE ADVOCACY, SOFT MONEY

Issue advocacy, typified by TV ads attacking candidates while tiptoeing around a "vote for" or "vote against" message, can be more formally defined in these terms:

> political speech that may mention specific candidates or political parties but does not "expressly advocate" the election or defeat of a clearly identified federal candidate through the use of words such as "vote for," "oppose," "support," and the like.[6]

As Richard Briffault explains more fully in Chapter Four, the concept has its origin in *Buckley* as a part of the Court's narrowing of the scope of FECA in response to arguments that it was unconstitutionally vague in defining what constituted campaigning. Most federal courts have hewed to a very narrow and literal interpretation of

Buckley that comes down to whether or not the magic words of advocacy are used. One court also struck down the attempt of FEC to define issue advocacy more broadly in an administrative rule.

Because issue advocacy is, by definition, outside the campaign and thus outside the reach of FECA, it is completely unregulated. Neither the expenditures for it nor the sources of the money that paid for it need be reported to the FEC. Moreover, issue advocacy can be funded by money raised outside the constraints of FECA. Those freedoms open issue advocacy to any individual, group, association, party, or PAC—whether or not it is registered with the FEC, whether or not it could be so registered. Corporations and labor unions, long prohibited from the direct funding of federal candidates, for example, may freely engage in issue advocacy.

Since no one reports spending on issue advocacy to the FEC, we cobble together a record of the practice mainly from court cases and reporting in the media. It is impossible to say when it began. A voter's guide published in 1978 by the Massachusetts Citizens for Life landed before the Supreme Court.[7] A 1992 television blitz by the Christian Action Network against the Clinton candidacy also eluded FEC action in a lower federal court.[8] But it was the proliferation of issue ads in the 1996 campaign that put the question on the public agenda. The AFL-CIO professed spending at least $25 million on television ads attacking Republican candidates for Congress. A business coalition responded with opposing issue ads, and groups such as the Sierra Club were also active. Both political parties used them as well, accounting for a combined $30–$40 million. The Democratic National Committee ran issues ads extensively in 1995 to bolster President Clinton's popularity in the national polls, and its Republican counterpart kept Bob Dole's campaign alive with issue ads after Dole had reached his spending limit in the 1996 presidential primary season. The cost of all issue ads in the congressional and presidential campaigns of 1996, according to informed estimates, reached at least $150 million.

Estimates on issue ad purchases in 1998 are more specific, but just as problematic. The Annenberg Public Policy Center of the University of Pennsylvania, by far the most systematic monitor of issue ads, reports a total of between $275 and $340 million, a range approximately double its calculation for two years earlier. These totals, however, include ads in national, state, and local campaigns, and comparisons with the 1996 estimates are complicated by the fact that there was a presidential election in 1996. Even if one posits a substantial increase in issue ads in state and local elections, it is very likely that those in congressional campaigns more than doubled, considering the absence of a presidential campaign in 1998. Moreover, there are indirect indicators of growth in issue ads in congressional campaigns. In 1997–98 the party campaign committees in Congress raised 39 percent more soft money than they did in 1995–96 ($107.3 million versus $77.3 million in the early reports), a likely sign since much of their soft money finds its way to state parties for the purchase of issue ads. Moreover, the decline in party independent spending in 1998's congressional campaigns (an early total of $1.5 million against the $11.5 million in 1996) suggests that issue ads were becoming the new "independent" expenditure of choice.

Soft money, on the other hand, has its roots in American federalism rather than the First Amendment. The two major parties are federated, in that they have both national (that is, federal) and state and local (that is, nonfederal) responsibilities. Party committees, both state and national, began to feel their way toward separate funds for these separate roles in the latter 1970s. Requests for advice from the FEC brought Advisory Opinions recognizing the separate funds. Moreover, the FEC appeared to legitimize the separation by approving allocation formulas for dividing costs when a party committee played both roles simultaneously—as in a campaign event for both state and congressional candidates. The informal practice grew in the 1980s; in 1984 the two parties raised an estimated total of $21.6 million in soft money for their nonfederal spending. That total doubled by 1988, and it doubled again (to more than $86 million) in 1992. In that year soft money already accounted for 17 percent of the cash receipts of the six national party committees.[9]

Soft money, by reason of being raised outside of FECA, has freer sources than hard money, but its uses are more constrained. Corporations and labor unions may give it, and they and any other U.S. citizen, permanent resident, or organization may give it in unlimited sums. Even though contributions at the seven-figure level are still rare, six-figure contributions are increasingly common. Raised without limit, their use is, however, limited: they cannot be spent on any campaign for federal office.

As of January 1, 1991, soft money became a publicly documented feature of American campaign finance. On order of a federal district court, the FEC in 1990 adopted regulations for soft money, ordering national party committees to disclose their soft money intake and spending beginning with the 1991–92 cycle. Therefore, the 1992 totals, $86.0 million, and those for 1994, $101.7 million, and 1996, $262.1 million, come from vastly more specific data than the estimates of the 1980s. And so we know that the soft money available to the national party committees more than tripled in the 1990s.

Much of the concern over soft money centers exactly on uses of soft money to affect, however indirectly, the elections on which, under FECA, only hard money may be spent directly. The strategic uses of soft money for such an indirect impact take many forms. For example:

♦   National party committees send soft money to targeted states that the party's presidential candidate has a chance of winning. Party committees in them can then intensify voter registration and get-out-the-vote drives.

♦   Soft money transmitted to the states shores up local party organization for the campaign. State and local activity help federal candidates by bringing the party's loyalists to the polls and encouraging them to support all the party's candidates on the ballot.

♦   Soft money spent on state legislative elections helps party turnout at the election and, the national committees hope, develops strong party candidates for future races for the Congress.

♦   Soft money sent to the states can free up the hard money state and local committees may have, thus enabling them to use the scarcer hard money for congressional or presidential campaigns in their states.

♦   National parties spend soft money themselves on issue ads that praise party candidates for national office or that criticize their opponents. Alternatively, they may transfer soft money to state committees for them to do the same thing.

There is, of course, a synergy between such strategies and the raising of soft money. The soft money gives the parties flexibility in devising and using the strategies, but the efficacy of the strategies also helps them raise the soft money.

INFLUX OF NEW PLAYERS

Beyond the impact of issue ads and soft money, the 1990s saw another outward expansion of FECA's boundaries: the arrival of new participants in the system. Until the 1990s the nongovernmental sources of money for federal campaigns were clear: party committees, individuals, and a category of contributors the statutes knew simply as "non-party committees." Virtually all of those non-party committees were PACs, the "multi-candidate committees" that raised money from at least fifty contributors and contributed to five or more candidates for federal office, thereby enjoying the favored contribution limit of $5,000 per candidate per election. Moreover, PACs adhered to FECA's rule that they could direct their campaign money to only four places: candidates, other PACs, party committees, and independent expenditures. Other non-party committees could, if they also registered with the FEC, choose those four options, but any contributions were limited to $1,000 rather than $5,000.

Sometime in the 1980s groups not registered with the FEC began, in the view of the FEC and many other observers, to spend directly in campaigns for Congress. They did not contribute to candidates but spent their money in ways that appeared to be campaigning. Some, such as corporations and labor unions, paid for issue ads that ran during campaigns while picturing and commenting on candidates. Others, such as the Christian Coalition, distributed voter guides that appeared so directly supportive of preferred candidates as to be in-kind contributions to them. Still others, such as nonprofit political think tanks, became avenues for helping like-minded candidates by waging issue ad campaigns against their opponents. In short, it had become evident that any organization, entity, or individual so motivated could easily find ways to influence presidential or congressional elections without restriction by FECA and with a good chance of remaining anonymous in doing so. An elaborate and effective science of pseudo campaigning thus developed under the protection of the First Amendment.

The new nonprofits were exemplified in the 1996 campaigns by the best-reported of the clan: Triad Management Services. A for profit political consulting firm, Triad raised money from conservative Republicans—more than $3 million in the 1996 cycle apparently—and then funneled the proceeds to its two affiliated nonprofit think tanks. They in turn bought issue ads supporting conservative Republican candidates for Congress. (As something of a sideline, Triad also referred contributors directly to sympathetic PACs and candidates.) Candidates and PACs could accept only hard money, but the nonprofits were free to take money from any source and in any amount. Nor did they have to report the original sources of the money or their spending of it to the FEC. In fact, the desire of some contributors not to be known was apparently one of Triad's great appeals.[10] So the possibilities for raising and spending unregulated soft money multiply. While party committees may still be the most important raisers of soft money, they are no longer its only ones.

Although harder to document, the decline of confidence in FECA—and respect for it—has been the final characteristic of FECA's third and current era. "Pushing the envelope" of the regulatory regime has become an insiders' sport, and the level of disregard for it rises steadily. Some campaign budgets now include contingency planning for enforcement costs and penalties, and "win at any cost" becomes more common. In part, all this resulted from the wild scurrying after money in the 1996 campaign, but it also reflected a loss of confidence that FECA or the FEC could constrain others in a timely way or that they could indeed reach, much less control, some of the major events and actors of the campaign. Consequently, one essential element of any regulatory regime—a high level of self-enforcement—was significantly diminished.

In sum, the third era of FECA, that of the 1990s, is more than just the next era in a sequence. To be sure, some of the qualities of the second era remain; individual contributors maintain their importance, accounting for 56 percent of the receipts of all congressional candidates in 1996 (versus 54 percent in 1988). Nonetheless, the third era was marked by transformation and change. Stimulated by greater electoral competition and by struggles for control of both elected branches of government, political activists pushed levels of getting and spending sharply upward. Political risk-taking increased as well, especially in contributors' willingness to support non-incumbent candidates. Whole new categories of activity appeared on the peripheries of FECA's regulatory apparatus. The "new" included new spenders (for example, non-PAC organizations), new sources of money (especially unregulated soft money), and new kinds of expenditures (for example, issue ads and independent spending by the parties).

Just as the third era marks a sharp break with the two that preceded it in the life of FECA, it also heralds the emergence of the full effect of *Buckley v. Valeo* a decade and a half later. Initially *Buckley* had destroyed a fully comprehensive regulatory system by removing constraints on campaign expenditures. While the Court struck down a set of regulatory tools, it required disclosure of expenditures and it did not alter the structure of the transactions regulated. The actors and campaigns regulated—minus expenditure limits—were pretty much as Congress defined them in 1974. But the *Buckley* precedent was available for the "envelope pushers," the more venturesome operatives in campaign finance, who wanted to do precisely that: to change the dimensions of the regulatory envelope. At the same time *Buckley* provided the First Amendment's rhetorical and legal cover for such adventures. Campaign practices that would have been scorned as blatantly illegal a decade ago are now proudly touted as the exercise of free speech.

To be sure, *Buckley* was available to the adventuresome for fifteen years before they began to exploit it. Why the delay? One explanation leads all others: the political instability of the 1990s. The new electoral competitiveness, the electoral aggressiveness of conservative groups, the public distrust of incumbents and politicians in general, the increasing movement of interest groups into electoral politics, the reborn strength of party committees as campaign funders, a volatile electorate either shifting or abandoning old party loyalties—all of this unsettled the stability of the 1980s and created new electoral opportunities for political activists. Suddenly control of both the legislative and executive branches was under contention, as were a greater number of individual seats in Congress. So, too, was the very future of the social welfare state. New kinds of newly militant actors and tacticians wanted to seize electoral advantage by persuading voters with increasingly expensive mass media campaigning. The expansion and health of the economy assured the flow of resources necessary for those campaigns.

Then, too, there is a pattern, a rhythm, to political innovation and change. In this case, adaptation to the new regulation of campaign finance began timidly and in small increments after 1974. It was a process both of political learning about new realities and of innovation in the interstices and weaknesses of the regulatory structure. That initial stage of adaptation yielded to a period of consolidation in the late 1980s, a time of stability supported by the absence of stimulating change in both the regulatory and the broader political environments. As the changes of the 1990s created new political opportunities, the resulting adaptation was bolder, more innovative than the first wave. Was it a result of learning in the first stage, or of the greater political stakes of the time, or of the greater political aggressiveness that feeds on both knowledge and elevated stakes? Yes, yes, and yes.

Always behind the innovation and learning, however, was the enabler, the First Amendment. At root the First Amendment, as interpreted and applied in *Buckley*, is anti-regulation. For the adventurous it was the great legal-constitutional protection, both a rhetorical symbol and a legitimization of attacks on the regime of FECA. The regulation of campaign finance was, moreover, one of those First Amendment issues that united both ends of the political spectrum, drawing on the left's traditional commitment to civil liberties and on the right's libertarianism in the use of one's wealth. That powerful, enabling alliance afforded an ideal legal environment for big and bold innovative steps.

III. The Resurgence of the Political Parties

The old exemplars of the second era of FECA, the incumbents, were exemplars no longer in the 1990s. Within a few short years they had yielded the place of preeminence to organizations better adapted to the new campaign finance: the national party committees.

Ironically, the passage of FECA in 1974 had coincided with the declining influence of the American political parties. By the 1970s more and more Americans chose to seek their political goals through narrowly focused groups rather than through the all-inclusive, somewhat unfocused parties. While PACs flourished in the early years of

FECA, the parties limped along in near futility. Indeed, the rise of PACs had greatly embarrassed and threatened them, for it marked the first broad-scale interest group invasion into what had long been the domain of the parties: the contesting of American elections.

The parties had, of course, dominated campaign finance in the first half of the twentieth century. They raised their money from the fabled fat cats, and they funded campaigns for the presidency with it.[11] But with the decline of the parties and the advent of television and campaign technocrats for hire, candidates began increasingly, in the 1950s and 1960s, to raise their own campaign funds and to manage (or pay for the managing of) their own campaigns. In the 1972 events that led to the Watergate scandals, for example, the Committee to Re-Elect the President (CREEP), not the Republican National Committee, was the committee implicated. So marginal had the national party committees become by 1972 that merely to finance their own day-to-day operations they were often reduced to levying support payments on the state parties—and often having to beg them to send the checks.

Candidates continued to dominate the campaigns under FECA, but in the late 1970s the parties slowly began to find a place in the new campaigning. The Republicans, under the leadership of national chairmen such as Ray Bliss and William Brock, led the way by developing campaign services that rivaled those offered by private consultants. The Democrats followed within a few years. The national party committees quickly became "service vendors," in the phrase of one expert.[12]

By perfecting direct mail solicitations, by drawing on major political figures for fundraising, and by using their access to potential major contributors, the national party committees soon surpassed the state committees as campaign funders. In 1978 state and local party committees reported receipts of $2.2 million from the national parties; in 1996 the DNC and the RNC transferred $38.2 million in hard money and $102.4 million in soft money to state and local committees of their parties.[13] Moreover, the majority of state committees in both parties were meekly ceding their FECA-given spending authority in federal campaigns to the national parties under "agency agreements." That is, while FECA permits all national party committees taken together and all state and local party committees in a candidate's constituency to spend equal sums "on behalf of" the candidate—that sum being beyond the committees' authority to make direct contributions to the campaign—those state and local committees may, and often do, delegate their spending authority to the national committees, thus doubling the sums the national party can spend. All in all, in less than a generation the national parties, no longer paupers, became the new princes of campaign funding.

The national parties were ideally crafted and adapted, therefore, to become the icons of the third era of FECA.

♦   They alone of the actors within the aegis of FECA could raise and transfer soft money, and with it they built up their infrastructures, supported state parties, and spent generously on issue ads.

♦   Their adeptness in raising hard money permitted new levels of party support for candidates and, beginning in 1996, permitted them to make their newly sanctioned independent expenditures.

♦   Their success in fundraising gave them the leverage with which to orchestrate national strategies in congressional and presidential campaigns and even to recruit candidates and support them in state races. All of this they did without major objection or interference by the now quiescent state committees.

♦   The federated structure of their hierarchies enabled them to use hard money with maximum efficiency, substituting soft money wherever it could do the job. In fact, reports surfaced in 1996 of party-run "markets" in which state parties could trade hard and soft money funds, always at exchange rates that reflected the greater "value" of hard dollars.

Thanks to *Buckley* and its offspring, the parties by 1998 were the only participants in FECA's original paradigm that could function both within its regulated regime and in the expanding precincts outside its walls. They became the only masters of both hard and soft money, of traditional campaigning and the new pseudo-campaigning, of partisan campaign spending and independent spending even on candidates carrying their labels, even of new alliances with politically oriented nonprofits as well as the old alliances with PACs. And as of this writing they are only one vote on the Supreme Court away from completely escaping FECA's limitations on their coordinated spending for party candidates, thanks again to one of *Buckley*'s progeny.[14]

The political parties also brought intrinsic organizational advantages to the campaign finance of the 1990s. PACs had enjoyed an early success because they were limited, single-purpose organizations, but in the politics of the 1990s the parties benefitted greatly from the very characteristics that separated them from PACs. They profited from their complex, federated structure, their sophisticated strategies and political knowledge, their ability to take risks without considering the interests of a parent body, and their undivided and unblushing commitment to electoral politics. And so they moved quickly and easily from service vending to masterminding campaigns.

The data on party resources document the party resurgence. The Democratic and Republican parties raised a hard money total of $445.0 million in the 1992 cycle, but they raised $638.1 million (43.4 percent more) in 1995–96. Their ability to attract soft money grew even more dramatically in the same four years: from $86.0 to $262.1 million, an increase of 205 percent. Indeed, by 1996, unregulated soft money accounted for 29.1 percent of the parties' receipts.[15] In total hard and soft money receipts, the two national parties raised a breathtaking $900.2 million in 1995–96. Even in a cycle without the excitement of a presidential campaign, the early totals of November 23, 1998, reached $627.7 million. PACs active in 1995–96 reported total receipts of $437.4 million, all of it hard money, of course, and only 13.5 percent more than the $385.5 million they raised in 1992.

Many academics, political observers, and public officials greet such party successes with enthusiastic approval. In campaign finance their pro-party views translate into arguments for why the parties are the preferred sources of campaign money—and especially why their funds are preferable to those of PACs.

The pro-party position in campaign finance works from the premise that party money is money cleansed of the interests of the people who gave it to the parties originally. Its proponents put it this way in a recent brief before the Supreme Court: "As a source of campaign funds, American parties probably constitute the cleanest money in politics. Recognizing that political parties are large aggregators of many contributions diffuses any real or perceived undue influence that might arise from a financial contribution. . . . Parties are too large and too diverse to be controlled by any special interest. The old rule of sanitary engineers applies: the solution to pollution is dilution."[16]

The argument, however, demands closer scrutiny, especially its assumptions about the cleansing mechanism. How is it that the political agenda of the contributor to the party is so magically erased, and how is it that the party's contributors, while known to the party, are not known to the candidates who, if successful in the campaign, hold legislative or executive office? How *does* the money become disinterested and the donor anonymous?

In fact, national committees of both parties solicit major contributors, whether individuals or PACs, with dinners, outings, receptions, or weekends that appeal to them precisely by removing their anonymity. Prospective contributors meet party leaders, important members of Congress, even presidential candidates. Such fundraising promises them that they will be known, that their agendas will be noted, and that the reasons for their contributions will not be lost or "diluted" in some larger aggregate. Moreover, when those contributors give, it is often abundantly clear that they give for specific policy goals and not to support a general party platform. They do not seek to control or dominate the party, as the brief suggests; they seek only success for a specific policy or a policy agenda.

However, the pro-party argument continues, the parties as a source of money exert their pressures on policymakers more benignly than do PACs. Even if the party is demanding and disciplining, its pressures will be on behalf of a broadly based, broadly supported party policy rather than the one particular interest of a PAC with a narrow constituency. Again, that is an argument hard to square with the realities of contemporary American politics.

Much of the pro-party enthusiasm of the last fifty or seventy-five years has assumed a grassroots, participatory political party acting on behalf of a unified party platform or program. Whether such a "golden age" of integrated, mass-based parties ever existed or was even imperfectly approximated, it is not in sight today. Most of the powerful local party organizations, with their armies of fervent activists, vanished years ago. The national party committees that dominate campaign finance in the 1990s have very few ties to local parties and local activists, even to the platforms and officials of state parties.

The legislative campaign committees of the national parties—the Democratic Congressional Campaign Committee (DCCC), the

Democratic Senatorial Campaign Committee (DSCC), the National Republican Congressional Committee (NRCC), and the National Republican Senatorial Committee (NRSC)—function even more autonomously. As campaign committees for their legislative candidates, they raise money and form campaign strategies very much as candidates do. Their program or platform for a campaign reflects in various mixes the preferences of the party's legislative incumbents, a residue of party ideology, issues calculated to win votes, and, to an extent hard to define, the goals of their financial supporters. The Contract for America, drafted by House Republicans in 1994, was only a formalized version of what usually remains informal. In all this cobbling together of a party campaign, the overriding goal of a legislative campaign committee is clear, limited, and precise: to maximize the number of the party's members in the legislative chamber.

Raising campaign money shapes the methods of all who raise it. Parties and candidates thus employ similar techniques, such as offering major contributors access to public officials and the attendant opportunities for influencing policy decisions. But party committees can offer them longer-run, personal relationships with important, even leading policymakers. Above all, they offer access to a whole cohort of party candidates and incumbents rather than access merely to a single candidate or incumbent.

Beyond the common need to raise voluntary contributions, both party committees and PACs contribute much of the money they raise to candidates. In those contribution decisions they both must attend to the preferences of their contributors as well as their own interests and agendas. But with one important difference. PACs have far fewer large contributors, by any standard, than do the parties. Thus the major contributors to party committees tend to be more important to them and the attainment of their political goals. They also tend to be more politicized and greatly more exigent.

If I have correctly assessed the role of the national party committees in this third era of FECA, what are the broader implications of party ascendancy for FECA's regime?

- ◆ It is hard to escape the conclusion that the expanded party role will mean greater access to party officeholders, whether presidents or members of Congress.

- Party ascendancy will certainly mean a sustained testing of the limits of FECA and its administration, even to probing for expanded First Amendment protections.

- The polarizing differences between the parties over FECA and its reform will, if anything, become firmer and harder-edged as the party stake in funding campaigns increases.

- If party control of campaign resources continues to grow, it will surely enhance the power of national party leadership in Congress as candidates, including even some incumbents, become increasingly dependent on party resources.

- The greater the party resources, the greater the competitiveness in congressional elections. To maximize the number of their partisans in Congress, parties channel their funds strategically either to bolster incumbents in trouble or to boost the chances of challengers with good prospects. They also flock to open-seat races for the same reason. With competitiveness, of course, comes the inevitable need for higher levels of campaign funding.

In short, the parties are poised to exploit and build on virtually all the innovations that mark FECA's third era.

IV. THE SPECIAL CASE OF PRESIDENTIAL CAMPAIGN FINANCE

The funding of presidential campaigns under FECA has evolved less than that of congressional campaigns. The continuity owes largely to the two public funding programs for the presidential campaign: the first for the presidential primary season before the nominating conventions, and the second for the general election campaign following them. There is no public funding for the presidential jockeying before January 1st of the election year, although would-be candidates can establish eligibility for it before then and then use their certificates of eligibility to secure bank loans until the public funds flow. The two programs remain substantially unchanged since 1974, and although voluntary, all leading candidates of the major parties except two—John Connally, a seeker for the Republican nomination in 1980, and Malcolm (Steve) Forbes, a Republican hopeful in 1996—have opted for public support from 1976 through 1996. In accepting public funds, they accepted the principal conditions attached to them: limits on both their campaigns' and their own personal expenditures.

In the primary season candidates acquire public funds on a matching basis: public dollars for every individual contribution of $250 or less up to a maximum of $5 million in 1974 dollars, *if* the candidate has established eligibility by raising at least $5,000 in at least twenty states in sums of no more than $250. (Since those sums are not indexed, eligibility has been progressively easier to establish as inflation has reduced the value of the 1974 dollar.) The total paid out from the U.S. Treasury in any year fluctuates wildly because the number of contenders for the two nominations fluctuates. If an incumbent president seeks renomination, the absence of competition in that party cuts the number of contenders sharply, and a strong front runner has the same effect in the other party. The sheer numbers of qualifying would-be-nominees in any one year, that is, is the major variable affecting the campaign money raised and spent.

In all of this prenomination volatility, however, there is one strong constant. Among the contenders for the two major party nominations, public funding tends to account for about a third of total receipts. Furthermore, candidates raise virtually all their other money from individuals subject to the usual $1,000 contribution limit. PACs do not often become involved in chancy campaigns for nominations, and party committees almost always avoid intraparty battles.

Moreover, the majority of contenders stay well below the spending ceilings, with the candidates who will be nominated most likely to reach the maximum (in 1996: $30.9 million). From 1976 through 1996 only thirteen Democratic and Republican candidates reached the statutory spending limit; ten were the eventual nominees of their party. Yet one cannot leap to the conclusion that these contenders won their party's nomination *because* they outspent their opponents. In many instances, they raised the greatest sums because they were going to be nominated. In most years the nomination is secured by April or early May—and the money continues to roll in long after.

Public funding for the presidential general election campaigns is simpler and more predictable. The official candidates of the two major parties—or of any party getting 25 percent of the popular vote in the previous presidential election—claim an indexed grant ($61.8 million in 1996), which is all they are permitted to spend. In addition, their national party committee may spend an indexed sum ($12.0 million in 1996) on their behalf, although the parties have not always hit the maximum.

Since all major party candidates, even opponents of public funding such as Ronald Reagan, have accepted public funds for the last six presidential campaigns, the sums spent by the two major parties and their candidates, therefore, have increased every four years, but somewhat behind the rate of inflation. In actual expenditures the sums spent in the major party presidential campaigns thus increased from $47.9 million in 1976 to $132.0 million in 1996, an increase of 176 percent. That rate of increase contrasts with the 667 percent increase in spending for congressional campaigns in the same period.

These totals, to repeat, are for public funding of major party candidates from 1976 through 1996. Ross Perot in 1992, a major if not *major party* candidate, spurned public funding. He was, therefore, able to spend without limit and draw without limit on his own substantial resources. Individuals, PACs, and party committees contributing to him were bound by the usual FECA limits: $1,000, $5,000, and $5,000 respectively. As it turned out the Perot campaign raised $67.5 million, $63.5 million provided by Ross Perot himself. In 1996 Perot chose public funding and received $29.1 million, a partial share of the public funding allotment based on the ratio of his 19 percent of the popular vote in 1992 to the vote percentages won by the two major party candidates.

All this describes the hard money campaigns for the presidency as FECA describes the "campaign." The one great destabilizing event in them has been the onset of soft money campaigns, a development many date to the 1988 campaign. Before and during the campaign, presidential candidates raise great sums of soft money that go to promote, however indirectly, their victory and that of other candidates. Ultimately soft money itself emerged as an issue in the 1996 campaign and as the centerpiece of the McCain-Feingold reform package in 1997–98. The reformers of 1974 did not anticipate a soft money campaign "supplementing" a publicly funded presidential campaign. Nor did they foresee the extent to which *Buckley*'s version of the First Amendment would sanction issue ads by spenders otherwise governed by FECA and by many others who are not.

The Supreme Court's major impact on this plan for funding presidential campaigns was to let it stand as Congress had enacted it. Its sweeping invalidation of all spending limits in *Buckley* extended to these as well, but with no great effect so long as major party candidates continue to opt for public funding and the spending limits attached to it. Left for the future is the potential impact lingering as long as *Buckley* does: a presidential campaign in which one major party candidate, supported by the party's organization and its fundraising prowess, chooses not to take public money and spends three or four times what the publicly funded opponent can.

Until then, these sections of FECA stand as testimony to legislative skill and expertise. Reform solutions of these kinds often are pragmatic and wedded to the status quo; the decision not to grant easy or full funding to minor party candidates is a clear case in point. And yet the Congress fashioned a viable public funding program that achieved its main purposes: a lid on spending and relative parity between the major party candidates.

The one grain of instability in *Buckley*'s holdings on public funding—that it must be voluntarily taken—has been manifest in state programs. Plagued by low rates of acceptance of their public moneys and the attached spending limits, states have tried to devise compensatory benefits for the publicly funded and thus constrained candidate whose opponent does not operate under a spending limit. At what point do the compensatory benefits create such disadvantages for the candidate not taking the money that he or she is in effect coerced into accepting it in violation of the free choice protected by the First Amendment? The following section on the states will take up that problem in fuller context.

V. CAMPAIGN FINANCE IN THE STATES: 1974 TO PRESENT

BUCKLEY SCUTTLES AN EXPERIMENT

Beyond their effect in Congress, the Watergate scandals released a burst of reformist energy in the states. Herbert Alexander reports that forty-nine states passed "new laws" on campaign finance between 1972 and 1976.[17] Some, to be sure, adopted limited reforms—requiring disclosure of contributions or expenditures or both, for instance—but some were full-scale reform packages modeled roughly on Congress's recasting of FECA in 1974. Indeed, by 1975 the editors of the *Harvard Law Review* identified thirty-six states with spending limits on candidates for one or more state office.[18] In five of those states the spending limits were attached to the candidate's voluntary acceptance of public funding, but in thirty-one the spending limits were freestanding and mandated by state law on all applicable candidates.[19] By 1976 the majority of states also had in place limits on the sums that groups or individuals could spend independently.[20] The states had volunteered once again to serve as "laboratories" for democratic policy making.[21]

The richness of their incipient experiments was as important as their sheer number. Their thirty-six different plans for limiting campaign expenditures prove that the states were not merely adopting a made-in-Washington template. Some states specified the spending limits in total dollars; those limits varied vastly, depending on state populations, the populations of the constituencies of the office campaigned for, and the competitiveness of the elections at stake. Other states defined limits in terms of cents per voter; most ranged from 10 to 40 cents per voter or resident. Some states applied the limit to candidate expenditures in the aggregate, while others imposed "sub-ceilings" on specific kinds of expenditures (for example, those on media ads). Some state limits applied not only to candidates but also to supporters and opponents of ballot propositions. Inevitably, state law differed widely in the range of campaigns covered; the race for the governorship was the one most commonly limited.[22]

With the Court's decision in *Buckley*, these experiments in expenditure control became the path not taken, the experiment not conducted. While the facts of the case were limited to FECA, the *Buckley* precedent also applied to the states. One can only speculate about the lessons lost. What kinds of administrative authority and funding are needed to oversee successfully 5 or 50 or 150 campaigns? Are those administrative burdens borne differently in various political cultures or traditions? Is the wiser regulatory course one of incrementalism or is it a total regulatory embrace of all state campaigns? More specifically, will money run from regulated to unregulated campaigns? And what is the feasibility, even the constitutionality, of singling out certain categories of spending for limits while not regulating other spending in the same campaigns? The irony, of course, is that expenditure control remains the favorite option of the reformers, and in part that is because we have no real evidence about its effectiveness, its consequences, its administrability. It remains the White Knight everyone admires but no one really knows.

ADAPTATION TO *BUCKLEY*

So the majority of states continued, post-*Buckley*, to regulate contributions to candidates for state office. Their experience was shared within the regulatory community via meetings, newsletters, the publication of data, and by an occasional scholarly foray into state campaign finance. On the other hand, *Buckley* denied reformers, legislators, and regulators a comparable body of knowledge about the one reform at the top of many agendas. Only a few states have had viable public funding programs with the acceptance of spending limits as a condition, and only one state, Minnesota, has developed comprehensive experience with a funding with-limits package in the large majority (in this case, over 90 percent) of state legislative campaigns. Minnesota's largely successful experience in containing spending, standing by itself, is often dismissed for merely demonstrating the state's "special" political culture—one proof of which is that it has the most pervasive system of public financing of campaigns in the first place! Such a conclusion illustrates the importance of the knowledge never acquired about spending limits.

Beyond the loss of spending limits, a small number of states also lost to *Buckley* their statutory limitations on candidates' financing of their own campaigns, either in contributions or unpaid loans to themselves. In the great dichotomy of *Buckley*—the difference between contributions and spending—the Court categorized self-financing as spending, even though most states treated it as a contribution. The Court also held that, since candidates could not corrupt themselves, limiting self-financing was outside of the legislature's legitimate interest in preventing corruption or its appearance. It is an old argument, that the candidate's own money is the cleanest money. The maxim is as old as wealthy candidates; Ross Perot's invocation of it in 1992 was in that time-honored tradition.

Why did only a few states have limits on candidate self funding in early 1976?[23] Two explanations suggest themselves: candidates commonly funded their campaigns in races for lesser state offices, and the general spending limits, extensive and very low in many states, would limit the need for candidate money in any event. By 1984 only three states had such limits, all of them voluntarily accepted as a condition of receiving public funds.[24]

What difference the loss of limits on self-financing made in the states is not easy to say. State data on candidate self funding are spotty at best, and even where they exist, state agencies fail to tabulate them in user-friendly aggregates. The celebrated, very rich candidates from populous states get media attention; Nelson Rockefeller of New York and John Y. Brown of Kentucky became two of the most famous statewide candidates in recent American history. We lack, however, systematic data for the rest of the country, now or at any earlier time. Nonetheless, two points about self-funding in the states are clear. First, it is heavily limited to challengers, and it helps many of them run competitive campaigns. Second, aside from statewide campaigns, it usually involves modest sums. Malbin and Gais report that challengers in races for the lower houses of four state legislatures contributed the following percentages of their campaign treasuries: 6 (Washington), 7 (Missouri), 8 (Wisconsin), and 14 (Kansas).[25]

Finally, *Buckley* greatly affected the states in a way unique to them. Exactly half of the states permit their voters to decide policy issues in the polling places, either in ballot initiatives or in referenda or both.[26] In later applications of its *Buckley* precedent, the Supreme Court held that the states could not regulate either contributions or expenditures in such ballot campaigns. Because it had stipulated the prevention of "corruption or the appearance of corruption" as the sole ground on which legislatures might regulate the protected transactions of campaign finance, limits on expenditures for ballot issues did not pass muster. No candidates for public office were chosen in these elections, and the Court could find no other agent or mechanism of "corruption."[27]

All experts agree that the number of initiatives, as well as the total of all kinds of ballot issues, is on the rise in the states. David Magleby tallies 120 referenda and initiatives in the United States in the 1970–79 period, 193 in 1980–89, and 353 between 1990 and a projected 1999.[28] In California, the consensus champion of the initiative, voters confronted 22 initiatives in 1970–79, in 1980–89 they saw 44, and between 1990 and 1997 voted in 48.[29] Moreover, campaigns

for them are progressively more expensive. Betty H. Zisk reports
that 50 "major" ballot issues in California, Massachusetts, Michigan,
and Oregon in 1976–80 had median campaign expenditures of
$237,500. In the same four states 22 major ballot issues in 1982
were contested for a median figure of $840,600.[30] Moreover, indi-
vidual contributions for ballot campaigns clearly reflect the absence
of regulation; in California, for instance, fully 80 percent of contributions to ballot measure committees in the early 1990s came in
sums of $10,000 and more.[31]

By removing limits on giving and spending in these campaigns,
the siblings of *Buckley* have made the most media intensive of all
electoral campaigns into the least constrained. In a short period, interests on both sides of a ballot question must try to mobilize majorities
almost from point zero, for in these campaigns there are no incumbents, no candidates with name recognition, and few anchors of party
loyalty. The contesting coalitions target voters who are as close to
"blank slates" as one finds in American politics. Especially in the
larger and most populous states, these statewide campaigns are likely
to succeed, when contested, only with the resources for massive
media, billboard, and direct mail campaigns.

In one of the grander ironies of campaign finance, initiatives,
despite their unregulated campaigns, have become the reformers'
method of choice for reforming campaign finance in the states. They
offer a handy vehicle for bypassing parties and legislatures either protective of the status quo or unable to agree on a single reform proposal.
Notwithstanding the impact of *Buckley*, the reformers have been successful with the initiative. Alexander and NyBlom report that of the
twenty-one state initiatives reforming campaign finance from 1972 to
1994 a total of fifteen passed.[32] The difficulties have been in the
courts. The Supreme Court's application of the First Amendment has
robbed the reformers of reform options with the greatest mass appeal.
Mandatory spending limits and limits on candidate self-financing
are out, and low contribution limits—especially in the $100 range—are
suspect.[33] The crafters of these initiatives walk a fine line between
plans that will attract voter support and those that will pass the
scrutiny of the courts.

Understandably, they err repeatedly on the side of winning popular majorities. An increasing number of initiatives win on election day
only to lose in court. Of the five state initiatives passed in 1996—in

Arkansas, California, Colorado, Maine, and Oregon—only those in Colorado and Maine stand intact in early 1999, and the one in Colorado is under adjudication, while the one in Maine may well be. In California a federal district court judge struck down Proposition 208, passed in 1996, on grounds that some of its contribution limits were too low and that, more generally, the proposition would not permit candidates to raise funding necessary for effective campaigns. In 1998 initiatives beginning public funding in return for candidate spending limits passed in Arizona and Massachusetts; their legal and constitutional futures are uncertain at this early date.

The initiative as a weapon of reform is, moreover, a two-edged sword. A successful initiative may make, and may be *intended* to make, the campaign finance regime less even-handed, less acceptable to political activists, and more partisan in its impact. Most recently a movement to prohibit labor unions from using dues of members for political purposes unless they have the members' written permission to do so has gained national momentum. (Virtually all labor money in both the states and the nation goes to Democratic candidates.) An initiative passed in 1992 in the state of Washington was its opening success. In 1998 a similar proposition lost in California, despite the campaign leadership of the state's Republican governor.

Overall, despite special circumstances in the states, candidates, parties, and contributors adapted to the post-*Buckley* regime in state politics much the same way they did in national politics. Of necessity, regulation rested heavily on a combination of disclosure and contribution limits, but with two great differences: disclosure in the states was rarely as effective as it is at the national level, and contribution limits were far less pervasive and constraining. Withal, the development of campaign finance systems in the states followed outlines similar to the regime of FECA. Spending levels increased, PACs became more important players, and individual contributors in many states began to give in higher average sums. But there was one great difference: the role of the parties.

THE SPECIAL CASE OF PARTY COMMITTEES

As it had for decades, the funding of state campaigns post-*Buckley* relied much more heavily on political parties than on other players. Initially that meant state protection of newly threatened party organizations. Between 1973 and 1976 nine states adopted programs of public funding for the parties, and another five began similar programs in the 1980s. Like the programs of public funding for candidates, the party-funding programs of the 1970s were largely funded by check-offs on the state income-tax return; four of the five adopted in the 1980s relied on voluntary additions to tax liability and consequently generated very small sums to disperse.[34] Generally, the parties in these states spent the unrestricted proceeds for general administrative costs and only secondarily to support candidates and campaigns.

More commonly, the states supported the party role in campaigns specifically by freeing them from limits on contributions to them or on their contributions to candidates. As of 1996 a total of twenty-four states imposed no limits on either contributions to party committees or contributions by them. Only eight set limits on both, and twelve limited party contributions.[35] Moreover, in those states with limits on both party and PAC contributions, the limits on party contributions were always equal to or higher than those on PACs.[36]

Data on party spending in federal and state campaigns reflect the greater state lenience. In the congressional elections of 1996 the party committees, in the total of their contributions to candidates and their coordinated spending on their behalf, accounted for only 5.3 percent of all the spending in the campaigns for the House and Senate—$40.8 million out of $765.3 million. In many states, party committees did much more in contributions alone. Of the seventeen states they report on, Gierzynski and Breaux find that at least one of the two major parties in seven states accounted for 10 percent of their legislative candidates' receipts in 1992; in thirteen of them at least one party's contributions accounted for 5 percent.[37] In Minnesota in 1994 the total party contributions made up 13 percent of all receipts for state lower house candidates; in the state of Washington it was 15.6 percent in the same year.

Beyond those direct contributions by state party committees lies the terra incognita of their spending of behalf of candidates, the equivalent of the coordinated spending of party committees under FECA. Both journalism and scholarship are largely silent about it, a silence that probably reflects the fact that it is not regulated and thus not reported to a state agency. Wisconsin has a law that limits a party committee to $500 in contributions to a candidate if it has made any coordinated expenditures on his or her behalf. Both Washington and Minnesota permit unlimited coordinated spending only when it is on behalf of three or more candidates; in both states, conveniently, the senatorial districts are divided into two districts for the lower house.[38] That, apparently, is the extent of regulation in the states.

The sums of such spending may at least be inferred from the reports that party committees must file in some states. Dwyre and Stonecash report substantial gains in spending by New York committees "on behalf of" candidates in the 1980s. By 1988, for example, the Republican campaign committee in the state Assembly was spending $1.17 million to elect Republicans, the Democrats $1.16 million, figures that were both above two-thirds of what the parties' Assembly candidates spent.[39] Other reports are rare, but one can venture two conclusions based on anecdotal evidence. First, what coordinated spending there is probably follows the same division of labor one sees at the national level: the legislative parties spend in legislative races, and the state committees spend in statewide races. Second, we confront here a kind of unregulated spending with tremendous potential for expansion, especially given the rising flow of soft money into state party treasuries.

The growth of spending by the legislative campaign committees (the LCCs) is by no means limited to New York. In some states these campaign committees are the party caucuses, in some states they are separate party campaign committees similar to the four committees in the U.S. Congress, and in a few states they are the party's legislative leadership acting directly. But whatever the organizational form, they function as adjuncts of the legislative party and its leadership.

Regardless of the form of the LCC, it benefits from the same loose control that the states accord the traditional party organizations. The result in some states, often the most populous ones, is a degree of party dominance of campaign finance unapproached, even unthinkable, at the national level. The four major party leaders in the Illinois legislature funneled more than 45 percent of all 1992 campaign receipts through their hands for dispersal to their party's candidates in targeted competitive races.[40] Illinois, not incidentally, is a state with no limits on contributions and with a disclosure system that was until 1996 conspicuously user-unfriendly. Those figures for Illinois are, of course, of the same magnitude as those for New York a few years earlier.[41] In California, before a reform initiative imposed term limits on state legislators and greatly limited the power of LCCs, the speaker of the California Assembly assumed the LCC role. In 1986 Speaker Willie Brown raised $2.52 million for Democratic candidates for the Assembly, almost one-fifth of all money raised for all Assembly candidates in that year.[42]

The sheer magnitude of their contributions, however, is only one part of the LCC story. Just as important has been where they put their money. Invariably and at whatever funding level they function, LCCs give more of their money to nonincumbent candidates than any other funding source. On that point all scholarship is in accord. In a number of states—New York for one—that interest may even extend to recruiting legislative candidates and supporting them in contested primaries, even against the candidate of the local party organization.[43]

REFORM OPTIONS

As the states adapted, perforce, to the constraints of *Buckley,* reform did not die, although initially it did not flourish. Several states were tempted into the "bargain" the Court offered in *Buckley:* make spending limits a condition of the candidate's choosing public funds, and the limits will pass constitutional muster. State plans, however, often relied on levels of funding or spending limits too low to induce widespread candidate acceptance. They also relied on unstable systems of funding for the program, most often one tied to the state's income tax. The revenue generated by taxpayer check-off declined as the percentage of participating taxpayers declined, and revenue from "add-ons" to taxpayer liability never generated enough money in the first place. The fundamental problem became clear: the lack of political support for public funding sufficient to raise enough money for it, either by increasing check-off sums or by tapping general tax resources. The problem was all the greater when Republicans, often ardent opponents of public funding, controlled state legislatures or governorships.

Gradually the states began in the 1980s and 1990s to build a more diverse, even innovative reform record. Different states began from different points of regulatory complexity, and thus many of the changes were mundane. Between 1980 and 1996 the number of states requiring disclosure went from forty-five to fifty, those putting limits on individual contributions rose from twenty-one to thirty-five, and those similarly limiting political parties went from eight to eighteen.[44] But even those basic reforms have not gone unchallenged. Pressures for lowering the contribution limits even to $100 for state legislative races would indirectly achieve limits on spending by drying up the funds to spend, not to mention the sharp limiting, perhaps elimination, of any media based campaigning. They also remind us that for some reformers reforming campaign finance is also reforming campaigning.

Some reforms have departed more radically from post-Watergate patterns. For example, some states have experimented with aggregate receipt limits—limits on how much a candidate can accept in toto from specified sources (usually sources the legislature believes represent "special interests"). Innovation also flourishes in "compensatory" public funding. For example, the state treasury may give campaign funds to candidates who are, under certain circumstances, the victims of independent expenditures urging their defeat or of the unlimited spending of an opponent not accepting public money. And proposals to limit out-of-state or out-of-district contributions neither die nor succeed widely.

At the same time, reform in the 1990s has often returned to the public funding option. A loose coalition of reformers in a number of states has coalesced around the "Clean Money Option" combining public funding, spending limits, and, often, reductions in contribution limits. Reforms in Maine and Vermont have been its signal successes. The Clean Money coalition includes old-style reformers such as Common Cause and the League of Women Voters, reformist foundations and think tanks, and newer players from the progressive-populist tradition: labor, Public Citizen, and some of the chapters of the Public Interest Research Group (PIRGs). Their commitment to a reduced scale of campaign funding as well as an all-out war on "special interest" money makes their proposals better suited for initiative campaigns than for battles in state legislatures. Nebraska has ventured down a lonelier road, trying to achieve public funding without public funds. Since public money goes only to candidates whose major party opponents will not (voluntarily) accept spending limits, and since the intention is for the threat to lead all candidates to accept the spending limits, the desired conclusion is no expenditure of public funds. The final words on the Nebraska plan will be said by the courts and the game theorists.

As always in the states, reform faces the uncertainty of judicial applications of *Buckley*. All the major sections of FECA have been reviewed by the federal courts, but the testing of state legislation has been spotty. Losing parties may choose not to bring the case to the Supreme Court, and if they do, the Court may choose not to take it. In 1995 or 1996, for instance, it denied certiorari to cases decided by the U.S. Court of Appeals for the Eighth Circuit, striking down compensatory payments to candidates who were "victims" of independent spending, contribution limits as low as $100, and the limiting of candidate carryovers of cash from one cycle to another.[45]

Cases from state courts fare no better. Wisconsin forbids any candidate for the state Senate to accept more than a total of $2,000 per campaign from PACs. That is to say, there are limits on one category of total receipts, transactions that are neither contributions nor expenditures. Even though at least three states used them in 1996 (all in different form), their constitutional status is not as yet finally established. The Wisconsin Supreme Court unanimously upheld that state's limit, but the Supreme Court refused to grant certiorari.[46]

In Summary

"Concluding" briefly about campaign finance in the fifty states over more than a generation would test anyone's skills of concision. The states have fifty different histories of campaign practices and funding levels. They also have fifty different regulatory regimes, ranging from regulation limited to minimal candidate reporting, to regulation whose texture and extent matches that of FECA, and finally to more extensive programs of public funding (for example, Maine and Minnesota) that go beyond anything tried at the federal level.

Thus the impact of *Buckley v. Valeo* on the states has been very uneven. Certainly it cannot be blamed for the minimal disclosure and complete lack of limits on contributions in states such as Illinois and Pennsylvania. *Buckley* creates no obstacles to timely and accessible ("transparent") disclosure. Nor does it prevent statutory limits on contributions, the regulatory step the states most widely adopt after disclosure. On the other hand, the Court in *Buckley* did rule out a number of options—candidate spending limits, limits on candidate self-financing, and limits on independent spending—that are a logical next stage once the regulatory foundation is built.

Most recently, *Buckley* now limits the states in fashioning responses to threats to their regulatory regimes: burgeoning soft money transfers to state parties, issue ads as campaigning, and independent spending by party committees. And while none is yet common in the states, they clearly have arrived. In Wisconsin, for instance, a large business association in 1996 spent more than $350,000 in radio and TV ads attacking members of the Wisconsin legislature it considered unfriendly to business. Those incumbents happened to be running for reelection.[47] Moreover, a number of state party committees have begun to raise their own "soft money"—money raised outside of the restrictions of state law and not available for direct campaign funding. Word of such developments reaches national attention slowly—more slowly, certainly, than it takes for word of political innovations to travel on the insiders' network. For promoting the diffusion of such innovations, furthermore, the political party, federated in structure and national in control, is the ideal agent.

Thus, the logic or aura of *Buckley* has narrowed and compressed the range of regulation in the states by eliminating options, variety, and imagination in those of them willing to press beyond the starter package of disclosure and contribution limits. In the longer run, *Buckley* has had a greater impact on the states than it has on FECA and the federal jurisdiction simply because some states have been more willing to reform campaign finance and to be more innovative in doing so.

Who then bears the rest of the blame for the failure of regulation in the states? In some states strong party organizations in the state or the legislature, happy with the status quo, have stifled reform. In others Republican dominance, or at least sometime dominance, has mattered, since many Republicans, whether out of ideology or out of self-interest, oppose reform in the states as vigorously as they do in Congress. Finally, reform may be stymied by the sheer complexity of state politics. It is certainly no coincidence that the states with heterogeneous and competitive politics, with high levels of campaign spending, with well-developed interest group systems—states such as California, Illinois, New York, Pennsylvania, and Texas—have persisted in rudimentary regulation. The political deadlock over reform in them looks very much like the deadlock in Congress, and so do its reasons.

VI. The Three Dynamics of a Campaign Finance Regime

The campaign finance system FECA created is exactly that—a system. It is an interacting set of components in which the parts—activists or institutions, for instance—all work to achieve some allocation of resources or other collective goals. In doing so any system develops, even institutionalizes, a number of internal mechanisms or processes. It has ways of working or operating, and in them one observes the relationships among the parts and between the parts and the whole and whether those relationships are or are not stable. No successful regulation of such a system is possible without a good understanding of the resource being regulated—money or cash in this case—and the processes, expectations, and decisions allocating it.

Cash was not always, however, the chief resource "paying" for most American campaigns. As the ancient tales of local party organizations, torchlight rallies, and door-to-door canvassing remind us, American campaigns were once paid for largely by labor contributed in varying degrees of voluntarism. As the politics of patronage and the neighborhood declined, and local party organization with them, a cash economy gradually replaced the earlier one of contributed, non-professional labor. The first national attempt to regulate money in campaigns—that of 1907—was thus an attempt to regulate only some of the resources of the campaign and at that, the resources used primarily in presidential campaigns. The task the Congress undertook in 1974 was one of regulating virtually all the resources of campaigns for all elective federal offices.

By any criterion, money is a very mobile resource. It changes hands or location in minutes, and it is quickly exchanged for any other resource for rent or for sale. The mobility of money undergirds its central dynamic: its aversion to regulatory confinement. The analogy to a hydraulic system is by now a commonplace. Campaign money flows freely within the confines of regulatory "plumbing," always finding the open spigots or breaking through the weakest walls in the system. Despite the heuristic insight, the analogy to the fluid resource is not altogether accurate. Water has intrinsic weight and force; money does not. The "force" in campaign finance is the activity of inventive, goal-seeking political actors. It is they who push money into new avenues and test for the weak spots in the regulations, and it is they who, operating with a mobile resource and within a vulnerable regulatory structure, make the regulatory task so difficult.

Like any other attempt at regulation, the regime of FECA has its points of vulnerable opportunity for those resisting it or adapting to it. Its weaknesses are too diverse for one to refer to them generically as loopholes. Some of them were intended weaknesses or exceptions framed at creation: for instance, the exemption of volunteered campaign labor. Some were in fact probably legislative bloopers— provisions of law that were flawed from the beginning. Topping the list is the failure to index the amounts taxpayers check off to provide the public funding in presidential campaigns while at the same time indexing the amounts paid out. (The consequence was repeated short-falls in the money needed to make payments to eligible would-be presidential candidates in the prenomination public funding program. Congress in 1993 raised the sum to be checked off from one to three dollars, postponing the day when indexed payouts would exceed non-indexed tax diversions.) Some resulted from Congress's failure in clairvoyance; the so-called soft money loophole is a case in point. And some were created by the federal courts in applying the First Amendment to FECA and a few FEC rules.

The continuous probing for weaknesses and opportunity in the regulatory structure, for ways of avoiding its hardest paths, may be thought of as the ordinary, natural dynamic of a system coping with regulation. A second and related dynamic centers on the rate or pace of challenges and the changes resulting from them. Through its first fifteen years or so, the testing of the regime of FECA proceeded at a steady pace, promoted by accumulating political experience and by growing political confidence. The pace was not rapid enough, the direction not radical enough, however, to disturb the basic stability of the system.

In the decade of the 1990s that stability gave way to an acceler-ated pace of challenge and innovation that produced something very much like an international arms race. As in the classic arms race and its analogs, the regulated added to an already potent arsenal of

conventional weapons an awesome pair of new ones: issue advertisements and independent spending by political parties, both protected by judicial applications of the First Amendment. For
candidates those initiatives were the military equivalents of opponents' opening new fronts that had to be defended or at least whose
defense had to be prepared. Spurred on by heightened stakes and
growing competitiveness in electoral politics, candidates and parties
raised increasing sums of money. New weapons, new expectations,
new fears, and newly raised political stakes produced their predictable results: the fervid, even panicky fundraising of 1996 that
increased in intensity with each acceleration in the arming for the
campaigns.

Of President Clinton's anxieties we know the most. His fear of
being outspent in his reelection campaign began before the 1994 elections were over. His political consultant, Dick Morris, shared and
fed those fears. The national Democrats had long lagged behind
Republicans in raising money and even though they closed the gap in
1992, the Republicans still showed a 1.5 to 1 margin in hard money.
Newly installed in office, the president was shocked at his party's
woeful performance in direct-mail soliciting. After the Republicans
widened the hard money gap to 1.8 to 1 in 1994, the president autho-
rized the use of the White House for coffees and sleepovers.
Democratic fundraising turned to new minority constituencies, both
ethnic and religious; the mobilization of Asian and Asian-American
friends is well documented. As the Republican financial edge grew in
1996, one can imagine Democratic fears when the Supreme Court
found a new use for the parties' hard money: independent spending.

Even into 1997 the president was still voicing the fears and psy-
chology of a classic arms race: "Every one of us who has participated
in this system, *even if we did it because we thought we had to do it to
survive or just to keep up,* has to take some responsibility for its
excesses. And I take mine."[48] The Clinton rhetoric of 1997's summer
continued the same theme in his defense of his fundraising in the
1996 campaign. "I'm proud of it . . . *I don't believe in unilateral disarmament.* . . . We have to raise enough to be competitive."[49] As it
turned out, the national Republicans increased their hard money
superiority to a 1.9 to 1 ratio in 1997.

At some point, ordinary change reaches a breadth and speed that
threatens not only the peripheries of the regulatory system but also the

very stability of the system itself. The arms race theorists describe destabilizing events leading to a destabilization of the system, the result of which is a lack of confidence in all limits, a declining sense of how much is enough, an escalating insecurity, and a consequent scrambling for more weapons. All of which only ratchets the race to a higher level in an upward spiral of getting and spending. The result, not infrequently, is overkill, the raising and spending of money out of all proportion to a reality-based assessment of need.

Ordinarily, regulatory regimes depend on a third dynamic to restore stability and the efficacy of regulation itself. It is the legislative response of repair and maintenance. When the regulated discover holes or weaknesses in the regulatory structure or when new practices in the regulated system raise questions not addressed in the regulations, the regulators react with remedial legislation. By patching and anticipating, they sustain the stability and the viability of the regulatory regime.

Since the final defining amendments of 1976, however, there has been no such revamping of FECA. The only significant subsequent legislation, that in 1979, came too early for "upkeep" and, indeed, created another small breach in FECA's boundaries by exempting some of the hard money expenditures of state and local parties (for example, sample ballots, yard signs, turnout drives) from their contribution or spending limits under FECA. Regulatory housekeeping has fallen to the same political deadlock that stymies all proposals for change in FECA. It has even suffered from opposition by some advocates of change who oppose any repair to FECA that is less than an all-matters-dealt-with reform package. So, in the race to maintain the regulatory regime, the regulators have fallen far behind the regulated.

In 1999 it is clear that the arms race in American campaign finance gallops on apace. The expansion of the campaign—in its broadest sense—in 1995–96 had its price; the total sums spent on issue ads and independent expenditures probably amounted to at least an extra 20 percent over the usual hard money expenditures in the cycle for campaigns for Congress and the presidency.[50] The likelihood of that percentage increasing hangs over the system. While the sums raised by the major party candidates in the 1998 general elections for Congress did in fact decline, the average sums raised edged up a bit over the 1996 averages. Moreover, the four party congressional campaign committees raised more money, soft and hard, than they did in the

1996 cycle: $260.7 million in 1996 and $288.7 in 1998. (The data for both cycles is from reports filed twenty days after the November election.) Finally, issue ads in those campaigns, even by the most constrained estimates, more than doubled over 1996.

In sifting through the causes of the destabilizing of the campaign finance system in the 1990s, two seem paramount: the intensifying competitiveness of national elections and the impact of the Supreme Court's progressive protection of parts of the perceived campaign from regulation under FECA. The Court began the destabilization in *Buckley* by diminishing what Congress intended to be total regulation of all actors and transactions of campaigns. By opening successive breaches in that regulatory structure, the Court freed the way ultimately for the unregulated money, actors, and campaigning of the 1990s. Beyond that, the Supreme Court made it harder for legislators to repair and maintain those structures. To be sure, political deadlock was the main culprit here, but the narrowing of repair options and the mobilization of First Amendment arguments against some of them made it more difficult to cobble together majorities. Finally, both in their decisions and in their rhetoric moving beyond *Buckley,* the federal courts have encouraged the envelope-pushing that is in itself a mechanism of instability. The campaign finance bar certainly notes, for example, the failure of the FEC's rule making to deal with issue advocacy and the anti-regulation votes in *Colorado Republican Federal Campaign Committee v. FEC.* There is, in short, a damaging aura of disease and weakness, an increasing expectation of failure, pervading FECA's regulatory regime.

VII. The First Amendment and Campaign Finance

No event in the history of FECA has been as profoundly formative as the Supreme Court's holding in *Buckley.* The applications and refinements of that ruling mark many of the turning points in the life of legislation. Before the law ever went into effect, the Court had struck down all limits on independent spending, on spending by candidates' campaign committees, and on spending by the candidates in their own behalf. Simultaneously, it also denied Congress the power to reach all parts of an intricately interlocked system. Without any limits on spending, moreover, it made the money chase of the 1990s more likely, perhaps even inevitable. In brief, the Court doomed FECA to a bad start and an even worse future.

Such assertions about the effect of a constitutional precedent—indeed about the primacy of *any* cause in a complex cause-effect relationship—are notoriously speculative. Certainly *Buckley* was not the only shaper of the future of FECA and American campaign finance. The vagaries of American electoral politics and electoral competition have had a significant impact, and so has the rise of interest groups to new levels of electoral importance. But those are causes within the ambit of campaign politics itself. For the catalog of causes outside it, there is, of course, the growth of the American economy and, especially, a new class of the very rich with new levels of disposable income. And that stealthy regulator, inflation, reduced all unindexed limits on contributions to one-third their 1974 purchasing power by 1990. Then there is *Buckley*.

Any summary of the impact of *Buckley* begins with the loss of spending limits, both those on total campaign expenditures and those on the candidates' own spending. While direct spending on presidential general election campaigns rose by 176 percent between 1976 and 1996—limited to increases only at the rate of rise in the CPI—the spending of all congressional general election candidates rose 667 percent in the same period. As for candidate self-financing, from 1986 through 1990 there were in each year either two or three congressional candidates who spent at least $1 million of their own on their campaigns; in 1994 and 1996, however, there were nineteen. Michael Huffington's two-step attempt to vault into the Senate brought national publicity to candidates of wealth. He spent $5.2 million of his own on a winning candidacy for a House seat in 1992, but lost, with 44 percent of the vote, in his attempt in 1994 to unseat Senator Diane Feinstein of California despite providing $28.4 million of the $30.0 million his campaign spent.

Conclusions about paths not taken do not come easily. Limits on self-financing are probably more feasible administratively if only because regulating one campaign resource is easier than regulating all the spending of an entire campaign. As daunting a task as regulating hundreds of legislative campaigns, or even gubernatorial or presidential campaigns, surely is, it has been done in presidential campaigns and in those states with substantial public funding tied to spending limits—especially, Michigan, Minnesota, and New Jersey. (In all these instances, of course, spending limits are voluntarily accepted as a condition of receiving public funds. The degree of control on spending, therefore, depends on the percentage of major party candidates choosing to take the public money and the spending limits it entails.) The cloud on the horizon concerns independent spending. While it has tended to increase when campaign spending was constrained, the spending stimulated has long been much less than the damping effect of the spending limits. The new independent spending by parties and issue advocacy by parties and groups may well afford a more attractive alternative to constrained candidate spending.

The loss of both of these spending limits, moreover, strikes at questions of the perceived integrity of basic representational processes. Large segments of the mass public see the issue of very wealthy candidates as the "buying" of public office with one's personal fortune. Conversely it signals the difficulty that a candidate of modest means will have in running a competitive campaign for office. As for campaign spending, it quickly becomes an issue of candidates absorbed by the need to raise large sums from interested PACs and affluent individual contributors. To a considerable extent, the merits of these perceptions are beside the point; popular sensitivities convert them to a loss of confidence in and support for the political system. Once again, *Buckley's* impacts are some of the most difficult ones to measure in any way other than in the usual democratic pressures for change.

As for the effect of the Court's ruling on independent spending, it seemed unimportant until 1996. After the initial flurry of attention to NCPAC in the 1980s, independent spending dwindled and never became a force in federal elections. In 1994 the independent spending, both for and against candidates for the House and Senate, was only $257,000, an infinitesimal figure beside the total of $726 million spent in all of those campaigns. In *Colorado Republican,* however, the Court found constitutional reasons why party committees should be permitted to make independent expenditures. In just a few months the parties made $11.1 million in independent expenditures in the 1996 campaigns for the Congress, eclipsing in those few months all the independent spending of all PACs, other groups, and individuals.

While the invalidation of statutory spending limits once seemed the most serious casualty of *Buckley,* one is less sure in 1999. The

Colorado decision authorizing independent spending by party committees combined with the federal courts' very narrow interpretation of "express advocacy"—both of which brought new kinds of campaigning into the campaign—will probably emerge as the most significant results of *Buckley*. And of those two innovations in First Amendment protections, I suspect the ultimate impact of issue advocacy will be far greater. Even if one assumes that only half of the Annenberg Center's estimated $300 million in issue ads in 1998 targeted congressional candidates, the $150 million total is about thirteen times the $11.6 million in independent expenditures spent to elect or defeat congressional candidates in 1998 (as of reporting by November 23, 1998). Unlike independent spending by parties, issue ads can be bought with soft money and can be employed by virtually any American citizen or group, and need not be reported to the FEC.

In short, *Buckley* permitted an expansion of the perimeters of a congressional campaign well beyond the power and reach of FECA and yet well *within* what both expert and ordinary opinion sees as campaigning. It created new categories of "pseudo-campaigning," done by both old and new types of committees, all of them safely outside the aegis of FECA. The consequences frustrate both the regulators and the public. For the latter, it bears noting that the resulting definition of campaigning has made the campaign finance system even more incomprehensible. And for those in the public able to comprehend it, the redefined reality becomes a cause for cynicism and even amusement. It is not easy to convince them that campaigning is not necessarily campaigning.

So much for the direct effects of *Buckley*, but what of the indirect effects, the effects on the participants in the system—the questions of who has been advantaged, who has been disadvantaged? Among the contributors, those giving large sums are clearly in greater demand at a time of rising spending levels; they enjoy greater leverage in the contributor-candidate relationship, whether or not they choose to use it. Therefore, PACs emerge as the greatest beneficiaries of *Buckley*'s striking of spending limits because of their FECA-conferred contribution limit of $10,000 per cycle and the absence of any limit on their aggregate contributions.

It is much less clear, however, that *Buckley* affected the distribution of campaign money. In simple terms, under FECA the receipts of Republican national party committees have consistently outdistanced those of Democratic committees by significant margins, but that was true also in the decades before 1974. Democratic candidates, on the other hand, maintained a margin of superiority over Republicans for much of the time since 1974, probably because of their control of the House and the Senate for longer periods. The advantage of the Republicans qua party appears when one compares their relative positions before and after the shift in control of Congress in 1994. Republican candidates for the House raised $174.3 million in 1992 against the $217.7 million the Democrats raised, but in 1996 the Republicans outdistanced the Democrats, $266.9 million to $233.1 million.

With that said, however, Republicans probably raise more money for reasons other than *Buckley.* Their party loyalists are on the average more affluent than those of the Democrats, or as the jargon of fundraising puts it, the Republicans have a larger donor base. FECA, passed by a Democratic Congress, was careful to put an annual limit on an individual's contributions to national party committees ($20,000 in aggregate) and on PAC giving to them ($15,000 per national committee). Those limits plus the comprehensive limits on contributions to candidates did not achieve party parity, but they kept Republican dominance under a measure of control. *Buckley* did not disturb those controls. Democrats, in using the power of incumbency and majority status in Congress and the White House, may well have had to work harder to raise competitive sums, however. That problem appears to lie close to the root of the arms race of 1996.

As for the distribution of money among incumbents and challengers, the years of FECA have been years of incumbent riches. For more than a majority of election cycles they enjoyed more than three to one ratios of superiority. Even in the hostile campaign of 1992, House incumbents still enjoyed a 3.1 to 1 margin of superiority over their challengers in money raised during the cycle. Part of this success resulted from the aggressive use of office and access in raising money, but their chief asset was the overwhelming odds of reelection, more than nine to one in House races, for example. The rising tide of money in the system never lifted the challengers until 1994 because they were largely foreordained losers. It was precisely because most open-seat candidates were not doomed to defeat that they consistently, except in overwhelmingly one-party districts, raised average sums of the magnitude that the average incumbent raised.

The incumbent dominance of congressional campaign finance persisted until 1994, but *Buckley*'s role in the dominance was limited. To be sure, the absence of limits on campaign spending may have encouraged incumbents to more aggressive fundraising, and it may also have diminished the perceived chances of challengers to make a competitive race against an incumbent. The political advantages of incumbency, however, largely sprang from other sources—legislative perks such as the franking privilege, easy access to the print and pictures of the media, and the ability to cultivate local support with constituent services and legislative pork.

Buckley's chief initial impact on campaign finance, therefore, was to stimulate the raising of increasing sums of money by creating unlimited opportunities for spending it. To raise ever greater sums, of course, required more and more effort by candidates, inevitably taking time away from the substance of the campaign or the business of public office-holding. At such a time of expanding cash demands, furthermore, the leverage of the contributor increases since candidates find it politically more costly to displease or discourage a contributor.

How was it then that the growth of campaign money stopped in the 1980s for a decade of stability? In part that happened because the surviving sections of FECA still limited contributions; moreover, inflation made those limits progressively more stringent over the life of FECA. More important, perhaps, the stability of the 1980s grew out of the stable two-party politics of the period. It was not until the 1990s that *Buckley* began to influence the distribution of campaign money between the parties and among types of candidates by permitting the creation of new and unregulated contributors and spenders as well as new and protected forms of campaigning. That effect, combined with the new electoral competitiveness of the time, produced the new campaign finance and all the fear and insecurity associated with it.

Beyond its effects on the flow of money within the system, *Buckley* greatly altered the rhetoric and the politics at the intersection of the First Amendment and American campaign finance. It did so by making a statutory-regulatory issue into a constitutional issue, by creating a coalition of First Amendment supporters of the left and anti-government ideologues of the right, and by reducing concerns about equity, accountability, and efficacy in American campaign finance to virtual irrelevance.

In *Buckley* the Supreme Court defined narrow grounds (that is, legitimate interests) to justify limits on the protected transactions of campaign finance. Legislators could act only in instances of "corruption or the appearance of corruption." In this and subsequent cases the Court made it clear that it had a narrow concept of corruption in mind, one centered on some form of a quid pro quo. The Court's definition of legislative authority thus addressed a problem not on the minds of the authors of the FECA revision of 1974 or on the minds of most reformers today, substituting its own choice—corruption.

The Court's focus on corruption may have come from a misreading or misapplication of the old Burroughs[51] precedent, upholding the disclosure requirements in the Federal Corrupt Practices Act of 1925. In that case, the Supreme Court clearly had elections on its mind; for example, "To say that Congress is without power to pass appropriate legislation to safeguard such an election from the improper use of money to influence the result is to deny the nation in a vital particular the power of self protection." The whole opinion is about the power of money to affect elections, not legislatures; it came, of course, at the end of an era in which the buying of votes was not uncommon in the United States, especially in many cities—nor were casting votes from the graveyard, coercing voters, or rigging ballot counts.

Perhaps it is just as important to remember just what the Court did *not* decide in *Buckley*. It bypassed the clear opportunity to concede a legislative interest in protecting the integrity of elections or the electoral process. The Court of Appeals had rested a good deal of its support of FECA precisely on that interest.[52] The Supreme Court's rejection of it makes all the more surprising its acceptance of a public funding program in FECA that limited the amounts and delayed the paying of public funding for qualifying third party presidential candidates. It was a provision intended to discourage third party or independent presidential candidates in the general election, and it can be justified only in terms of protecting the orderliness and efficacy of the American presidential election—that is, the health and integrity of that part of the electoral process.

Finally, the Supreme Court also rejected all egalitarian concerns with a lofty dismissal and an infelicitous formulation of the issue:

The concept that government may restrict the speech of some elements of our society in order to enhance the relative voice of others is wholly foreign to the First Amendment, which was designed "to secure 'the widest possible dissemination of information from diverse and antagonistic sources.' "[53]

All questions of widespread access to candidacy, of candidates contesting on reasonably equal terms, of viable options or alternatives for voters—all the issues so central to the meaning of elections in a mass, popular democracy—were summarily bypassed. And so, too, were the questions of mass support for and belief in a fair and healthy electoral politics.

That issue of the integrity of the electoral processes addresses only the first of the overriding issues in American campaign finance. The second involves the representative processes, especially questions of access to and influence on the policy-making of elected public officials. The public fears undue political influence on public policy and the opportunity for achieving it by funding campaigns for public office. Contributors routinely seek access to public officials whose campaigns they have funded, and those officials and their parties openly offer it in campaigns as an inducement to contribute. Weekend briefings, Washington dinners, even coffee klatches bring contributors together with major party and official figures. Candidates get to know their most generous supporters informally, but very well. As Jonathan Krasno and I have written:

> Regardless of contributors' success or failure in exploiting access, however, the main issue remains the availability of extra opportunities to persuade. Such opportunities resulting from campaign contributions corrupt the central relationship of mass democratic, representative government by permitting some citizens to acquire a preferred representational avenue, to be listened to more promptly or more intently or more often. While it is inevitable in a large popular democracy that influence will not be evenly distributed, it is not inevitable that avenues or opportunities to influence—the very heart of the representational processes—will be skewed by campaign contributions.[54]

In short, the case for a legislative interest in protecting the basic electoral and representational processes of American democracy and for balancing them against the imperatives of the First Amendment is a compelling one.

By rejecting the argument that a legislature must have the ability to protect the core processes of a representative democracy—and by limiting those legislatures to a pseudo-problem of hard core corruption or its appearance—the Court created for campaign finance an application of the First Amendment that was functionally absolute. No matter that the Court long ago rejected the absolutist notion that the First Amendment bars any infringement on speech, that is precisely what we are left with when the Court rejects legislative findings about the need for regulation in favor of a stipulated "legislative interest" that fails to address the problems of the real political world.

Moreover, in so doing, the Court transformed the policy problem and the policy process in campaign finance. Its First Amendment jurisprudence distracts all reformers from the issue of the effectiveness and administrability of proposed legislation and forces them instead to focus on what will pass judicial testing. In some instances, indeed, it has encouraged them to play fast and loose, however unfortunately, with judicial precedents. In others it has forced them to embrace unwanted policy options (for example, public funding) in an effort to achieve top priority goals (for example, spending limits). To make a policy issue, even in part, into a constitutional issue is to alter it fundamentally, at least to the extent of making it less of a policy issue.

Buckley has also reshaped the politics of campaign finance by creating a new and powerful coalition opposed to regulation. It has brought the civil libertarian left into alliance with the libertarian right; the American Civil Liberties Union and the Cato Institute stand shoulder to shoulder in opposition to regulation. Right-to-Life groups, the Christian right, and conservative Republicans now rush to the standard of the First Amendment in opposing the McCain-Feingold reform package in 1997–98 for its attempt to regulate issue ads and soft money. For some of them, surely, it is an embrace of convenience; many admit that they fear the loss of the new opportunities, especially the issue ad option, that flowed to them from the words or logic of *Buckley*. But political advantage aside, to enable regulated interests to shift their defense from self-interest to the much higher ground of constitutional principle is to drastically alter their standing in the debate.

At the same time the invocation of the First Amendment has also neutralized some support for new reform or regulation, especially in the mass media. On one level the media finds campaign finance a difficult story to tell; the relatively bloodless tale of dollar sums and arcane categories of campaign money never had any appeal for consumers of the news and, if truth were told, for many of its reporters. The lack of visual appeal has, moreover, made the story anathema to television. The newly important constitutional dimension to the story only complicates the already complex. Even prestigious newspapers manage to write about the regulatory wreckage in the aftermath of 1996's campaign finance without mentioning the federal courts or the First Amendment.[55] On the editorial level, that constitutional dimension has muted some former support for reform as editorial boards confront the dissonance between their loyalty to the First Amendment and their support for campaign finance reform.

Because campaign finance raises questions of the integrity of elections and the integrity of representative processes, *Buckley* has had an impact on the very nature of American democracy. The impact began by diminishing the power of legislatures to act on what are classic issues of a viable representative democracy—the kind of indirect, representative democracy that the Founding Fathers called a republic. The First Amendment is by its nature anti-government ("Congress shall make no law . . . "), but it does not have to be applied in ways that ignore the wisdom and judgment of elected legislatures in the kinds of political issues they know a great deal about. The Court in *Buckley* undermined legislative authority to regulate campaign finance in another way. It has, willy nilly, come down on the side of a concept of democracy that very much looks like the direct democracy of American populism. Its decisions have stimulated extravagant campaigns on a growing number of ballot issues in the states. Furthermore, the issue ads it protects and thus encourages become issue plebiscites, the more so as the battles of issue ad versus issue ad threaten to overshadow the campaign of the candidates. And what indeed could be more empowering to the direct action of organized interests than to sanction their unregulated campaign messages if only they will place a fig leaf over them? With the flourishing of direct persuasion and direct mobilization in campaigns comes a kind of populism and direct democracy of the affluent. All of these are, in short, new and potent ways around the role of representative institutions.

Ultimately, the dominance of First Amendment concerns over legislative policy on campaign finance may very well lead to proposals for a constitutional amendment restoring some or all of those powers. Already, such respected members of the House as Morris Udall and David Obey have authored amendments to restore pre-*Buckley* powers, although neither their amendments nor others have yet passed either house of Congress. One can, however, imagine a scenario in which, after another scandal of Watergate dimensions and judicial invalidation of radical reform legislation, an amendment restoring Congress's power would have far greater appeal than it has had thus far. The nation might very possibly find itself embroiled in a serious, even perilous debate over amending the First Amendment.

The passage of FECA and the decision in *Buckley* came at an awkward time for constitutional jurisprudence. Great changes in the American political landscape were only in their early stages—the expansion of interest group influence, the alliance of campaigns and the electronic media, the aversion of the electorate to the business and people of politics, the decline of powerful state and local party organizations, the pervasiveness of costly, candidate-centered campaigning. *Buckley,* especially, seems in hindsight crafted for an older, simpler political order, one closer to the elegant campaign speeches of an Adlai Stevenson and the political reserve of a Dwight Eisenhower than to the lavishly financed, media-repetitive attack politics of the 1990s. Perhaps there was no way for the Court to foresee the future, but deciding the fate of campaign reform legislation before it could serve even a single set of campaigns certainly did not help. Not only did the Court lack foresight, it also crafted a precedent without much headroom for new and unanticipated conditions.

To some extent, the Court may also have been lulled into complacency by the early history of compliance with *Buckley.* The campaign finance system and its actors managed to cope with it. There were shudders when the power of PACs increased so dramatically and when independent expenditures caused a flutter for a few years, but matters settled down in the latter 1980s into what appeared to be a stable accommodation between the political world and the Court's vision of the First Amendment. Under later triggering events and conditions, what had been a benign precedent transformed American campaign finance. A constitutional precedent, crafted with little concern for the political realities the Congress was attempting to regulate, failed the tests of adaptation. It now stands as testimony to the danger of the Supreme Court's wandering into the political thicket without a map of the terrain.

2

FREE SPEECH AND THE DIMENSIONS OF DEMOCRACY

Ronald Dworkin

I. INTRODUCTION

AMERICAN POLITICS AT CENTURY'S END

Our politics are a disgrace and money is the root of the problem. In Chapter One Frank Sorauf described an ailing democracy. Our politicians need, raise, and spend more and more money in each election cycle. The candidate who has or raises the most money, as the 1998 midterm elections demonstrated once again, almost always wins. Officials begin raising money for the next election the day after the last one, and often put more time and industry into that task than into those for which they were elected. They spend the bulk of the campaign money they raise, moreover, on television ads that are often negative and nearly always inane, substituting slogans and jingles for argument.

The more money politicians need to be elected, the more they need rich contributors, and the more influence such contributors then have over their political decisions once elected. Federal law does limit how much individual citizens and groups can give to political campaigns. But, as Chapter One shows, new and larger loopholes make these limits less and less effective year by year. In recent years candidates and anxious donors have exploited the "soft money" loophole, which permits donors—not just individuals but corporations and unions, which are otherwise prohibited from making political contributions—to make unlimited donations to political parties or committees. The parties spend that money on so-called issue-advocacy media campaigns that do not technically, in explicit terms, urge a vote for or against any candidate, but praise or denounce candidates with uninhibited vigor, and often end by advising their audience to tell the denounced candidates to mend their ways. Richard Briffault shows, in Chapter Four, how the issue-advocacy device has eviscerated long-standing legal controls on political contributions. In the 1996 presidential election both major party candidates used that loophole to avoid not only the contribution limits but also their legal obligation to observe voluntary spending limits on campaign expenditures in return for federal funding, and the *New York Times* called that election, for that reason, one of the most corrupt in American history.

The staff of the Federal Election Commission recommended that the Clinton and Dole campaigns both be forced to refund contributions, but the full Commission refused to accept the staff's advice, and their decision helps to guarantee that the 2000 presidential election will see yet another major escalation of the "soft money" device. Would-be presidential candidates in both parties have established political action committees of their own so that corporations, unions, and rich private individuals can donate huge sums to run issue ads for them and against their primary or general election opponents.

Other democracies, appalled by the overweening importance of money in American elections, wonder why we do not simply place a ceiling, as they do, on the total amount that a candidate may legally spend in a particular election campaign. The most effective way to prevent money from dominating politics, and to prevent powerful corporations, unions, and other groups from receiving favors for contributions, is to lessen politicians' need for money, and the most effective way to do that is to limit what the politicians may spend. Congress did enact expenditure limits in 1974, following the Watergate scandals. But in just over a year, in *Buckley v. Valeo,* the Supreme Court ruled that expenditure limits are unconstitutional because they violate the First Amendment of the U.S. Constitution, which provides that Congress shall "make no law" abridging the freedom of speech or association. Prohibiting politicians or anyone else from spending as much money as they wish to express their political convictions and policies, the Court said, is restricting their freedom of speech. Several of the essays in this volume, including Richard Briffault's, point out that regulation of campaign expenditures would have raised many problems even if the Court had upheld spending limits. But the experience of the other democracies I just mentioned, which do severely limit election expenditures, shows that such limits are workable.

Many constitutional scholars (though by no means all) believe that the *Buckley* ruling striking down expenditure limits was a mistake, and they hope that it will be overruled. The contributors to this volume have agreed to assume that the decision has indeed been overruled, so that expenditure limits are not automatically deemed unconstitutional: We were asked to consider what regulatory regimes, built around expenditure limits, would then be attractive, effective, and constitutional. I shall begin, however, by exploring one of the premises of that supposition, which is that *Buckley* was so wrong, as a matter of constitutional law, that it should now be overruled after a quarter century of life. For if we are to assume that the decision has been overruled, we must make some further assumptions about the arguments that have led to that result, and we should assume that it has been overruled for the right reasons. It is concededly optimistic to suppose, moreover, that *Buckley* will be flatly overruled, as least for some time. It is more plausible to imagine that as conviction spreads that the decision was a mistake, it will be reinterpreted and narrowed so as to permit more regulation. If so, then the argument that lawyers settle on for regretting the decision will determine the way in which it is narrowed.

The most important reason for pausing over the question why *Buckley* was a mistake, however, is that much of the criticism of the decision ignores the most powerful arguments in its favor. Until we identify those arguments we cannot understand why the decision, which seems so wrong to so many scholars and lawyers, seemed so right to the Supreme Court and to so many other scholars and lawyers who continue to defend it. In fact, the legal and political disagreement over *Buckley* is both deep and important, because whether we think the decision right or wrong depends on how we conceive the character of American democracy and the role of the First Amendment in defending and perfecting that democracy. Our answer to a philosophical question—What is the best conception of democracy?—is likely to be decisive of whether we endorse or reject, not only campaign expenditure limits, but also the other ways of regulating our electoral process that this book explores on the assumption that *Buckley* has been reversed or marginalized.

THE ARGUMENT TO COME: AN ADVANCE SUMMARY

The strongest case for *Buckley*'s ruling that expenditure limits are unconstitutional depends on a popular strategic assumption about the best way to realize and protect democracy. I call this assumption (following the famous federal judge, Learned Hand) the "democratic wager." It holds that democracy is best protected by a principle that forbids government to limit or control political speech in any way for the purpose of protecting democracy. So it forbids laws that attempt to make elections fairer by limiting what rich candidates or parties can spend. That principle may seem paradoxical: How can it improve democracy to prevent government from restricting political speech when government believes that the restriction will itself improve democracy? But the wager supposes that constraints on political speech are likely to harm democracy even when they are enacted with the intent, real or feigned, of improving it. That is what Hand called the bet "on which we have staked our all." So it adopts the prophylactic technique of forbidding government to attempt to make our political system more democratic through that device. Even though government may regulate and restrict speech for other reasons—to protect national security, for example, or private reputation—it cannot regulate or restrict it for that particular reason. As the Court said in *Buckley*, in as explicit a statement of the democratic wager as any in the legal record, restricting "the speech of some elements of our society in order to enhance the relative voice of others is wholly foreign to the First Amendment."

If we accept the democratic wager, then we must acknowledge that very strong argument for the *Buckley* ruling. Should we accept it? Perhaps we should if we conceive democracy, as many political theorists have, only as a political arrangement designed to enforce the will of the majority. But if we reject that majoritarian conception of democracy in favor of a different and more ambitious one that understands democracy as a partnership in collective self-government in which all citizens are given the opportunity to be active and equal partners, then we should reject it. We should adopt instead a more fine-grained and discriminating, though still rigorous, test for deciding when government should be permitted to regulate political speech in the interests of democracy. That test would permit reasonable expenditure limits on political campaigns; it would make plain why *Buckley* was wrong in principle and should now be overruled.

I am not supposing that freedom of speech has only instrumental value, that it is nothing but a means to a more important end. On the contrary, that freedom is in itself a fundamental human right. Free speech and democracy are connected not instrumentally but in a deeper way because the dignity that freedom of speech protects is an essential component of democracy rightly conceived. We cannot hope fully to understand either free speech or democracy, or properly to interpret the First Amendment as part of the Constitution as a whole, unless we interpret those values together, trying to understand the role each plays in a full account of the other.[1] The assumption that the two ideas are bound together in that way is itself part of American constitutional practice: we treat the Constitution as constructing a distinctive form of democracy and we assess the First Amendment as both contributing to and helping to define that form. Of course, free speech serves other purposes as well. Many people suppose, as John Stuart Mill did, that a society that adopts the free market strategy will be more effective in discovering truth, for example, than a society that rejects or qualifies it. But it is the connection between free speech and democracy that has been the nerve of First Amendment jurisprudence.

Since this essay is intended to supply a general jurisprudential background for the other essays in the volume, it must necessarily be somewhat abstract. But I shall try to mitigate the abstraction in two ways. First, I shall describe, at the outset, the general form of various of the proposals that critics have made for reforming American election law. The proposals can serve as both illustrations and tests of principles I discuss, and we can consider, at the end, how we might evaluate these proposals if Buckley were no longer an obstacle to their implementation. (I describe these proposals in very general terms because that is sufficient for that exemplary purpose, but some of them are made more concrete and detailed by other essays in the volume.) Congress is not likely to enact any of these proposals, I fear, in the present political climate. But it will nevertheless be revealing to examine how the choice among the different conceptions of democracy that I shall describe affects the desirability, in principle, of reforms of these different kinds. Second, my discussion must be concrete in another way as well. We need to ask not merely which conception of democracy, and of the role of free speech in protecting democracy, is superior as a matter of abstract political morality, but which conception and role offers a better interpretation of American constitutional and legal practice. So I shall illustrate and refine the theoretical claims by attempting to interpret selected Supreme Court decisions, including but not limited to Buckley, in their light.

II. Proposed Reforms

Familiar proposals for reform can be grouped under four headings.

- *Expenditure caps.* Overall expenditures by parties and candidates should be limited to stipulated sums during each election period. The expenditure ceiling must be generous enough to enable little-known candidates and parties to bring themselves and their positions to the public's attention, but low enough so that candidates and parties without access to enormous funds are not driven from the field.

- *Contributions and coordinated expenditures.* Individuals should continue to be limited in their contributions to political campaigns and parties, and expenditures that are coordinated with a particular candidate's campaign must count against that limit. Coordination is defined, for this purpose, to include any consultation with or solicitation of advice from a candidate's advertising, polling, and strategic organizations, as well as other parts of the campaign staff. The "soft-money" loophole should be eliminated.

• *Independent expenditures.* Individuals and PACs should of course continue to be free to spend their own funds on political advocacy. But during an election period, each individual's expenditure on advocacy that mentions a political party or a candidate for national office should be subject to a further and distinct limit. Such expenditures made during an election period by an advocacy committee or group to which an individual has contributed should be charged, to the extent of that contribution, to that individual's overall limit.

• *Conditional Public Funding for Political Broadcasts.* Generous public campaign funds should be made available to candidates and parties, but only to those who agree not to run, during the election period, ordinary campaign commercials—the short advertisements run in breaks in regular programming on radio or television that have become a staple of our elections. Those who accept such funds would be free, however, to run longer, more substantive political broadcasts on behalf of a candidate or party during that period. Such political broadcasts would be freestanding programs, not broadcast in commercial slots within other broadcasts, of at least three minutes' duration, in which a candidate or officer in a political party speaks to camera or microphone for the bulk of the broadcast. Such funds should be offered, subject to that condition, equally to the major parties, and to other parties in a proportion fixed by evidence of public support.

The first three proposals directly address the role of money in our elections by imposing limits on campaign expenditures and contributions. The fourth proposal goes further, because it imposes conditions designed to affect the form of electronic media politics. It draws a line between some media of expression—television and radio—and the rest, and it aims not just to reduce the impact of money on elections overall, but to improve the character and quality of the political debate by eliminating sound-bite political commercials. The last proposal is therefore more troublesome than the first three, because the

First Amendment is particularly hostile to efforts to regulate the content of political speech, and encouraging politicians to substitute substantive argument for sound bites might be considered an attempt to regulate content. Though expenditure caps do limit the quantity of political speech, they are nevertheless neutral as to the form of the political messages that the permitted expenditures may be used to publish. The conditions imposed in the last proposal are not, however, neutral in that sense. They pick out electronic media for special restriction—not through flat prohibition, to be sure, but as a condition on a public grant—and the restriction is designed to affect the form of political speech by making it more argumentative, though not to discriminate in favor of or against any particular political party or position or conviction. The last proposal raises First Amendment issues that might well be thought grave even if Buckley were overruled.

III. What Is Democracy?

Democracy is extraordinarily popular now, around the world. But people disagree about what democracy is. When these disagreements cross cultures, they are often formidable: some leaders claim, for example, that a one-party state with only state-controlled press and media, whose elections are formalities, comes closest to realizing the democratic ideal. Even within the mature Western democracies, however, the disagreements are considerable. Some Americans believe that judicial review of legislation by courts, which have the power to declare such legislation unconstitutional, undermines democracy; others that judicial review helps to perfect it. Americans and Europeans disagree about whether proportional representation, or federalism, or voter initiatives of various kinds, make representative government more or less democratic.

The near universal agreement that democracy is the only acceptable form of government hides deeper disagreements of that character. Many of the disagreements among constitutional lawyers about the proper understanding of the First Amendment, including the argument about the constitutionality of campaign expenditure limits, are best explained as consequences of these more general disagreements about democracy. Of course, few lawyers have formulated an explicit conception of democracy; they rely on an intuitive sense of what democracy is. But some of these intuitive understandings are strikingly different from others because they differ in the following fundamental respect.

Democracy, we all say, means government by the people rather than by some family or class or some tyrant or general. But "government by the people" can be understood in two radically different ways. On one view—the majoritarian conception—it means government by the largest number of the people. On this majoritarian view, the democratic ideal lies in a match between political decision and the will of the majority or plurality of opinion. We can construct different versions of that general account of democracy. One is a populist version: A state is democratic, according to that version, to the degree to which government enacts the law or pursues the policy that is actually favored by the largest number of citizens at the time. A more sophisticated version of the *majoritarian* conception, however, insists that the majority's opinion does not count as its will unless citizens have had an adequate opportunity to become informed and to deliberate about the issues. A state is democratic, on that more sophisticated account, when its institutions give citizens that opportunity, and then allow a majority of citizens to select the officials whose policies match their will. That sophisticated account is plainly more attractive than the populist one, and I shall have the sophisticated account in mind when I refer, in the rest of this essay, to the majoritarian conception of democracy.

I shall call the rival, very different, conception of democracy the *partnership* conception. According to the partnership conception, government by "the people" means government by *all* the people, acting together as full and equal partners in a collective enterprise of self-government. This is a more abstract and problematic conception than the majoritarian one, and, as we shall see, it is more difficult crisply to state what it takes to be the democratic ideal. But we should note, immediately, one fundamental and relevant difference between the majoritarian and partnership conceptions of democracy.

Citizens play two main roles in a mature democracy. They are, first, the judges of political contests whose verdicts, expressed in formal elections or in referenda or other forms of direct legislation, are normally decisive. *Public opinion* means the relevant opinions of citizens acting in this capacity. Citizens are also, however, participants in the political contests they judge: they are candidates and supporters whose actions help, in different ways, to shape public opinion and to fix how the rest of the citizens vote. The majoritarian conception of democracy pays exclusive attention to the first of these roles. It insists, in the more sophisticated version I described, that, so far as this is feasible, the informed and reflective opinions of the largest number should be decisive of who is elected to government and of what government once elected does. But it says nothing further about the role that individual citizens and groups must be allowed to play in shaping the opinions of others. The partnership conception recognizes both roles, because it supposes that in a true democracy citizens must play a part, as equal partners in a collective enterprise, in shaping as well as constituting the public's opinion.

IV. Democracy and Free Speech

Free Speech and the Majoritarian Ideal

Free speech plays an evident role in the majoritarian conception. That understanding of democracy requires that citizens be given an opportunity to inform themselves as fully as possible and to deliberate, individually and collectively, about their choices, and it is a compelling strategic judgment that the best way to provide that opportunity is to permit everyone who wishes to address the public to do so, in whatever way and at whatever length he wishes, no matter how unpopular or unworthy the government or other citizens deem the message to be. Of course, that strategy cannot be absolute. Free speech must sometimes yield to other values, including security and, perhaps, a private interest in reputation. In such cases, laws forbidding or regulating speech may have the incidental result of influencing the public's verdict on officials or their policies. But this is a regrettable side-effect of constraints adopted for reasons quite independent of that effect.

Regulations that are intended to improve democracy, however, like the various proposals for electoral reform that I described earlier, deliberately aim at changing public opinion in some way. They do not aim that the public reach a different overall verdict in any particular election. But since they attack what they take to be defects in the formation of public opinion, they do aim that the content of public opinion be different from what it would otherwise have been. Reformers want to limit campaign spending, for example, because they think that rich candidates and groups now have too much power to mold public opinion their way. They therefore assume that limiting what the rich can spend would make a difference in what at least some members of the public come to believe or want. Such limits would not, perhaps, favor one party or one political perspective: they might well be, in the language of constitutional lawyers, viewpoint neutral. But they would certainly alter public opinion. That is, after all, their point. So the proposals raise the following question for the majoritarian model: Is it consistent with that conception of democracy to permit legal restrictions that decrease the overall volume of electoral speech when such restrictions have, as their goal, that public opinion be different from what it would be without such restrictions?

The majoritarian conception tests any proposed electoral structure by asking whether that structure reveals what a majority of citizens would choose after the fullest possible opportunity for information and reflection. If we are to make that test workable, however, we need to specify more precisely what conditions provide that fullest possible opportunity. What structure of public debate and argument would be ideal for that purpose? How close does any particular structure come to meeting that ideal?

We might consider a result-oriented answer: ideal conditions, we might say, are those that make it most probable that citizens will vote in accordance with their true or authentic interests. We can make some sense of this suggestion if we limit our concern to citizens' narrow economic interests. We might think that certain tax or other economic policies would actually work against the economic interests of most citizens, for example, even though we know that politicians with enough money to spend on advertising might persuade them of the contrary, and we might intelligibly consider which forms of electoral regulation would best guard against such deception. It is hard to predict what such a result-oriented study might indicate. We might decide, for example, that a scheme that gave all parties and candidates equal time to argue their case would give citizens the best chance of reaching the right conclusions. Or we might reach some more surprising and unattractive conclusion—for instance, that a scheme that disqualified rich candidates from speaking at all would provide the best protection. We need not pursue these possibilities, however, because in any case a result-oriented strategy could not take account of the interests and convictions citizens have beyond their own narrow economic self-interest—it could not take account of their convictions about economic justice, or foreign policy, or abortion, for instance. For it makes no sense to think that there is an underlying fact of the matter about what a particular citizen's true or authentic political or social or moral convictions are, a fact that can be determined without answering a question or voting. Since any such poll or vote must take place after a particular, even if minimal, public discussion, we cannot establish which structure of discussion is most likely to produce true answers without begging the question in favor of some such structure.

So we need a different strategy for refining the test the majoritarian conception deploys, and we must seek this in some combination of two areas: first, assumptions about the conditions of good reasoning generally and, second, assumptions that underlie the majoritarian conception of democracy itself. We know from experience that certain intellectual practices and environments are more likely than others to produce good reasoning about a wide variety of matters. Scientists, historians, and people facing practical decisions all do better, for example, when they base their conclusions on a wide rather than a restricted set of pertinent data, and when they have reflected on and tested these conclusions over time rather than settling on them precipitously. We have no reason not to assume that these general conditions of good reasoning apply to political judgments as well as everything else. So the majoritarian conception can endorse any government intervention in the political process—subsidies for publicizing underfinanced or unpopular opinions, for example—that provides the public with access to information, argument, or appeal that it would not otherwise have.

It might seem tempting to use a similar argument in favor of expenditure limits: we might argue that the public will reason better if it hears no more from one side than from any other. But that argument, on reflection, is very weak. True, we can imagine circumstances in which limiting the advertising of a rich candidate would prevent voters from being misled in some way: such limits might prevent a well-financed candidate from broadcasting mendacious advertisements in so many areas that less-well-financed rivals could not reply to all of them, for example. But we can as easily imagine circumstances in which such limits would prevent some voters from receiving information they would value. Even a political message endlessly repeated on television is seen on each repetition by at least someone who had not yet seen it, and that message might seem valuable to that voter. So we cannot say, in general and in advance, that reducing the overall quantity of political information in order to make the influence of all candidates more equal would improve the ability of voters to think clearly.

In any case we could not support that suggestion, as we can support the idea that the more information voters have the better, by appeal to general principles about good methods of reflection. No scientist or historian or practical decision maker would avoid reading all material arguing for one hypothesis or decision just because more literature was available for that hypothesis or decision than for its rivals, even if he knew that the group that had produced more literature was for some irrelevant reason better financed. He might well take that latter fact into account in evaluating what he read, but he would not limit his reading for that reason. He would trust his own tutored judgment.

It is true that in some contexts—appellate legal arguments and formal debates, for example—each side is given equal time. But those contexts are special in two pertinent ways. First, the overall time set aside for an appellate argument or a formal debate is fixed, so that time taken by one side is necessarily lost by the other. In contrast, though as a practical matter the time any particular voter has available for politics is limited, no such limit is formal or rigid, and allowing rich candidates to broadcast more often does not mean that voters are unable to pay as much attention to whatever advertising a poorer candidate can offer as they could if expenditure were equal. Second, equal-time regulations in legal arguments and formal debates are mainly justified by independent concerns about fairness to the parties or participants: it is fair to the participants that no side have a greater opportunity to make its case than any other. That concern for fairness is distinct from any concern for accuracy or good reasoning. It is recognized by the partnership conception of democracy, but not by the majoritarian conception whose implications we are now considering.

The second body of ideas on which a majoritarian conception might draw to help define ideal conditions of political argument is democratic theory itself. The democratic claim that the people must be left free to judge for themselves, and not have their minds made up for them by any official or caste, means that citizens must have that freedom as individuals. It is not consistent with that assumption to allow the legislature, even representing the will of the majority, to dictate to individual citizens what it is appropriate for them to attend to in considering how to vote. It is not consistent for the legislature to prevent individual citizens from watching as many political advertisements of a particular candidate as that candidate is willing and able to provide. The *Buckley* Court put the point, once again, with the clarity that makes its decision such a crisp endorsement of the majoritarian conception. "In the free society ordained by our Constitution it is not the government, but the people—individually as citizens and candidates and collectively as associations and political committees—who must retain control over the quantity and range of debate on public issues in a political campaign." On the majoritarian conception, the only argument for limiting the quantity of political debate is the paternalistic and unacceptable one that people will think more clearly if government limits what they hear. (No such assumption is necessary on the partnership conception, because that conception justifies expenditure limits by appealing to an independent concern for fairness among political contestants, which that conception—unlike the majoritarian conception—recognizes.)

So neither of the two grounds that a proponent of the majoritarian conception might consider for accepting expenditure limits—general assumptions about the conditions of good reasoning and general presumptions embedded in the majoritarian conception itself—offers any persuasive argument for such limits. On the contrary, together they make a powerful—and some might think a compelling—case for the democratic wager that I described earlier, the wager on which the *Buckley* decision was premised.

THE PARTNERSHIP CONCEPTION: THE THREE DIMENSIONS OF DEMOCRACY

The majoritarian conception of democracy is very popular—it is the conception most frequently endorsed by political scientists and philosophers—and it is therefore hardly surprising that the *Buckley* ruling against expenditure limits should have struck many lawyers and judges as correct. The equally widespread impression that the *Buckley* ruling is wrong, however, suggests that many other lawyers and laymen reject that conception of democracy, at least intuitively. I have elsewhere argued that the majoritarian conception is radically defective. Almost all of us think that democracy is a valuable, even indispensable, form of government. We think that it is worth fighting and perhaps even dying to protect. We need a conception of democracy that matches that sense of democracy's value: We need an understanding that shows us what is so *good* about democracy. The majoritarian conception fails to do this, because there is nothing inherently valuable about a process that allows a larger number of people to impose its will on a smaller number. Majority rule is not fair or valuable in itself: it is fair and valuable only when certain conditions are met, including requirements of equality among participants in the political process through which majority will is determined.

So we must now explore the rival partnership conception of democracy that I briefly described, which insists on recognizing these conditions as essential to true democracy. On the partnership conception, institutions are democratic to the degree that they allow citizens to govern themselves collectively through a process in which each is an active and equal partner.[2] That aim, as I conceded, is a very abstract one, and it might be realized, more or less well, through very different packages of institutions. British democracy is differently structured from American democracy, and both are differently structured from South African democracy. But they all grant some measure of partnership democracy, even though none of them grants a full measure. We test how well any society has succeeded in creating a partnership democracy not by holding its institutions to a single standard, like the standard I constructed to illustrate the majoritarian construction, but against a more complex set of ideals encompassing different dimensions.

The first dimension of partnership democracy is popular sovereignty, which is a relation between the public as a whole and the various officials who make up its government. Partnership democracy demands that the people rather than the officials be masters. The revolutionary slogans that demanded equality when modern democracy began in the eighteenth century had that kind of equality in mind: Democracy's enemy, then, was privilege by inheritance or caste. The majoritarian conception demands popular sovereignty too, but it defines this not as a relation between the people generally and their officials but as the power of the largest number of citizens finally to have their way.

The second dimension of partnership democracy is citizen equality. In a democracy, as I said earlier, citizens though collectively sovereign are also, as individuals, participants in the contests they collectively judge. Citizen equality demands that they participate as equals. The distinct importance of that dimension of equality became evident only later in democracy's story, when it was no longer controversial that the people as a whole rather than some monarch or despot should have the final power of government, but it nevertheless remained unclear how that collective power should be distributed among citizens individually—who should be allowed to vote and speak in the various processes through which collective political decisions are made and public opinion and culture are formed. It is now settled among mature democracies that, in principle, all mature citizens, with very few exceptions, should have equal voting impact.

The majoritarian conception of democracy insists on equal suffrage because only in that way can elections hope to measure the will of the largest number of citizens. The partnership conception insists on equal suffrage too, but it requires that citizens be equal not only as judges of the political process but as participants in it as well. That does not mean that each citizen must have the same influence over the minds of other citizens.[3] It is inevitable and desirable that some citizens will have greater influence because their voices are particularly cogent or moving, or because they are particularly admired, or have devoted their lives to politics and public service, or have taken up careers or investments in journalism. Special influence that is gained in these ways is not in itself incompatible with the partnership understanding of democracy.[4] (On the contrary, democracy could not succeed on its third dimension, which I introduce in the next paragraph, unless it encouraged special influence on at least some of those grounds.) But partnership democracy is damaged when some groups of citizens have no or only a sharply diminished opportunity to appeal for their convictions because they lack the funds to compete with rich and powerful donors. People cannot plausibly regard themselves as partners in an enterprise of self-government when they are effectively shut out from the political debate because they cannot afford a grotesquely high admission price.

The third dimension of democracy is democratic discourse. Genuine collective action requires interaction: if the people are to govern collectively, in a fashion that makes each citizen a partner in the political enterprise, then they must deliberate together as individuals before they act collectively, and the deliberation must center on reasons for and against that collective action, so that citizens who lose on an issue can be satisfied that they had a chance to convince others and failed to do so, not merely that they have been outnumbered. Democracy cannot provide any genuine form of self-government if citizens are not able to speak to the community in a structure and climate that encourages attention to the merits of what they say. If the public discourse is crippled by censorship, or collapses into a shouting or slandering match in which each side tries only to distort or drown out what the others say, then there is no collective self-government, no collective enterprise of any kind, but only vote counting as war by other means.

This brief account of partnership democracy is a tripartite idealization, of course. No nation has achieved or could achieve perfect control of officials by citizens, perfect political equality among citizens, or a political discourse unsullied by irrationality. America does not have full popular sovereignty because our government still has great powers to keep dark what it does not want us to know. We do not have full citizen equality because money, which is unjustly distributed, counts for far too much in politics. We do not have even a respectable democratic discourse: our politics is closer to the war I described than to any civic argument. But we must keep the tripartite ideal in mind in judging, as now we must, what role the First Amendment could sensibly be assigned in improving democracy on the partnership conception, in bringing it at least closer to the unattainable pure case of that form of government.

FREE SPEECH IN A DEMOCRATIC PARTNERSHIP

Each of the three dimensions of a nation's democracy, on the partnership conception, is affected by the constitutional and legal arrangements it makes to encourage and protect political speech.

Popular sovereignty demands that the people rather than officials have final power of government. But if officials are allowed to punish criticism of their decisions as sedition, or to forbid the publication of information that might lead to such criticism, or to shut down new parties or newspapers who might expose their mistakes or crimes, then the people are not, or not fully, in charge. So a constitutional structure that guarantees freedom of speech against official censorship protects citizens in their democratic role as sovereigns.

Free speech helps to protect citizen equality as well. It is essential to democratic partnership that citizens be free, in principle, to express any relevant opinion they have no matter how much those opinions are rejected or hated or feared by other citizens. Much of the pressure for censorship in contemporary democracies is generated not by any official attempt to keep secrets from the people, but by the desire of a majority of citizens to silence others whose opinions they despise. That is the ambition of groups, for example, who want laws preventing neo-Nazis from marching or racists from parading in white sheets. But such laws disfigure democracy, because if a majority of citizens has the power to refuse a fellow citizen the right to speak whenever it deems his ideas dangerous or offensive, then that citizen is not an equal in the argumentative competition for power. We must permit all citizens whom we claim bound by our laws an equal voice in the process that produces those laws, even when we rightly detest their convictions, or we forfeit our right to impose our laws upon them. Freedom of speech enforces that principle, and so protects citizen equality.

Some argue that the expression of opinions derogatory of a race or ethnic group or gender—often called "hate speech"—itself injures citizen equality because it not only offends the citizens who are its targets but also damages their own ability to participate in politics as equals. Racist speech, for example, is said to "silence" the racial minorities who are its targets. The empirical force of that large generalization is uncertain: it is unclear how great an impact such speech has and on whom. But in any case it would be a serious misunderstanding of citizen equality, and of the partnership conception of democracy in general, to suppose that allowing even psychologically damaging political opinions free circulation offends the equality in question. Citizen equality cannot demand that citizens be protected by censorship even from those beliefs, convictions, or opinions that make it more difficult for them to gain attention for their views in an otherwise fair political contest, or that damage their own opinion of themselves. We could not possibly generalize a right to such protection—a fundamentalist Christian, for example, could not be protected in that way—without banning speech or the expression of opinion altogether. We must collectively attack prejudice and bias, but not in that way.

Citizen equality does require, however, that different groups of citizens not be disadvantaged, in their effort to gain attention and respect for their views, by a circumstance as remote from the substance of opinion or argument, or from the legitimate sources of influence, as wealth is. Experience has shown—and never more dramatically than in recent elections—that any group's political success is so directly related to the sheer magnitude of its expenditures, particularly on television and radio, that this factor dwarfs others in accounting for political success. That is the heart of the democratic argument for expenditure limits in political campaigns.

The connection between freedom of speech and the third dimension of democracy—democratic discourse—is also complex. Some regulations of speech that a government might be tempted to adopt, including laws limiting the investigative powers of the media, would damage the democratic discourse by denying it information and diversity. But the degradation of our public discourse by moronic political commercials that make no arguments beyond repetitive slogans and jingles also compromises the argumentative character of our discourse, and certain forms of indirect regulation of that discourse, such as the last proposal in my list, might help to arrest that damage.

So the connection between a constitutional guarantee of free speech and the quality of a partnership democracy, on its different dimensions, is a complicated and delicate one. If we were constructing such a guarantee as part of a new constitution, we would have to choose among three strategies: the democratic wager I described earlier, a "balancing" approach that would permit regulations of political speech that damaged democracy on one of its dimensions but improved it on another when the combined effect was thought to enhance democracy overall, or a more discriminating approach that combined elements of each of these two strategies.

Should we permit a balancing approach that allows regulations that impair democracy on one dimension when these are calculated to improve democracy overall? The case for such balancing might seem, in the abstract, a strong one. A guarantee of free speech cannot, in any case, be absolute: we cannot prohibit otherwise reasonable regulations that are necessary to protect national security or, perhaps, private reputation. We would be likely to sustain regulations for less urgent reasons, moreover: we would presumably permit "time and place" restrictions, like those forbidding broadcasting from sound trucks at night. If constraints like these are acceptable because they serve a useful purpose and do not detract from democracy overall, then why should we not make exceptions for other regulations that actually improve democracy overall?

But there are two powerful answers to that simple argument. First, the different dimensions of democracy cannot be collapsed into one overriding goal that allows trading off violations on one dimension for overall gains. In particular, citizen equality is a matter of individual right, and we could not justify violations of that right—by censoring racists on the ground that this would improve democratic discourse, for example—through any aggregating calculation. Second, any such exception would be peculiarly open to abuse: there would be a standing danger that government would attempt to crush strident new parties or powerful critics in the name of democratic discourse or citizen equality, as, after all, totalitarian governments have often done elsewhere. Congress or a state legislature might disqualify a party whose message it declared dangerous to popular sovereignty because it was confusing, for example.

These fears justify rejecting a balancing strategy. Should we then accept the democratic wager? Are the dangers I just described so great that we should insist that though government may regulate political speech for a number of compelling reasons, it may never do so in order, in its judgment, to improve democracy itself? Our Constitution, we might say, should commit us to the prophylactic judgment that democracy is best served, in the long run, by a rule that forbids government any power to try to improve it, from time to time, by compromising the freedom of people to say what they like when and as often as they like. Justice Scalia set out that argument in characteristically vivid language in 1990. He referred to the idea that "too much speech is an evil that the democratic majority can proscribe," and he declared that that idea "is incompatible with the absolutely central truth of the First Amendment: that government cannot be trusted to assure, through censorship, the 'fairness' of political debate."[5] If we accepted this caution, we would make the democratic wager part of our constitutional law.

This argument for the democratic wager has two parts. The first is a diagnosis of danger: that the most significant threat to democracy, even now, lies in government's desire to protect itself, and to cheat citizens of their democratic sovereignty, by filtering and choosing what the public may watch or read or learn, and by attempting to justify that illegitimate control by claiming, as many tyrannies have indeed claimed, that this control is necessary to protect democracy on some other dimension. The second part is a maxim of strategy: it supposes that the best protection from that threat lies in prophylactic overkill, that is, in a doctrine that absolutely forbids government to appeal to that kind of justification for constraining speech even when the legitimacy of the appeal seems obvious. But though history supports both the plausibility of that fear and the wisdom of such a strategy, we can no longer afford to ignore the opposite dangers—particularly in the electronic age—of a wholly unregulated political discourse. We must compare the danger that a less rigid constitutional guarantee will allow an ingenious government to cheat the public of information and argument it should have, even if the courts are vigilant to prevent such abuse, with the rival danger that more rigid protection will allow wealth and privilege grossly undemocratic power, and allow the political discourse to be so cheapened as to lose its argumentative character altogether.

The signs of exactly that decay are now too obvious to be set aside: we have as much a parody of democracy as democracy itself. In the 1996 and 1998 elections, political expenditures ballooned to formerly incredible sums, and politicians at every level, including the president and vice president, were forced to abase themselves before rich donors. Politicians continue the relentless and draining chase for money even while they call for rules that would make this unnecessary. For many politicians the situation is a classic prisoners' dilemma. Each would prefer expenditures to be limited, but if they are not limited, each must struggle to raise and spend as much as possible. Poorer would-be candidates are driven from the field at every level, and groups representing convictions unpopular among the rich are not able even to begin assembling wide political support. Elected officials must begin the search for fresh money the morning after their election, as I said, and the intense and continuing effort seriously erodes the time they have for the public's business. The money these politicians raise is spent under the direction of pollsters and consultants who have no interest in principle or policy and whose skills lie only in the seduction of consumers by repetition, jingle, and sound bite.

The consequence is the most degraded and negative political discourse in the democratic world. Public participation in politics, measured even by the number of citizens who bother to vote, has sunk below the level at which we can claim, with a straight face, to be governing ourselves. The public traces its own disaffection to the process itself: it reports that the power of money in politics has made it cynical and that the coarseness of television politics has made it sick. The prophylactic overkill of the democratic wager is now far too expensive in genuine democracy. It is now foolish rather than cautious, blind rather than wise.

So we have powerful grounds for trying to construct a strategy for the protection of political speech that has something of the flexibility but not the danger of the balancing strategy. The *discriminating* strategy (as I shall call it) acknowledges that danger and forbids any regulation of speech that appreciably damages either citizen sovereignty or citizen equality. It does not allow government to compromise popular sovereignty by forbidding the press to discuss the sexual lives of officials, for example, even though it is highly plausible that the third dimension of democracy—democratic discourse—would be improved by that constraint. It rejects, as incompatible with citizen equality, the argument I mentioned that racist or sexist speech should be forbidden in an effort to avoid "silencing" minority groups or women or to improve the character of political discourse.[6]

But the discriminating strategy does permit regulations of political speech that improve democracy on some dimension when the defect that they aim to repair is substantial, and when the constraint works no genuine damage to either citizen sovereignty or citizen equality. So it permits ceilings on campaign expenditures when these help repair significant citizen inequality in politics, provided the ceilings are set high enough so that they do not dampen criticism of government, and so that no new inequality is introduced by foreclosing unfamiliar parties or candidates.

V. The Legal Record

The Issue Framed

I have been examining the philosophical basis for the "democratic wager" on which the Supreme Court based its *Buckley* ruling. That prophylactic strategy flows naturally from the majoritarian conception that takes the nerve of democracy to lie in government according to the informed and reflective will of the majority. Some critics of *Buckley* have said that the decision represents a return of the *Lochner*[7] mentality that once led the Supreme Court to reject progressive social and economic legislation on the ground that people had a right to use their property and spend their money as they wished. But the *Lochner* analogy misunderstands the true appeal of the prophylactic reading, which rests, not on the almost universally rejected view that people with money should always be free to spend it as they wish, but on the much more popular idea that democracy means government by majority will. If democracy has only that single dimension, then the democratic wager might well be deemed a good bet.

The majoritarian conception is not, however, the only available conception of democracy. The partnership conception is a more attractive alternative: that conception offers at least three dimensions on which democracy must be tested, and it recommends not the democratic wager but the more discriminating interpretation of free speech that I described. If we were constructing a new constitution, on a clean slate, we would have powerful reasons for constructing it with a partnership democracy in mind, and for drafting a discriminating protection of free speech. But we are not drafting a new constitution. We are attempting to interpret the Constitution we have, and the history of practice and adjudication under it. So we must ask: Which conception of democracy provides a better interpretation of our own constitutional structure and practice?

I have elsewhere argued that the partnership conception does, because that conception explains, while the majoritarian conception cannot, the Constitution's provision of individual rights against a democratic majority. True, some of those rights could be explained as necessary to create and protect even a majoritarian democracy.[8] If we read the First Amendment as incorporating the democratic wager, then we could treat a citizen's right to free speech as a right protecting a majoritarian democracy in spite of the fact that it limits what a democratic majority can do. But the Constitution contains individual rights—like the right to equal protection of the laws as this has been interpreted by the courts—that cannot be reconciled with the majoritarian conception of democracy in that way.

We would do well, however, for this occasion, to frame our interpretive question more narrowly. We should confine ourselves to First Amendment jurisprudence and distinguish between two readings of the free speech clause. The first is a prophylactic reading modeled on the democratic wager. It declares that political speech may never be restricted or regulated in the interests of democracy. The second is a more flexible reading drawn from the partnership conception. It allows regulation of free speech that improves citizen equality provided it meets the rigorous standards of the discriminating strategy that I described. Which of the two readings seems better to explain what the Constitution says or what the courts have done about free speech?

TEXT AND RHETORIC

We get little help, in choosing between those two interpretive readings, from the Constitution's text. The First Amendment provides that "Congress shall make no law . . . abridging the freedom of speech." It is possible to read that language in an absolutist way as forbidding regulation of speech for any reason whatsoever. But both the democratic wager and the discriminating strategy reject that absolutist interpretation, as do almost all scholars and judges, and the text provides no further guidance as to the choice between those two readings. If the text permits regulation of speech to protect national security, or the peace and quiet of neighborhoods, then it also permits, just as a matter of the bounds of language, regulation to protect or perfect democracy.

Nor is judicial rhetoric decisive in either direction. The flat declaration in *Buckley* that concerns for equality are "foreign" to the First Amendment is, as I said, a clear endorsement of the democratic wager. But we can find even better-known statements that equally clearly endorse the rival discriminating strategy. Chief among these is Justice Brandeis's famous statement in his *Whitney* opinion.

> Those who won our independence believed that the final end of the state was to make men free to develop their faculties, and that in its government the deliberative forces should prevail over the arbitrary. They valued liberty both as an end and as a means. They believed liberty to be the secret of happiness and courage to be the secret of liberty; . . . that the greatest menace to freedom is an inert people; that public discussion is a political duty; and that this should be a fundamental principle of the American government.[9]

This statement recognizes the importance of popular sovereignty. But it also lays particular emphasis, as part of an overall justification of the First Amendment, on the other dimensions of democracy: on the importance of citizen equality and, above all, on the value of a deliberative democratic discourse. It declares that the point of freedom of speech is not just to stop government from oppressing the people but to allow individual citizens to develop their faculties, that liberty is for this reason a democratic end as well as a means to other democratic purposes, and that civic deliberation with others is a "political duty" that stands beside the duty, as citizen-sovereign, to vote. It would be bizarre to accept that strong endorsement of the varied goals of the First Amendment and yet to insist that it must never be interpreted or applied to further those goals.

So we must look beyond text and rhetoric to evaluate our rival readings as interpretations of judicial practice. We must look to the actual decisions in those cases in which the two readings compete. There are not many such cases: most First Amendment decisions are consistent with both readings. Both readings justify *New York Times v. Sullivan,*[10] the *Pentagon Papers* decision,[11] the *Skokie* case,[12] the flag-burning cases,[13] and most of the other great First Amendment landmarks. I shall concentrate on a number of those relatively few cases in which the two readings do pull in opposite directions, to see which reading's gravitational force proved the stronger in each case. That question is not settled by the language of the opinions in question, which almost never addresses our question directly. We shall have to look at what American courts have actually done in these cases, against the background of the facts presented to them, to judge which of the two readings better explains what they did.

CONTRIBUTION LIMITS

As we have already seen, one part of *Buckley*—its holding that expenditure caps are unconstitutional—is supported only by the prophylactic reading. The Court declared, in its argument for that holding, that the purpose of the First Amendment is limited to protecting popular sovereignty—to providing the public with "the widest possible dissemination of information from diverse and antagonistic sources"—and it specifically rejected the argument that government could regulate speech to protect citizen equality. We must take the same view of some of *Buckley*'s progeny—the cases, like *Colorado Republican*,[14] that were decided by appealing to that *Buckley* ruling as a precedent.

But another ruling was also part of the *Buckley* decision—the Court's ruling that permitted Congress to impose limits on the contributions that people might make to political campaigns of others—and that ruling is just as much a part of the constitutional record. It presupposes not the prophylactic but the discriminating reading, because it can be justified only on the assumption that Congress has the power to limit the political activity of some people in order to safeguard the citizen equality of others. The Court denied this rationale for its decision: it said that preventing people from speaking indirectly, by contributing as much as they wish to help finance the speech of other people, is different from preventing them from spending their own money to speak for themselves, and that contribution limits were therefore subject to a lower constitutional standard than expenditure limits. But that supposed distinction is illusory, as Justice Thomas pointed out forcefully in the *Colorado Republican* case.

The most effective means most people have of expressing their political convictions is contributing to an organization or campaign dedicated to publicizing or acting on those convictions. Contribution limits offer as great—or as little—a threat to popular sovereignty as expenditure limits. If the rich are prevented from contributing all they would wish to political campaigns, then politicians will not be able to broadcast their messages as often as they would like, and citizen-sovereigns will not hear a message they would otherwise have heard. Government would have limited the flow of campaign information and appeal just as directly as it would have done had it limited what the politicians might spend. Though contributors conceivably could spend as much in other ways and forums as they would have contributed to particular campaigns, had they been allowed to do so, few are likely to take up that option—for a variety of reasons, including the evident fact that independent expenditures are less likely to attract the gratitude of powerful public officials. Nothing in the prophylactic reading justifies testing laws limiting political contributions by a less exacting standard than laws limiting direct expenditures.

The conclusion that many commentators have reached—that the *Buckley* Court sought a compromise by striking down expenditure limits and accepting contribution limits—seems irresistible. But it was a compromise of the wrong kind, a checkerboard compromise that applies one reading of the First Amendment to the first of these issues and a different reading to the other. The *Buckley* decision, which in one aspect is the strongest available authority against the discriminating reading, is in its other aspect a strong argument for it.

FAIRNESS DOCTRINE

The First Amendment is pertinent not only when government seeks to stop publishers from printing or broadcasting what they wish, but also when it forces them to publish what they otherwise would not, because in such a case government also intervenes in the political discourse by altering what information is available to citizens, and that, too, offends the principle of popular sovereignty that government must not choose what citizens hear. In *Red Lion*,[15] however, the Supreme Court upheld the FCC's "fairness doctrine" then in force, which required broadcasters who chose to editorialize on a controversial political issue to present opposing views as well. The Court cited the "First Amendment goal of producing an informed public capable of conducting its own affairs," and said that it was perfectly consistent with that goal for government to require more balanced programming. That idea fits comfortably with the discriminating reading of the First Amendment. But it is anathema to the prophylactic reading, because it rests on exactly the kind of judgment—that citizens are better informed and more responsible if opposing views are presented to them by the same broadcaster than if they are left to seek out opposing opinions on their own if they so wish—that the prophylactic reading condemns.

It is often said, however, that the *Red Lion* decision was based on what is called a "scarcity" rationale: that because only relatively few broadcast stations can operate within any particular geographical area, government has a stronger interest in forcing those few outlets to broadcast opinions contradicting their own. If so, then the decision would be inapplicable in the cable and satellite age, when a much larger number of outlets is available throughout the country. But a concern for scarcity could not have figured in the decision in any way that suggests a prophylactic reading, because scarcity is not pertinent under that reading. If it is in principle wrong for government to attempt to control the flow of political information and argument to the public, then the fact that the outlets it seeks to control are scarce, or that it has licensed the use of those outlets, would be beside the point. For it would nevertheless be government that had decided what information and argument would flow out of that scarce medium rather than the combined force of individual decisions. Since government had the option of licensing broadcast bands without such intervention, the First Amendment, on the prophylactic reading, would demand that it do so.

In fact the Court cited scarcity only to support the proposition that entry in the broadcast medium is very expensive—it cited the commanding position of early entrants, which, it said, was minatory even when gaps in the spectrum were still available. But of course speakers who are denied the use of television for these economic reasons are free to seek other, less scarce and in any case less expensive media through which to publish their views. The Court's argument actually depended on the assumption, almost explicit in its opinion, that it is unfair and undemocratic when access to a medium so dominant in politics as broadcasting had become is restricted—*either* by license grant or by economic power—to a very few and therefore very powerful people, and that government therefore had a right to intervene to make the political process more equal. The decision presupposes the discriminating reading: that citizen equality in politics is so central to the Constitution's overall conception of democracy that the First Amendment must recognize that improving equality is sometimes a compelling reason for appropriate regulation.

Of course it does not necessarily follow, even if we accept the discriminatory reading, that the *Red Lion* Court correctly applied that reading. Someone might argue that citizen sovereignty is significantly impaired when broadcast editorialists are dissuaded from stating controversial opinions because it would be expensive or otherwise distasteful for them to allow conflicting views to air, and that the decision was wrong, even assuming the discriminating reading, for that reason. That is not a powerful argument in the case of broadcast companies, whose editorial content rarely constitutes a significant part of their programming in any case, however, and I believe that the decision was correct. In other circumstances, however, such an argument would be more persuasive: in the *Tornillo* case,[16] for example, the Court struck down a Florida law requiring newspapers to grant equal space for a response by candidates they had criticized. Since judges might well think that such a law would have a chilling effect on the critical zeal of newspaper editors, that decision is consistent with the discriminating reading as well as the prophylactic one.

MUST CARRY RULES

In the two *Turner* decisions,[17] the Supreme Court upheld so-called must carry regulations requiring cable companies, under certain circumstances, to carry broadcast stations. Justice Breyer provided the swing vote in a 5–4 decision in *Turner II*, and he began his analysis by remarking that First Amendment interests were to be found on both sides of the case. It is difficult to make sense of that claim on the prophylactic reading. The First Amendment, on that reading, commits the nation to the strategy of protecting democracy by keeping government out of the various decisions that determine what the public is offered by way of speech. If so, then there is a First Amendment issue only on one side—on the side of the cable companies who wish to be free of government's interference in their decision as to what mix of programming to offer; the consideration Breyer stressed—that requiring cable companies to carry broadcast stations improves political discourse because it provides local news and argument that cable subscribers would otherwise have to seek elsewhere—is irrelevant.

According to the discriminating reading, however, Breyer was right, because that reading acknowledges the democratic importance of informed discourse and accepts that government may intervene in media decisions to help secure it. He embraced the discriminating view when he declared that the policy in question "seeks to facilitate the public discussion and informed deliberation which, as Justice Brandeis pointed out many years ago, democratic government presupposes and the First Amendment seeks to achieve." He underlined his reliance on the discriminating reading, moreover, by citing not only Brandeis's *Whitney* opinion but *Red Lion* as well.

It is true that Breyer's was only one opinion in *Turner II*, and that he did not participate in *Turner I*. But his opinion makes much more sense than the plurality's opinion, which relied on economic analysis, as Justice O'Connor remarked in her dissenting opinion in *Turner II*. The complicated *Turner* litigation is best read, overall, as recognizing one of the most basic claims of the discriminating reading: that government may intervene in the powerful electronic media in order to improve the public political discourse when the intervention favors no point of view, popular or unpopular, and does not otherwise compromise citizen sovereignty or citizen equality.

Campaign-free Polling Zones

In *Burson*,[18] the Supreme Court upheld state election laws forbidding political canvassing on election day within a stipulated distance from polling places. Though the Court attempted to justify its decision in the way that a prophylactic reading of the First Amendment would require, the decision can in fact be supported only on a discriminating reading. The Court said that barring political speech from a large area around voting booths on election day was not neutral, because it touched only political and not other forms of speech or solicitation. But it also said that the regulations met the exacting "compelling justification" standard for overriding the First Amendment's prohibition on such content-sensitive regulation, because a state has a compelling interest in election procedures that eliminate intimidation. This argument has the right form for the prophylactic reading because it does not appeal to informed discourse, or to any other dimension of democracy, to justify a constraint on political speech. It appeals instead to people's distinct interest in not being intimidated.

But though that argument has the right prophylactic form, it is a silly argument, and it was properly ridiculed by Justices Stevens, O'Connor, and Souter in their dissent in the case.[19] The state did not need to prohibit political speech over an area of 30,000 square feet (or, in the case of some states, over 750,000 square feet) in order to prevent intimidation. Once again, the decision is much better justified if we suppose that the Court actually rejected the prophylactic reading and embraced the discriminating one. If we read the First Amendment to permit regulations of speech that further its assumed goal of protecting democracy, by improving citizen equality or the character of political discourse, the case becomes an easy one. It is fairer to citizens as participants not to allow any candidate or group the special and unseemly advantage of a last-second appeal at the crucial moment of voting, and it improves democratic deliberation to allow citizens a space for final reflection, free from importuning, before they vote—to allow them freedom *from* politics when that freedom is most important.

The First Amendment, on the discriminating reading, does not prohibit government from intervening to aid citizens in that way, so long as such regulations do not offend the core principles of political impartiality or any other aspect of popular sovereignty. The importance of that qualification is underscored by an earlier decision in which the Supreme Court struck down a state law that might initially seem similar to the one it upheld in *Burson*. In *Mills v. Alabama*,[20] the Court declared unconstitutional a law forbidding newspapers to publish editorials endorsing or opposing any candidate on election day. That law would have deprived citizens of a traditional source of political argument and advice that could be read and reflected on at home, away from the bustle of the actual voting booth, even on election day. Its impact on consumer sovereignty was therefore greater, and its contribution to deliberative deliberation nonexistent.

CORPORATE ELECTIONEERING

In *Austin v. Michigan Chamber of Commerce*,[21] the Court upheld a statute that prohibited corporations from using their general assets to support or oppose political candidates, though it permitted them to use segregated funds they raised expressly for political purposes. The Court's argument almost explicitly endorsed the discriminating reading and rejected the prophylactic one. It conceded that, according to *Buckley*, states need a "compelling" interest to justify constraints on political speech, and acknowledged that the only such interest recognized in that case was an interest in protecting against corruption. But, the Court said in *Austin*, the kind of "corruption" that states may guard against is not limited to the familiar contribution-for-favors kind, but also includes "a different kind of corruption in the political arena: the corrosive and distorting effects of immense aggregations of wealth that are accumulated with the help of the corporate form and that have little or no correlation to the public's support for the corporation's political ideas."

The "distortion" in question has nothing to do with the familiar kind of corruption. It is not a compromise of popular sovereignty: the fact that a political commercial has been paid for by a corporate contribution does not make the information or appeal it contains any less valuable to the public watching that commercial. The "corrosive" impact of large corporate spending is entirely its impact on citizen equality, that is, on the dimension of democracy that *Buckley*'s prophylactic interpretation of the First Amendment declared irrelevant. Nor does it matter, from the perspective of that prophylactic understanding, how the corporation's profits are earned. It is irrelevant, on that understanding, that these profits do not reflect popular political convictions: the value of the information to the public as sovereign is the same whether the corporate contributions are from a segregated political action fund or from the corporation's general treasury. That is not, however, irrelevant to the discriminating reading, because that reading permits government to regulate electoral speech so as to protect citizen equality when the regulation does not damage democracy on any other dimension, and citizen equality is seriously impaired when corporations are free to use their vast general wealth to wield political influence that few if any individual citizens can.

The discriminatory reading provides not only a persuasive justification for *Austin,* but also a persuasive distinction between that decision and an earlier decision that has struck many commentators as contrary to *Austin* in spirit. In the *Bellotti*[22] case, the Court declared unconstitutional a Massachusetts statute forbidding corporations to spend any funds at all campaigning for or against a state ballot initiative. That restriction posed a much more serious threat to citizen sovereignty than the statute upheld in *Austin* did, because it threatened to deprive citizens of information that might not otherwise be available to them. Many ballot initiatives concern complex economic issues, and corporations often have an incentive that individuals lack for presenting a particular side of the argument. The *Bellotti* statute did not allow such corporations even the use of segregated funds raised specifically to present that argument. The *Austin* statute, on the contrary, was limited to elections, in which political parties and other groups have a lively interest in offering any argument for their candidates and against their opponents, and it did permit corporations the use of segregated funds to make whatever case for or against a candidate they believed had not been effectively made by others.

VI. The Epistemic Argument

So the discriminating reading that I associated with the partnership conception of democracy fits the pertinent precedents as well as the prophylactic reading associated with the majoritarian conception. If the analysis of the last section is sound, it fits those precedents, on the whole, even better. Constitutional interpretation, however, is not just a matter of fit: a compelling interpretation should not only fit the record but justify it as well. Is the prophylactic or the discriminating reading superior on that score? It is true that the discriminating reading is at least marginally more open to abuse by a government anxious to protect itself from criticism or to solidify its position. Such a government might regulate political speech claiming to protect democracy when it is really only protecting itself. But the discriminating reading runs no serious risk of such abuse, because, unlike the balancing reading I distinguished, it does not permit regulations of political speech that damage either citizen sovereignty or citizen equality in any significant way, and, in any case, the risk of abuse is more than outweighed, as I said earlier, by the evident damage to democracy that the prophylactic reading requires us to bear.

But the prophylactic reading might seem more appealing for a very different reason. It is a popular rationale for the First Amendment that freedom of speech helps the public not only to govern but also to discover the truth about how best to govern. Proponents of that claim often refer to John Stuart Mill's argument that a competition of ideas, from which no idea is excluded, is the best means of discovering truth across both science and value—not just truth about what people want but truth about what they should want. The prophylactic reading seems more deeply committed to such a competition, because it rejects any regulation of speech in the supposed interests of improving democracy. So Mill's epistemic hypothesis might seem to argue for that reading. In fact, however, both readings find support in Mill's epistemic claim, though the claim takes different forms in the two readings and is actually more plausible under the discriminating reading than the prophylactic one.

If we accept Mill's claim as a justification for the prophylactic reading, we must take that claim to endorse the sheer *quantity* of speech as having, in itself, epistemic value. On this view, the value of a public debate is overall improved, at least in the long run, by enforcing the principle that the more speech-acts the better, so that repetitions of substantially the same claims or ideas are to be valued as contributing, at least marginally, to the epistemic promise of the debate, and by rejecting any qualification of that principle designed to improve the *quality* of the argument. If we offer the claim as a justification for the discriminating reading, on the other hand, we emphasize the epistemic importance of a principle holding, not that no speech-act be excluded, but that no *idea* be excluded. On this different view, what is important is the cognitive and emotional mix of what is presented, not the quantity in itself, and it is mix rather than quantity that is served when we declare, as the discriminating reading does, that no speech may be censored or constrained because what it says or expresses is deemed dangerous or offensive. Rigorously enforcing *that* principle is the best way of ensuring that the debate is exposed to the widest variety of ideas possible; it is not also necessary to maximize the sheer quantity of speech.

The discriminating reading permits an expanded and even more plausible epistemic claim to be made, moreover, which is that a discourse from which no idea is formally excluded is even more likely to secure truth if the discourse is further structured to encourage ideas to be inspected on their merits. The prophylactic reading cannot make that expanded claim because it insists on the sole epistemic virtue of the highest quantity of speech unstructured by any regulation at all. That idea—that quality as well as quantity counts—is widely accepted in other contexts, as in appellate arguments or formal debates where we insist on argument rather than multimedia performances. The prophylactic model, on the contrary, places all its epistemic eggs in one unsound basket: it must rely, for any claim that its rigidity serves the discovery of truth, on the hugely doubtful assumption that an unstructured debate is more effective as a means of discovery than a structured one with just as many ideas but fewer speech-acts.

VII. THE PROPOSALS REVISITED

The discriminating reading of the First Amendment allows legislation that limits and regulates political speech when such legislation does not keep information or argument from the public that would otherwise be available to it, when it is not designed to favor government or to favor any party or ideology or policy over any other, when it does not reflect any assumption about the truth, falsity, danger, or offensiveness of any message or display, and when it is likely to improve the democratic character of public political discourse by making participation available to more citizens on an equal footing, or by improving the quality of public discourse, or both.

It would be difficult to defend the constitutionality of any of the proposals set out at the start of this essay, including the limits on campaign contributions already in force, if we accepted the prophylactic reading of the First Amendment. We must now examine those proposals against the discriminating reading I have been defending. It might be helpful to notice, first, that though some of the proposals might seem radical to Americans, they are familiar in other democracies. Adopting all the proposals would make the American system much more like the British electoral scheme, for example, which according to general international opinion works very well. It is true that elections in a parliamentary system, with strong party control, are in many ways different from those in our own complex federal system, which separates executive and legislative offices. But the differences do not defeat the comparison. President Clinton, calling for campaign reform, recently suggested that the election in which Tony Blair defeated John Major was both fairer and better reasoned and argued than the one in which he defeated Robert Dole.[23] The proposals would also bring our electoral system closer to those in place in the other major democracies. None of these allows unlimited expenditure, and all regulate television and radio politics.

The proposals that limit campaign expenditures are, of course, contrary to the *Buckley* holding. The premise of this book is that *Buckley* has been overruled. If we presume that it has been overruled in deference to the discriminating reading, then the First Amendment would permit expenditure ceilings high enough so that they do not increase the advantage that incumbents already have over challengers and do not prevent candidates with no name recognition or groups with novel policies from securing enough public interest to engage the attention of journalists and other broadcasters. Unless these conditions were satisfied, expenditure limits would compromise citizen equality, and they would injure popular sovereignty, too, because the public would be denied the ideas that such candidates or groups would offer if they could. The discriminating reading does not permit significant damage to any dimension of democracy. In Chapter Five, Burt Neuborne suggests, in fact, that *Buckley* was probably right on its facts: The limits Congress imposed in the 1974 Act that the Court struck down would not have been enough, he points out, to allow the purchase of a single quarter-page ad in the *New York Times*. We should therefore assume that any overruling decision would insist that the limits be reasonable and fair to challengers and unknown candidates.

The final proposal grants generous public funds for political campaigns but prohibits candidates who accept those funds from running political commercials on radio and television, except in the form of political broadcasts whose format encourages argument and discourages subliminal and other nonargumentative techniques. This proposal is more novel and unsettling, and would be controversial even if the discriminating reading had been recognized and adopted. It is true that the legislation would prohibit nothing. It would merely impose conditions on the use of public funds and leave any politicians who prefer to pay for ordinary political commercials out of their limited campaign budgets free to do so by refusing any public funds. But the pressure on both candidates and broadcasters to accept the public's shilling would be so strong, particularly on the assumption that other candidates and broadcasters have done so, that the conditions imposed would have a coercive bite. The discriminating reading therefore requires proponents of these proposals to show that they would not, in practice, damage democracy on any of its dimensions.

It might be objected, for example, that a grant program that imposed such conditions would offend citizen sovereignty because it would induce politicians not to produce political appeals in the form that the public prefers. After all, politicians swamp programming with thirty-second negative sound bites, not out of personal taste, but because they judge that such advertising has the most impact. We must be careful to distinguish, however, between what the public deems appropriate by way of political discourse and what it in fact responds to—the advertising industry is largely built on the difference between these two phenomena. We learn, from polls as well as politicians, that the public disapproves the genre of political commercials, and that distaste, as I said, is thought to be in part responsible for the alienation of so many people from politics.

That does not, however, fully answer the objection, because it remains true that in consequence of the condition imposed on public financing, at least some people will not have political appeals available to them in the volume and form they prefer and that politicians would otherwise provide. But it is a mistake to think that citizen sovereignty, or either of the other two dimensions of democracy, requires that every citizen be entitled to receive political information in his preferred form. Even on the prophylactic reading, government is permitted to regulate the "time, place and manner" of political appeals. Some citizens might prefer political appeals delivered by sound truck at home at three o'clock in the morning: that might fit their occupational schedule or diurnal rhythm perfectly. But democracy is not compromised by regulations that make that unlikely or impossible, so long as these regulations in no way diminish the information that is ultimately and reasonably available to each citizen. The political broadcast regulations I described have only the same limited effect. They do not diminish the information or argument that will be available to any citizen who is willing to make a reasonable effort, by tuning in on political broadcasts at the scheduled time, or by watching other election coverage, to learn what a candidate or group has to say. The First Amendment hardly demands, on any reading, that a citizen too unconcerned to make that effort must be offered a cheap and inadequate substitute in time-out commercials while watching his favorite football team at work.

It might now be said, however, that the restrictive conditions on the use of public funds for electronic politics, which are designed to make politics more argumentative, offend citizen equality because they are not after all neutral among political perspectives. They favor an elitist form of political discourse. Once again, however, we must be careful not to misunderstand the form of neutrality that citizen equality, properly understood, demands. It does not demand that political procedures be constructed so that bad arguments can be as effective as good ones and jingles as powerful as reasons, or so that candidates without knowledge or convictions or qualifications have maximal opportunity to hide those embarrassing failings. The neutrality at which we should aim is almost exactly the opposite: it requires a scheme that allows citizens to judge the structure, merits, and appeal of all candidates and ideas, including the worst financed and initially most unpopular of these, and the proposed scheme would serve that conception of neutrality much more effectively than unregulated television and radio politics can. I do not mean now to claim that the discriminatory reading would plainly permit that scheme, but only that the argument that it should is both more complex and plausible than it might first appear to be.

VIII. Conclusion

I began by reporting the widespread view that our democracy has been seriously damaged by the curse of money. We can use the different dimensions of the partnership conception of democracy that we have now distinguished to make that charge more explicit. It is not obvious that unlimited campaign expenditures, which give the rich more influence in politics because they can finance vast media advertising campaigns, offend citizen sovereignty. Their money is spent in forming majoritarian opinion, not in evading what majority opinion commands. It is arguable that vast disparities of wealth can mislead the public into thinking it wants what is not in its real economic interests, narrowly defined, to want. But we have no basis for supposing that its votes would more accurately reflect its authentic overall convictions if campaign expenditures were limited, in part because we have no independent way of defining or discovering those authentic convictions. So if popular sovereignty were our only concern it would seem reasonable to allow the public as much information or advertising as anyone wished and was able to supply to it, and then to rely on the public to discount repetitive or misleading messages, and to seek out information about small and underfinanced candidates through journalism and less expensive media like small cable stations. Popular sovereignty is not threatened by such a policy, and whatever appeal the *Buckley* ruling has lies in the policy's apparent reasonableness.

When we adopt the partnership conception of democracy, however, we add two more dimensions to the democratic metric, and on each of these two further dimensions the defects of our present democracy are evident. Citizen equality is destroyed when only the rich are players in the political contest, and no one could mistake our huckster politics for democratic deliberation. The partnership conception makes plain, too, what is at stake in these defeats. We take pride in the democratic legitimacy of our form of government: we pride ourselves that ours is a nation in which the people govern themselves. But self-government means more than equal suffrage and frequent elections. It means a partnership of equals, reasoning together about the common good. We can never fully achieve that ideal—no nation could. But when politics are drenched in money, as our politics now are, then we risk not simply imperfection but hypocrisy. The issues taken up in this book are of great practical and intellectual importance, but they are of the first moral importance as well.

3

ELECTORAL EXCEPTIONALISM

Frederick Schauer and Richard H. Pildes

In *Arkansas Educational Television Commission v. Forbes,*[1] the Supreme Court held that candidate debates are special for First Amendment purposes. Because "candidate debates are of exceptional significance in the electoral process," the Court concluded that the First Amendment principles that apply to state-sponsored candidate debates are different from those that apply to any other form of broadcasting.

The case involved a state-owned television station which decided to exclude a ballot-qualified independent candidate for Congress from a candidate debate it was sponsoring. The public television station allowed two other candidates—a Democrat and a Republican—to participate. But the station concluded that this particular candidate should not appear in the debate, offering as a justification the assertion that the candidate was not sufficiently likely to win the election. The candidate, however, insisted that this was tantamount to being excluded because the station disapproved of his unpopular political viewpoint.

At the heart of the case was the difficult question whether state journalism was best seen as the state or as journalism, or some hybrid of the two. The excluded candidate insisted that the public television station was an arm of the state, and hence subject to stringent First Amendment rules prohibiting "viewpoint discrimination"—the purposeful exclusion of certain ideas solely because the excluder disapproves of the message conveyed by those ideas.[2] In contrast, the public station insisted its activities should be treated as journalism, the consequence being that its editorial judgment—including the right to favor some viewpoints over others—was fully protected by the First Amendment.[3]

The Court concluded that the state-owned television station should be treated like a private station engaged in journalism, with essentially the same editorial latitude and the same immunity from the First Amendment demands of viewpoint neutrality. But the Court then went on to add an intriguing qualification, holding that candidate debates, because of the special role they serve in democratic politics, were to be treated as an exception to the Court's newly announced principle. "Deliberation on the positions and qualifications of candidates is integral to our system of government," the Court observed, "and electoral speech may have its most profound and widespread impact when it is disseminated through televised debates."

In the end, the Court articulated a general rule and an exception. In general, a public television station, like other branches of the press, is permitted to prefer certain viewpoints over others, even when it is engaged in political programming. When the station runs a candidate debate, however, it may not discriminate on the basis of viewpoint.

Our goal in this chapter is not to deal with the question of state journalism, nor even with the surprising claim, which ultimately determined the result in *Forbes,* that excluding a candidate from the debate based on judgments about the likelihood of his winning the election was not a form of viewpoint-discrimination. Rather, we want to explore the implications of the Court's holding that candidate debates are *special* for First Amendment purposes, and that the First Amendment principles that might apply to candidate debates are different from the First Amendment principles that would otherwise have been applied. More broadly, we want to explore a possible extension of this principle. If candidate debates, because of the special role they serve in democratic politics, might be subject to special First Amendment principles, then is it possible that the Supreme Court, or at least the six members of the Court who constituted the *Forbes* majority, might also believe that *elections* themselves—because of the special role that elections serve in a democracy—could also be the subject of special First Amendment principles?

I. THE RHETORIC OF EXCEPTIONALISM

The position we take up is one we will label *electoral exceptionalism.* According to electoral exceptionalism, elections are (relatively) bounded domains of communicative activity. Because of this boundedness, so the argument goes, it would be possible to prescribe or apply First Amendment principles to electoral processes that do not necessarily apply throughout the domain of the First Amendment. If electoral exceptionalism prevails, the courts, in evaluating restrictions on the speech that is part of the process of nominating and electing candidates, would employ a different standard from what we might otherwise characterize as the normal, or baseline, degree of First Amendment scrutiny.

What we call electoral exceptionalism has begun to surface both in public debate and in the First Amendment literature within the past several years.[4] In this book alone, Ronald Dworkin, Burt Neuborne, and Richard Briffault all subscribe to versions of the principle as the foundation for an argument against *Buckley v. Valeo.* Each accepts the principle that one may spend one's own money to promote one's own ideas as good First Amendment law in general.[5] But each concludes, for different reasons, that this principle ought not to be taken to be good First Amendment law when the cause that one is promoting is the cause of a candidacy for public office. Operationally, therefore, the most common version of electoral exceptionalism would permit restrictions on communicative activity in the context of elections—spending caps for Dworkin and Neuborne, disclosure and fundraising restrictions for Briffault—that would not be permitted in what we might call the general domain of public discourse.

Some might immediately suggest that electoral exceptionalism is an argument for weaker First Amendment protection in the context of elections than would otherwise prevail throughout the precincts of the First Amendment. But this is an oversimplification. Consider the arguments that campaign finance regulation would increase voter and candidate participation, or decrease the influence of money compared to other sources of influence. If so, it is hardly clear which way the values underlying the First Amendment cut, for those values might support regulation more than they support speaker (or candidate) immunity from regulation. More broadly, it is not self-evident that the values of the First Amendment—such as democratic deliberation, guarding against the abuse of power, searching for truth, and even self-expression—are best served by treating government intervention as the unqualified enemy. Such a negative conception of the First Amendment is not the only option. Consider, for example, the numerous debates about public access to the press and press access to the corridors of government.[6] These debates have made clear that sometimes First Amendment values may be better served by allowing to the state a limited positive role of fostering the proliferation of voices in the public sphere,[7] or of increasing the roles of the content of the message and the effort of the speaker by decreasing the comparative advantage of wealth. Of course, the negative conception of the First Amendment generally, and freedom of speech in particular, have held sway both in the literature and in the case law over the past several decades.[8] Nevertheless, it still may be too early in the First Amendment day to assume that the possibility of a positive conception of the First Amendment, and thus of a positive but limited role for the state, have no claim to recognition as the legitimate bearer of the free speech banner. Accordingly, it strikes us as somewhere between premature and erroneous to assume that the allowance of greater state intervention in the circumstances of electoral communication is necessarily to be thought of as antithetical to the values underlying the First Amendment—and, therefore, exceptional.

Put another way, whether we view elections as exceptional for First Amendment purposes might well depend on our understanding of the more general nature of the limitations on the First Amendment. Accordingly, we might distinguish between internal and external limitations on the First Amendment. External limitations, typically thought of in "conflicts of rights" terms,[9] arise when some right or value external to the First Amendment and its values, such as the right of a criminal defendant to a fair trial, the right of a nation to protect against treason or violent crime, or possibly the right to equality, is thought to override the First Amendment even within the ambit of its coverage. When a court suspends the right to speak on the ground that a "compelling" governmental interest outweighs that right, or on the ground that the speech presents a "clear and present danger," the court is typically applying an external limitation on the First Amendment.

By contrast, internal limitations, which might be better thought of as "defeating conditions," hold that rights should not be enforced when the reasons for their existence do not obtain. Those who argue for First Amendment–inspired rights of access, or for First Amendment–inspired limitations on campaign spending, are best seen as arguing for internal rather than external limitations on what might otherwise be the effect of the First Amendment.[10] For them the purposes of the First Amendment itself internally limit the extent of the First Amendment's application, and in these cases the question of overriding never arises.

Moreover, even if elections were to be treated as exceptional, it would not follow that this view would necessarily support greater governmental intrusion. The position we label electoral exceptionalism has ordinarily been associated with greater power of state intervention, and thus with what some commentators might characterize as a weaker First Amendment protection with respect to elections. But electoral exceptionalism could be taken to support the opposite result. In other contexts, the First Amendment allows civil and criminal restrictions on some lies,[11] some threats,[12] some invasions of privacy,[13] some indecency,[14] some misrepresentations,[15] some verbal assaults,[16] and some incitements to unlawful violence.[17] But when it comes to political discourse, the doctrine tolerates few such special rules. A different cast on the claim of electoral exceptionalism, therefore, might conclude that official restrictions on communicative activity in the electoral process are especially risky, largely because it would be in the electoral process that the self-interest of potential governmental restricters in retaining their own positions and power would be the greatest.[18] Consequently, so the argument would proceed, restrictions that would in other or more "normal" contexts be permissible should be impermissible in the electoral context, rendering the First Amendment even closer to absolute in the context of elections than it is in various other contexts.[19]

This latter argument does not, to our knowledge, have any adherents, largely because the First Amendment is so protective generally that it would be difficult to develop election-specific rules that are even more protective. Still, the argument is worth noting, if only for the purpose of making the analytic point that the argument for electoral exceptionalism is distinct from the valence of that exceptionalism. We could decide that elections constituted a distinct domain for First Amendment purposes without committing to what we would do within that domain. Exploring the former possibility is our primary goal here.

II. The First Amendment as an Exception

It is widely believed that there is some "normal" or "standard" conception of what First Amendment doctrine does. This off-the-rack understanding of the doctrine, centrally informed by such icons of the First Amendment tradition as *Brandenburg v. Ohio*,[20] *New York Times Co. v. Sullivan*,[21] *New York Times Co. v. United States* (the *Pentagon Papers* case),[22] *Cohen v. California*,[23] and *Texas v. Johnson*,[24] is thought to represent the standard form of First Amendment protection. Departures from this, generally departures in the direction of less rather than more stringent protection, are routinely denigrated as exceptions.[25] In the context of the regulation of campaign-related speech and First Amendment-surrounded campaign expenditures and other electoral activity, we often hear the following three propositions from the Supreme Court and others: first, these and other cases prohibit government regulation unless the government has a "compelling" interest for regulation.[26] Second, the compelling interest standard is for all practical purposes unattainable.[27] Third, any proposals for regulation of campaign-related speech or for regulation of campaign expenditures would be tantamount to making an exception to the First Amendment.

This argument is part of a rhetorical discourse with strong support in the recent American political tradition. As many of the recent debates about pornography and hate speech demonstrate, the argument from free speech is often a more persuasive argument, in this political culture at this time, than the argument from equality. One way of seeing many modern debates is as a contest to see who can claim the rhetorical high ground of the free speech position. Conceivably, one reason for the persistence of *Buckley v. Valeo* is that its supporters have succeeded in claiming this high ground, hardly an inevitable outcome in a situation in which the opposite result could have been characterized in First Amendment terms.[28] Indeed, the "silencing" argument, which occupies center stage in much of the feminist antipornography literature,[29] could be seen in political or rhetorical terms as an attempt to translate the politically disfavored equality argument into a more politically favored free speech argument. If free speech itself is seen as embodying equality values, however, as Ronald Dworkin suggests in Chapter Two, then this tension plausibly disappears, albeit with the consequence of allowing some restrictions on speaking that are demanded by the goals of equality even though the same restrictions might not be permitted by an equality-free conception of freedom of speech.

While the argument that campaign finance regulations are exceptions to the First Amendment often appears to be quite persuasive, on closer examination the argument appears to be long on rhetoric and short on substance. In the first place, the argument does not address one of the central arguments against *Buckley* and its progeny—that there is nothing about the fact that money will be spent on First Amendment activities that makes the regulation of the expenditures a First Amendment problem. The regulation of lead paint or education or even traffic might have a secondary impact on activities protected by the First Amendment[30]—for example, by imposing costs on newspaper publishers or by preventing some people from teaching—but that does not convert such a regulation into a First Amendment issue.[31] So too the same argument might be made in the context of regulation of campaign financing generally, and campaign contributions and expenditures more particularly: the regulation of campaign contributions and expenditures has a secondary impact on political speech, but that should not necessarily convert the regulation into a First Amendment issue.[32]

But the argument over whether "money is speech" is not our concern here. What is our concern is the *structure* of the argument against *Buckley*, for the argument maintains that the activity at issue—raising and spending money—lies outside the ambit of the First Amendment altogether. And if this is the structure of the argument, then the claim that allowing the regulation of campaign contributions or expenditures would be tantamount to making an exception to the First Amendment is largely beside the point. The First Amendment does not cover all human activity, nor even all activity whose regulation has some effect on the quantity or incidence of First Amendment activity, and so the argument that this is an activity not covered by the First Amendment cannot plausibly be characterized as an argument for an exception to the First Amendment.

Even if we accept the claim that money is speech,[33] it hardly follows that identification of a restriction as a restriction of speech necessarily puts us within the domain of the First Amendment. Almost all of the law of contracts, warranties, labels, wills, deeds, trusts, fraud, and perjury, as well as much of antitrust law, securities law, and consumer law, is accurately seen as a regulation of speech in the literal sense of that word, yet exists without even a glimmer of First Amendment scrutiny. In most of these instances, the claim that the First Amendment is even relevant would generate little more than judicial silence, or perhaps a judicial laugh.[34] And once we see that the overwhelming proportion of speech is not covered by the First Amendment, and the overwhelming proportion of speech regulation not touched by the First Amendment, we can see the rhetorical sleight of hand implicit in the standard talk of "exceptions" to the First Amendment.[35] In reality, the First Amendment itself is an exception to the prevailing principle that speech may be regulated in the normal course of governmental business. To be sure, the First Amendment is a vitally important exception, but the argument that the First Amendment covers all speech acts, let alone all acts that have an impact on speech acts, makes no sense at all.

III. THE UNITARY FIRST AMENDMENT

The fact that the argument from an "exception" is a bad one does not mean that there are not better ones. And one of the better arguments recognizes that the First Amendment does not cover all speech, but insists that it is inappropriate to create different levels of First Amendment protection within the realm the First Amendment does cover.[36] In the past few years the Supreme Court has been urged to subdivide existing First Amendment doctrines in order to take account of economic, structural, or technological differences among various media; it has been urged to develop one First Amendment for television, another for cable, and yet another for Internet communications.[37] But for the most part the Court has resisted the invitation. The argument for a unitary First Amendment within its otherwise circumscribed coverage appears to have a sound foundation in the modern American First Amendment tradition, and indeed a sound foundation in much of American legal theory in the more general sense.[38]

When applied to campaign finance regulation, therefore, the argument now takes on a different cast. This is *political speech,* so the argument goes, and at least with respect to political speech we are now in the domain of highest First Amendment protection.[39] Indeed, so the argument continues, political speech in the context of elections is the paradigm case for the First Amendment,[40] and thus the argument against an exception for such speech is particularly strong.

Yet even in the context of political speech, the argument against exceptionalism is fragile. For with respect to political speech, the degree of that protection is highly institution-dependent. There is one form of protection for political speech on government property,[41] another for political speech on the broadcast media,[42] another for political speech in the public schools,[43] another (indeed, several others) for political speech by government employees,[44] and so on. What this suggests, therefore, is that the idea of a standard, normal, or off-the-rack conception of even political speech is an egregious oversimplification. Although the First Amendment is properly understood to make irrelevant features of particular speakers or speeches that might in other contexts be important (think, for example, of the way in which free speech doctrine makes Nazism or racism irrelevant[45]), it is clear that the contexts or domains in which the speech occurs remain quite relevant. And if this is correct, then it is equally clear that there is no standard conception of free speech to which electoral speech would be considered the exception. Rather, elections are one of numerous settings in which political speech occurs, such as billboards,[46] posters,[47] signs in windows,[48] schools,[49] colleges,[50] government employment,[51] polling places,[52] and so on. In each of these contexts, putative regulations are measured by domain-specific, institution-specific, sometimes media-specific, and generally context-specific principles.

IV. Elections as Bounded Spheres

Thus, the argument against electoral exceptionalism cannot be defeated by the specious argument that all communication (or even all political communication) is protected by a single, highly protective standard, and this argument cannot be defeated by the more plausible but still unsound argument that exceptionalism is itself disfavored. Instead, the argument against exceptionalism must rely on the view that elections are not in any important way different from the larger domains of First Amendment–protected communication. Thus, it might be argued, as the Supreme Court indeed concluded in *Buckley* itself and numerous other cases,[53] that the form of advocacy that advocates the election of one candidate over another is indistinguishable in First Amendment terms from the form of advocacy that advocates the round-earth over the flat-earth position, or flat taxation over progressive taxation, or pro-choice over pro-life, or socialism over social Darwinism.

In considering this position, let us accept for the sake of argument that the existing American libertarian approach to freedom of speech is the proper lens through which to view potential restrictions on advocacy in the general domain of public discourse. In other words, we will assume that government may not guard against market failure in the marketplace of ideas. Government may not, for example, rectify an imbalance when Philip Morris is competing with the American Cancer Society, or when racism is competing against tolerance. The notion that government may play such a role has never held sway in the United States, and so does not accurately characterize the American approach to freedom of speech and freedom of the press. Consequently, even a minimal respect for the American First Amendment tradition demands that it not be the task of government to rectify any financial, political, or rhetorical imbalance between the proponents of competing arguments.

The ultimate question in this book, then, is whether some degree of government intervention in the service of structuring an appropriate mode of remedying the pathologies of electoral discourse, or even just of remedying the specific pathology of the undue influence of wealth (and thus leaving all other electoral pathologies in place), might be permissible—even if that same degree of government intervention would be impermissible to remedy the parallel pathologies of nonelectoral discourse. Several chapters in this volume address this question and conclude that there are, in fact, good reasons to develop First Amendment rules that are unique to the electoral context. We, however, are interested in exploring a slightly different question: Does a plausible argument for a governmental role in the marketplace of electoral ideas founder because of the difficulty of drawing a *boundary* around elections? Only if electoral speech can in some way be distinguished from nonelectoral speech, so the argument goes, can we even get started in justifying First Amendment rules that are different in the electoral and the nonelectoral domains.

In considering this argument, we confront the familiar tropes of the American First Amendment tradition: Where do you draw the line? Who decides? A foot in the door. "The camel's nose is in the tent."[54] The thin edge of the wedge. The slippery slope.[55] With these and other slogans and metaphors, the tradition counsels us to avoid even justifiable regulations of communications for fear of being unable to draw the line between the justifiable and the unjustifiable, and for fear of a causal relationship between justifiable regulation now and unjustifiable regulation later.

In the context of campaign finance regulation, the line-drawing cluster of questions often arises in the context of the distinction between candidate advocacy and issue advocacy—the line that Richard Briffault grapples with in Chapter Four. If the tradition to which we have just referred demands that a libertarian approach be applied to public advocacy about issues and policies, and if there is no clear line between promoting an issue and promoting a candidate who promotes that issue, then will any attempt to allow the regulation of the latter but not the former be futile?

The least plausible version of the argument relies on nothing more than the "Where do you draw the line?" rhetorical ploy. It is of course true that the line separating electoral speech from nonelectoral speech would necessarily be both fuzzy and porous, and it is equally true that this would limit the effectiveness of any election-specific principles. But there is no reason to suppose that this line would be either more fuzzy or more porous than any number of other lines the Supreme Court has drawn to distinguish one type of speech from another. Consider, for example, the line between commercial speech and other forms of speech protected by the First Amendment.[56] The Supreme Court permits the regulation of commercial advertising under standards that are more easily satisfied than the standards for the regulation of "core" First Amendment speech. For the special set of rules to work, the Court has had to draw a meaningful boundary between commercial advertising and other speech. That boundary is neither clear nor impermeable, but neither some fuzziness nor some permeability renders the line worthless. The Court has stood by the doctrinal line between commercial and noncommercial speech, even though cigarette advertising could carry some implicit political content, and even though Mobil's political advertising might incidentally sell a bit more gas. Consequently, there is no a priori reason to believe that a doctrinal line between election-related speech and non-election-related political speech would be any less clear or any more permeable. True, election-related speech often serves to promote political causes unrelated to elections, and political advocacy unrelated to elections often serves to promote the election of candidates who subscribe to those political causes. But if we can live with an imperfect boundary in the context of commercial speech, we can live with one in the context of elections.

The "Where do you draw the line?" argument is not the most serious objection, however. More serious is the possibility that drawing a line between electoral speech and nonelectoral speech, with the likely consequence of permitting less regulation of the latter than of the former, would itself influence behavior and would thus be self-defeating. The model here seems to come from the consequences of obscenity law in the late 1960s. When the Supreme Court held in 1966 that material could be obscene only if it were "utterly without redeeming social value,"[57] it became the routine practice of producers of otherwise obscene material to include a sentence or two, or an image or two, of political commentary, usually commentary about the obscenity laws or about the First Amendment, at the beginning or end of their films.[58] This often served to immunize the films from prosecution, while in no way diminishing the effects that the promoters of obscenity laws thought that those laws were supposed to prevent.

In the context of electoral speech, therefore, one conceivable worry might be that the domain of election-related—and therefore more regulable—speech would be defined in such a way that it could be easily evaded. If one could depart from the domain of election-related speech by something like "Vote for Jane Smith, but even if you don't then support public housing," then any attempt to specify distinct principles for electoral speech would be too easily avoided to make any sense at all.

More plausibly, however, the domain would likely be defined in terms of inclusion rather than exclusion, with the standards for inclusion likely dependent on the presence in a statement of a named candidate and an existing election. Alternatively, the domain might be defined in terms of something like the "express advocacy" standard in existing law, or in terms of some demarcated period of days, weeks, or months prior to an election. And it is also possible that the domain would be defined in terms of actors, as with the existing law that often distinguishes among private individuals, associations, and corporations.[59] Richard Briffault summarizes a variety of proposed definitions that take each of these forms.

Any of these boundaries could of course be overcome. One can promote a candidate without identifying the candidate by name, and one could advertise more heavily just prior to a demarcated time period. But unlike the case of the modification of a sexually explicit film to bring it into technical compliance with obscenity doctrine, the modifications at issue here would come at some price. Advertising that does not name a candidate is not totally ineffective in garnering votes, but is generally less effective than advertising that does include the name. So too with time periods. Advertising far in advance of an election, although of some effect, is of less effect than advertising on or close to the eve of an election. And as long as the costs of compliance are sufficiently high, then there is no reason to believe that doctrinal separation would be totally ineffective. Insofar as the worry is that doctrinal separation would induce migration of behavior to the less regulable side of the doctrinal line, the extent to which that behavior is less effective would either be a barrier to migration (better to be regulated with effective advertising than unregulated with ineffective advertising), or would still produce a desired consequence of less of the most problematic behavior.

All the foregoing appears relevant to Briffault's conclusion that drawing the line between elections and politics is "in some sense, logically and practically impossible." Yet whether it is possible to draw a line depends upon the standard for a successful line. And since the idea of the line is to keep some things in and other things out, it is useful to think of a line in the same way that we think of a lock. We are fully aware that there are hundreds of thousands of people in the

United States who could unlock our locked cars and drive off without a key in a matter of minutes. Yet this does not lead us to give up on locks, or to leave our cars unlocked with the key in the ignition. And that is because the measure of a lock is not the bipolar question of whether it is successful by keeping out everyone or unsuccessful by keeping out no one, but rather the scalar question of whether the barrier is sufficiently great, or the cost sufficiently high, that it reduces the number of transgressions by enough to justify the cost of the barrier. As long as it is much less likely that our cars will be stolen if we lock them than if we leave them unlocked with the key in the ignition, we will continue to lock them, even as we know that what we do will be ineffective against the clever and determined criminal.

So too with doctrinal lines. As long as a doctrinal line operates as a barrier to migration across it in a sufficient number of cases (unlike the obscenity case, in which the cost of migration was so low that the line served as a barrier to no one), it is not self-evident that the barrier is ineffective. So if an election-specific principle served effectively to allow some otherwise beneficial regulation consistent with that principle, and if the difficulty of avoiding the regulation and retreating to more First Amendment–protected territory was sufficiently high, we might conclude that the line was successful, even if far from perfect.

V. THE CONSEQUENCE OF ABANDONING PROHIBITION

The preceding discussion is especially true if we stay clear of what might be called the Legal Prohibition Model. Under this model, familiar from the regulatory regimes of the 1960s and 1970s, policymakers, confronted with a practice that they desired to stop, simply legislated prohibitions banning the practice—racial discrimination in employment, for example. In this approach, Congress enacted nationwide bans on primary conduct—command-and-control regulation—that assumed that centralized, first-order prohibitions on conduct would be effective in practice.

Experience since the 1960s and 1970s, however, has brought more sophistication about the actual relationship between formal law and private behavior. Law can alter the incentives various actors face, and changed incentives can channel conduct along new routes. But if the structural pressures to reach a certain end state remain, private actors will seek to reach that state through the channels that remain open. Moreover, the effectiveness of law depends in part on how the law interacts with the relevant social norms that surround it. Law whose effectiveness depends on constant monitoring and enforcement by government officials will, absent massive commitment of public resources, be far less effective than law that can enlist social norms to assist in enforcement.

Although regulatory practice has in many respects advanced beyond the Legal Prohibition Model of the 1960s and 1970s, it is worthwhile remembering that the 1960s and 1970s were also the formative period of modern First Amendment doctrine. Legal prohibition was the primary method of regulating speech during that period. So it should come as no surprise that modern First Amendment doctrine evolved around the central task of invalidating certain legal prohibitions, and in many respects, that focus is still with us. It is no coincidence that *Brandenburg, Cohen,* and numerous other cases of the era were criminal prosecutions, and that the primary argumentative device in noncriminal cases such as *New York Times v. Sullivan* was the quick (some would say too quick) analogy to the criminal prosecution.

Just as regulation theory has begun to advance beyond the Legal Prohibition Model, so too has the First Amendment theory that was premised upon the Legal Prohibition Model. Illustrative are cases from the 1970s such as *Young v. American Mini Theatres, Inc.,*[60] which upheld zoning restrictions that govern adult establishments, and *FCC v. Pacifica Foundation,*[61] which upheld the FCC's "zoning" of "indecent" radio broadcasts to hours when minors were less likely to be listening. More recently, in a similar vein, *National Endowment for the Arts v. Finley*[62] upheld congressional restrictions on awarding federal funds to support indecent or offensive art. These cases exemplify an increasing trend in which the Court is resisting the temptation to treat any content-based regulation as if it were equivalent to a criminal law prohibition. Instead, the Supreme Court has begun to recognize that different forms of regulatory structure might justify different First Amendment responses. If some regulatory structures, for example, will not induce *ex ante* fear in people contemplating engaging in some behavior, then there is no reason to deploy the heavy artillery of a variety of doctrines that are premised on the possibility that actors will seek *ex ante* to avoid *ex post* punishment. It makes perfect sense, for example, to interpret the First Amendment to require a legislature to define with painstaking precision the type of speech that is regulated, if the consequence of crossing the regulatory line would be a prison term. Otherwise, the prohibition might create an excessive "chilling effect": speakers will refrain from engaging in protected speech for fear of prosecution. And in the context of criminal prohibitions, it makes sense to allow a speaker to invoke the so-called *overbreadth doctrine,* allowing attacks on a law based on arguments that the law would violate not the speaker's own First Amendment rights but the First Amendment rights of other hypothetical speakers.[63] In each context the First Amendment doctrine is premised upon the need to protect against punishment for speech. Yet that justification is all but eliminated in numerous other regulatory approaches.

What this suggests, therefore, is that the constitutional permissibility of electoral exceptionalism might also depend upon the particular regulatory model employed. Even if the Supreme Court were properly wary of drawing a line between elections and other forms of political speech for the purpose of determining what forms of communication might be subject to criminal punishment or civil fine, the same might not be true in other regulatory modes, some of which might specify different rules for different media as well as differentiating between elections and other types of speech. Ronald Dworkin's proposal in Chapter Two, for example, to apply special restrictions to campaign speech in the context of electronic media, might be easier to sustain than an absolute restriction on uttering certain words or a restriction on spending money on certain types of messages. Similarly, Richard Briffault is almost certainly correct when he observes in Chapter Four that the First Amendment might tolerate a broader and less precise definition of *election-related* if the consequence were to require disclosure of the spending covered by the definition rather than to impose restrictions on the spending.

VI. THE DOOR IS OPEN

It is uncontroversial that American free speech doctrine is unique, although it is more controversial whether the uniqueness of American free speech doctrine is a good thing. Even after decades of American influence on the development of free speech principles throughout the world, no country has come close to following the American model to the full extent of its free speech libertarianism. Nations that few would consider oppressive—Canada, New Zealand, and contemporary South Africa, to name just three—have free speech and free press principles dramatically less speaker-protective than those in the United States. Canada permits the punishment of Holocaust-deniers, New Zealand criminalizes incitement to racial hatred, and South Africa allows its common law of defamation to develop largely independent of the specific free speech and free press guarantees in its new constitution, and thus largely independent of the authority of its Constitutional Court. In the extent to which it immunizes speakers and speeches from state regulation, the United States stands alone.

Americans debate whether this state of affairs is to be applauded or condemned, but there is little likelihood that it will change. And as long as American free speech doctrine and culture remain so intolerant of the regulation of speech, any attempts to permit the regulation of electoral speech must confront the question of whether the domain of electoral speech can be distinguished from the larger domains it might be thought to inhabit. If the regulation of electoral speech cannot be distinguished from these larger domains, then the regulation of electoral speech would be constitutionally doomed even were *Buckley v. Valeo* no longer the law. But if electoral speech can be seen as a relatively distinct domain, then it would be plausible to consider various proposals to regulating it with less threat to the uniqueness of American free speech culture. The justification of a separate domain for electoral speech is thus a necessary task for any potential regulator of campaign speech who recognizes the futility of wholesale changes in the American approach to freedom of speech and freedom of the press.

As we have argued here, justifying this special domain need not entail the rhetorical burden many anti-regulation advocates would seek to impose. First Amendment doctrine is not a monolith to which the separate treatment of electoral speech would be a dangerous exception. Rather, recognition of the multifariousness of speech and of the multifariousness of the regulatory environments in which it exists points the way to seeing that developing distinct principles for electoral speech would not be appreciably different from the existing terrain of First Amendment doctrine. If there are arguments against electoral exceptionalism, they cannot be arguments against exceptionalism per se, because exceptionalism in the First Amendment is the rule and not the exception.

Our task here has thus been narrow but, we believe, necessary. In a post-*Buckley* world, the possibility would exist of greater regulation of campaign contributions and expenditures than now permitted. Such greater regulation may or may not be a good idea, and would depend on consideration of more dimensions of the financial and empirical electoral environment than we can address here. But if such regulation is indeed a good idea, then its permissibility would depend on the ability to develop First Amendment principles permitting such regulation while still prohibiting regulations that would be troublesome were they applied to the general domain of public discourse.

Yet even if we have avoided the issue of the desirability of campaign finance reform as a policy question, and even if we have avoided the issue of the positive case for election-specific First Amendment principles, we have confronted directly one primary impediment to both of those tasks—the argument that the election-specific First Amendment principles that are the necessary condition for campaign finance reform are inconsistent with essential features of the First Amendment itself. By showing this argument, in all of its variations, to be unsound, we believe we have opened the door to which all attempts to ground campaign finance reform, both as a policy matter and as a constitutional matter, must pass. Whether to walk through the door is a question we leave for others.

4

DRAWING THE LINE BETWEEN ELECTIONS AND POLITICS

Richard Briffault

I. THE ISSUE ADVOCACY PROBLEM

In the closing weeks of the 1996 election, Montana's airwaves were flooded with the following television advertisement about congressional incumbent Bill Yellowtail:

> Who is Bill Yellowtail? He preaches family values, but he took a swing at his wife. Yellowtail's explanation? He "only slapped her," but her nose was broken. He talks law and order, but is himself a convicted criminal. And though he talks about protecting children, Yellowtail failed to make his own child support payments, then voted against child support enforcement. Call Bill Yellowtail and tell him we don't approve of his wrongful behavior. Call (406) 443–3620.[1]

The anti-Yellowtail ad, financed by an organization with the cryptic name of Citizens for Reform, is a classic instance of what has come to be called "issue advocacy." It is called an *issue ad* not because it discussed any issues but because it avoided specific words of "express advocacy" of Democrat Yellowtail's defeat or the election of Rick Hill, his Republican opponent. The ad featured harsh criticism of Yellowtail by name, was broadcast on the eve of the election, and was paid for by an organization that spent $2 million supporting Republican candidates in elections across the country.[2] But it carefully refrained from any call to vote against Yellowtail or for Hill. As a result, it was exempt from regulation under the Federal Election Campaign Act, even from the provisions requiring the sponsor to disclose who paid for the ads.

Ever since the Supreme Court decided *Buckley v. Valeo* in 1976, the world of campaign finance regulation has conventionally been divided into two parts—contributions and expenditures. The earlier chapters of this book focus almost exclusively on these two categories of electoral activity, devoting considerable attention to the legal and philosophical arguments why government might regulate both within the framework of the First Amendment. But campaign finance regulation in today's world is really composed of three parts—contributions, expenditures, and issue advocacy. Increasingly, as Frank Sorauf demonstrates in Chapter One, the contribution/expenditure distinction pales in significance when compared to the difference between issue advocacy and all other election-related transactions, whether they come in the form of contributions or expenditures. Contributions and expenditures are both subject to reporting and disclosure requirements, and contributions and expenditures by business corporations and labor unions may be (and, under federal law, are) prohibited. By contrast, under current law, reporting and disclosure laws may not be applied to issue advocacy campaigns, and there can be no restriction on corporate or union issue advocacy. Moreover, although contributions to candidates, to political parties, and to organizations that make contributions to candidates may be subject to dollar limitations, contributions for issue advocacy may not be subject to such limits. A federal court even recently held that the statutory ban on campaign contributions by foreign nationals does not apply to contributions to issue ad campaigns.[3]

Issue advocacy, like soft money, is campaign activity that is beyond the scope of federal regulation. Soft money and issue advocacy are often intertwined, and soft money pays for much of the issue advocacy undertaken by political parties. But whereas the soft money exemption is largely the product of legislative and administrative action, the exclusion of issue advocacy from regulation is a matter of constitutional interpretation. In any event, any assessment of the constitutional rules governing issue advocacy must take into account the variety of political players—from candidates to advocacy groups to political parties—that might pour money into such messages.

The express advocacy/issue advocacy distinction grows out of the need to draw a line between *election campaign* spending and *general* political spending. Such a line is needed so long as we operate under a constitutional regime that simultaneously (1) protects political speech from government regulation and (2) treats political spending as a form of political speech, but (3) permits regulation only of political spending that is election-related.

These three characteristics define the present campaign finance regime under *Buckley v. Valeo*. But they would also frame campaign finance regulation under either of the principal alternatives to *Buckley*. If the Constitution were reinterpreted to permit greater regulation of election-related speech and to permit limitations on expenditures by candidates and by independent committees—as this book posits—there would still be a need to determine what is an election-related expenditure and what is not. By the same token, if the Constitution were reinterpreted to elevate contributions to the status of expenditures, to invalidate all dollar limitations on campaign finance practices, and to rely exclusively on disclosure laws to guard against corruption or undue influence[4]—as one Supreme Court justice has proposed—it would still be necessary to determine what constitutes the election-related activity that could be subject to disclosure requirements.

Either way, the Constitution demands that we draw a line between elections and politics. But to do so is also, in some sense, logically and practically impossible. Elections are—or ought to be—about political issues and ideas; politics, in turn, is often focused on elections. Election-related speech will typically refer to political issues, and political speech will frequently refer to elected officials or candidates for office. *Buckley* put it well:

> The distinction between discussion of issues and candidates and advocacy of election or defeat of candidates may often dissolve in practical application. Candidates, especially incumbents, are intimately tied to public issues involving legislative proposals and governmental actions. Not only do candidates campaign on the basis of their positions on various public issues, but campaigns themselves generate issues of public interest.

Yet campaign finance regulation necessarily requires a distinction between *election-related* spending and other political spending.

To say that we need to draw some line between elections and politics does not, of course, tell us where the line should be. *Buckley,* in a holding that is less well known than the spending limits ruling that has occupied the other authors of this book, drew the distinction between express advocacy and issue advocacy. The Court concluded that only "expenditures for communications that in express terms advocate the election or defeat of a clearly identified candidate" may be subject to regulation. By way of example, a footnote in Buckley listed "'vote for,' 'elect,' 'support,' 'cast your ballot for,' 'Smith for Congress,' 'vote against,' 'defeat,' [and] 'reject'" as examples of "express words of advocacy," but the Court has not strictly limited express advocacy to these particular words.

This definition of regulable election-related speech appears to reflect three concerns. First, despite, or perhaps because of, the close connection between election-related and other political speech, *Buckley* sought to establish a standard that clearly distinguishes election-related spending from other political spending. To avoid vagueness *Buckley* requires the line between elections and politics to be sharply drawn. Otherwise the definition would yield the sort of chilling effect the First Amendment abhors—self-censorship by speakers who stay far clear of the line for fear of unwittingly crossing it.

Second, the Court seemed worried about unwelcome administrative or judicial probing of the intentions of speakers. Extensive intrusion into the internal communications of an organization or the inner workings of a speaker's mind—to determine, for example, whether the sponsor intended to influence an election—would raise serious First Amendment problems. That is one of the reasons *Buckley* grounded its standard on the content of the communication. Whether a message is campaign-related must be assessed according to its words.

Third, the Court's definition of election-related speech appears intended to maximize the protection of general political speech and minimize the degree to which election regulation may encroach on political speech. Election-related speech must be defined very narrowly, even though this will enable some election-related speech to evade regulation, in order to ensure that no general political speech is restricted. Defining election-related speech as speech that expressly advocates the election or defeat of clearly identified candidates creates the narrowest possible exception to the general immunity of political speech from regulation.

It is unclear whether the Supreme Court intended to declare that only *Buckley*'s definition of "election-related" could pass constitutional muster. For the most part, the lower federal courts have behaved as if the First Amendment prohibits any attempt to regulate political spending that refrains from using *Buckley*'s "magic words" of express advocacy. A lot rides on whether the Supreme Court would sustain this prevailing view, for it allows all manner of political players to skirt any campaign finance regulations, even disclosure rules, that might be devised.

This chapter offers an alternative constitutional doctrine that addresses both the practical realities of contemporary political campaigns and the free speech concerns that worried the Court in *Buckley*. I begin by recounting how the doctrine has evolved and the dangers it raises. The chapter then turns to the reasons for redefining what qualifies as regulable election-related spending. Next, the chapter presents and defends a definition of election-related speech that respects both the First Amendment, particularly the three concerns that seemed to move the Supreme Court in *Buckley*, and the values the Court has recognized that justify campaign finance regulation.

II. The Current Doctrine
and Its Consequences

The Doctrine

The Supreme Court has said little that sheds further light on whether it is open to a more flexible approach than the one it adopted in *Buckley*. In *FEC v. Massachusetts Citizens for Life, Inc. ("MCFL")*,[5] ten years after *Buckley*, the Court offered its first, and only, explication of the definition it adopted. Before the Court was a "Special Edition" of an anti-abortion group's newsletter, which listed state and federal candidates contesting an upcoming primary, identified the candidates' positions on three litmus test issues, provided photographs of those with 100 percent favorable voting records but not of other candidates, and exhorted readers to vote for anti-abortion candidates. The Court concluded that the Special Edition constituted express advocacy. The newsletter never explicitly called for votes for a particular candidate, but it could not "be regarded as a mere discussion of public issues that by their nature raised the names of certain politicians. Rather, it provided in effect an explicit directive: vote for these (named) candidates." *MCFL* thus modestly broadened *Buckley*'s definition of what constitutes express advocacy, but the case is consistent with *Buckley* in relying exclusively on a close examination of the content of the message and, especially, on the presence or absence of exhortations to vote for clearly identified candidates.

Most of the lower courts have followed suit with a restrictive definition of express advocacy. This tendency is illustrated by the decisions in *FEC v. Christian Action Network*.[6] That case considered a 1992 television advertisement that (as described by the federal district court) referred to Bill Clinton's support for "'radical' homosexual causes," presented a "series of pictures depicting advocates of homosexual rights, apparently gay men and lesbians, demonstrating at a political march," and combined "the visual degrading of candidate Clinton's picture into a black and white negative," "ominous music," and "unfavorable coloring" in a manner that "raised strong emotions" among viewers. Both the district court and the court of appeals concluded that the message did not constitute express advocacy of Clinton's defeat. Although the advertising named Clinton and used his picture, was broadcast in the weeks immediately preceding the November 1992 general election, and was "openly hostile" to the gay rights positions it attributed to Clinton, the ad was "devoid of any language that directly exhorted the public to vote." Indeed, the court of appeals determined that the message fell so far short of express advocacy that it slapped the FEC with attorneys' fees and costs for bringing the case.[7]

Only the Ninth Circuit has sought to consider the impact of such a narrow definition of "express advocacy" on the effectiveness of the Federal Election Campaign Act. In *FEC v. Furgatch*,[8] the court found that a newspaper advertisement published on the eve of the 1980 presidential election was express advocacy when it combined heated criticism of President Carter's record with the caption and exhortation "Don't Let Him Do It." Although the ad made no reference to voting against Carter, the court found that "'Don't let him' is a command. The words 'expressly advocate' action of some kind." Voting against Carter in the upcoming election "was the only action open to those who would not 'let him do it.'" *Furgatch* emphasized the need to look not just at the magic words cited in *Buckley* but also at the communication "as a whole . . . with limited reference to external events," such as the timing of the ad, in determining whether the message constituted an exhortation to vote for or against a candidate.

Furgatch constitutes only a modest expansion of *Buckley*'s definition of express advocacy. The Court stressed that a message could constitute express advocacy only so long as it is "susceptible of no other reasonable interpretation but as an exhortation to vote." The message must be "unmistakable and unambiguous, suggestive of only one plausible meaning." If "reasonable minds could differ as to whether it encourages a vote for or against a candidate or encourages the reader to take some other kind of action," it is not express advocacy.

All other federal courts that have considered the issue have rejected *Furgatch*'s slight broadening of the definition of express advocacy and, especially, *Furgatch*'s call to consider whether a message as a whole, with some reference to its timing, constitutes an exhortation to vote for or against a candidate. They have, instead, rigidly insisted on the presence of words that explicitly call for the election or defeat of a candidate.[9] In the view of these courts, any standard that turns on administrative or judicial interpretation of a message—even a standard of no "reasonable minds can differ"—is too vague and poses too great a danger of chilling protected political speech. Thus the First Circuit Court of Appeals and a federal district court in New York have struck down an FEC regulation codifying *Furgatch*'s definition of express advocacy.[10] The Fourth Circuit, in *Christian Action Network*, sharply chastised the FEC for attempting to find express advocacy in "the combined message of words and dramatic moving images, sounds and other non-verbal cues such as film editing, photographic techniques, and music, involving highly charged rhetoric and provocative images . . . taken as a whole," rather than in explicit words of advocacy.

These courts have been both candid and strikingly nonchalant in their recognition that the magic words approach will exclude much election-related spending from regulation. Even as it punished the FEC for its effort to look to the meaning of the broadcast rather than for explicit words of advocacy, the Fourth Circuit in *Christian Action Network* acknowledged, quoting from the commission's brief, that "metaphorical and figurative speech can be more pointed and compelling, and can thus more successfully express advocacy, than a plain, literal recommendation to 'vote' for a particular person." The federal district court in Maine agreed that "language . . . is an elusive thing" and that communication depends "heavily on context"; yet, in the same breath, it held that the FEC's effort to define express advocacy with some reference to context was unconstitutional. Judge Hornby acknowledged that "the result is not very satisfying from a realistic communications point of view and does not give much recognition to the policy of the election statute to keep corporate money from influencing elections," but concluded that such an unrealistic express advocacy standard was constitutionally required.

The Consequences

For both pragmatic and principled reasons, the express advocacy/ issue advocacy distinction articulated in *Buckley* and elaborated by the lower courts must be reconsidered and a new standard for distinguishing election-related spending from other political spending must be developed. Pragmatically, the current test is an open invitation to evasion. It is child's play for political advertisers and campaign professionals to develop ads that effectively advocate the cause of a candidate or make a powerful case against the candidate's opponent but fall short of the formal express advocacy that would permit regulation. The most common tactic for political advertisers is to include some language calling for the reader, viewer, or listener to respond to the message by doing something other than voting. In *Christian Action Network,* for example, the ad called on viewers to telephone the sponsor "for more information on traditional family values." Other ads urge voters to telephone the candidate targeted by the sponsor and ask him why he opposes tax cuts or term limits.[11] A survey by the Annenberg Public Policy Center of 107 issue advocacy advertisements that aired on television or radio during the 1996 election cycle found that 54 percent urged the viewer or listener to contact either a public official or the advocacy organization sponsoring the ad about their views concerning a particular policy position.[12] (Less than a third of the ads urging the audience to communicate its views actually provided a telephone number or address for the audience to contact.) By combining sharp criticism of a candidate with an exhortation to call the sponsor or the candidate criticized, these ads can inoculate themselves against the charge that they constitute express advocacy.

The combination of a crabbed legal definition of express advocacy and the ingenuity of politicians and interest groups eager to exploit opportunities for circumventing campaign finance regulation has led to an explosion of issue advocacy. The Annenberg report estimates that in the 1996 elections between $135 million and $150 million was spent on issue advocacy. The numbers are necessarily imprecise, and the identities of the sources of funds unknown, because issue ads are not subject to reporting and disclosure requirements. Issue advocacy continues to grow in importance. According to news accounts, issue ads dominated the airwaves in the two special congressional elections held in 1997 and the winter of 1998.[13] A second Annenberg Public Policy Center study estimated that $275 million to $340 million was spent on issue advocacy in connection with the 1998 congressional elections—roughly a doubling from 1996 and a remarkable increase in spending from a presidential to a nonpresidential election year.[14]

Issue ads are increasingly indistinguishable from advertising intended to elect or defeat candidates—except perhaps that they are more likely to have "attack" messages[15]—and the organizations sponsoring the ads are often closely tied to particular candidates or to the major political parties. In the first Annenberg study, less than 5 percent of the issue ads that aired in the 1996 campaign actually called for support or opposition to pending legislation. By contrast, nearly 90 percent of the ads referred to public officials or candidates for office by name, and nearly 60 percent of the television ads included pictures of officials or candidates. The second Annenberg study found that more than 80 percent of the issue ads aired between September 1 and Election Day 1998 named candidates.[16] Only rarely did issue advocacy campaigns interject new, independent opinions or reflect the views of political outsiders. The 1996 Annenberg study found that more than 97 percent of issue advertising was aligned with either Republican or Democratic positions.

Journalists have documented how various groups that engaged in issue advocacy expenditures work with the parties and candidates in crafting and placing their messages. According to Elizabeth Drew, for example, issue ads for both Clinton and Dole "were prepared, written and produced by their own campaign apparatus."[17] "Clinton campaign ads were discussed and chosen at the regular Wednesday night political meetings in the White House residence, which were attended by Clinton and his political advisers, top White House officials, and also Cabinet officials who had been in politics," she reports. Many of the leaders of issue advocacy organizations made their careers in party politics. Most notable among them are former Reagan political director Lyn Nofziger, whose Citizens for the Republic spent more than $2 million on attack ads in the 1996 congressional election; Angela "Bay" Buchanan, who participated in Nofziger's effort while serving as campaign manager for the presidential primary bid of her brother, Pat Buchanan; and former Reagan political chair Peter Flaherty, who, as head of Citizens for Reform, ran the anti-Yellowtail ad that opens this chapter.[18] In some cases, the political parties provided the issue groups with the funds they needed to pay for their advertising. Americans for Tax Reform funded its $4.6 million issue advocacy program in 1996 out of a transfer from the Republican National Committee.[19] And, of course, the two major parties each spent tens of millions of dollars on issue advocacy in 1995 and 1996. Indeed, the two parties together appear to have accounted for more than half the total of issue advocacy spending in the 1995–96 election cycle.[20] In the 1997–98 election cycle, political parties accounted for 70 percent of the issue ads aired after September 1, 1998. Similar patterns have developed in state races.[21] As a pragmatic matter, then, the current express advocacy/issue advocacy distinction serves not to assure a place for independent debate concerning vital issues ignored by the major party candidates but rather facilitates the wholesale evasion of campaign finance laws by the candidates and parties.

Principle also calls for a reexamination of the express advocacy/issue advocacy distinction. The current doctrine implicitly treats the regulation of campaign finances as an obnoxious, minimally defensible exception to the general rule of unrestricted political speech. The failure of campaign finance rules limited to express advocacy to actually reach critical campaign finance activities is almost celebrated as an illustration of just how unrestricted political speech is. But as Frederick Schauer and Richard Pildes illustrate in Chapter Three, this misses the distinctive role that elections play in our system of democratic self-governance, as well as the role campaign spending plays in elections. Elections are our central form of collective political decision making and our most important mechanism for securing democratically accountable government. Campaign communications are a crucial part of elections, and, as the Supreme Court has indicated, may be regulated to advance the goals of deliberative, democratic decision making. The Court has repeatedly determined that reporting and disclosure requirements, contribution limitations, and restrictions on the political activities of corporations vindicate the ability of elections to function as an institution of democratic self-governance.

Campaign finance regulation ought to be seen not as a disfavored exception from the general rule of unregulated political behavior but rather as part of the electoral process—a process that, by its very nature, requires a considerable degree of regulation. Both the regulation of elections and the protection of speech reflect important constitutional values. The placement of the election/politics line should not focus exclusively on the values on the politics side of the line but should attend to the vital interests at stake on both sides of the line. The same analysis that leads Ronald Dworkin in Chapter Two to conclude that a more discriminating reading of the First Amendment would support spending limits leads inevitably to the conclusion that the First Amendment, correctly read, should tolerate a more realistic definition of election-related speech.

III. THE REGULATION OF ELECTIONS

INDIVIDUAL RIGHTS AND COLLECTIVE CHOICE

There is a distinctive jurisprudence of elections that attempts to reconcile strong protection of individual rights of political participation with the collective social interest in organizing the process of public choice. Elections deal with the most precious of all political rights, the right to vote. The right to vote, according to the Supreme Court, provides "a voice in the election of those who make the laws under which, as good citizens, we must live."[22] As the Supreme Court noted in *Reynolds v. Sims,* "undoubtedly, the right of suffrage is a fundamental matter in a free and democratic society. . . . The right to exercise the franchise in a free and unimpaired manner is preservative of other basic civil and political rights."[23] Consequently, restrictions on the right to vote are subject to exacting judicial scrutiny under the Equal Protection Clause, and the First Amendment also protects political activity incident to an election.[24]

Yet the Supreme Court has "emphasized on numerous occasions the breadth of power enjoyed by the States in determining voter qualifications and the manner of elections."[25] The right to vote is not simply a matter of individual political participation. It takes on its significance because of its role in our system of democratic collective governance. As the Court has observed, "the right to vote is the right to participate in an electoral process that is necessarily structured to maintain the integrity of the democratic system."[26] Government regulation of the electoral process is not antithetical to freedom of political expression and association. Rather, "reasonable regulations of parties, elections and ballots," the Court has declared, is necessary to make an election work as a mechanism for aggregating diverse preferences into results that reflect majority sentiment, command public support, and produce an effective, accountable government.[27]

Unlike general political activity, an election produces a result that binds an entire polity. People can and will disagree about matters subject to debate; majority views must coexist with dissenting opinions. But electoral outcomes govern the entire polity, the losers as well as the winners. Elections choose the public officers who make, enforce, or adjudicate laws, or, in the case of ballot propositions, they actually enact laws directly. The election's outcome directly affects what government does thereafter. That is, of course, the whole point of having an election. Elections transform a multiplicity of voices into an instrument of governance. Freedom of expression and association are a vital part of the electoral process. Voters must be free to put forward and consider a range of alternatives, and to seek to persuade their fellow voters concerning their electoral choices. But the fact of winners and losers, and the binding effect of electoral outcomes on both, creates the need for rules that not only protect the rights of individuals but also ensure the fairness and integrity of the process as a whole and enhance the democratic legitimacy of the government that results.

Elections also have a distinctive timing. The marketplace of ideas is always open. A speaker whose views are rebuffed by society today may continue to articulate those views and seek acceptance tomorrow. But elections occur at a moment in time. In our nonparliamentary system that moment is fixed and regular. For all federal and most state offices Election Day is at the beginning of November in an even-numbered year. Primary Election Days vary from jurisdiction to jurisdiction but the day is usually fixed and regularly recurring within a particular jurisdiction. Once Election Day passes the election is over and the question of who will be a party nominee, who will hold a contested public office, or whether a ballot proposition is adopted is resolved, at least for a period of time.

Like binding effect, the precise temporal nature of an election places a premium on rules that promote careful and considered choice, the fairness and effectiveness of the electoral process, and the political legitimacy of the result. New developments, changes in opinion about election issues, even new information about old events that comes to light after Election Day can change voters' minds about what should have happened in the election, but cannot change the election results.

Moreover, the regular, fixed temporal location of Election Day serves to concentrate public attention on election-related concerns in the weeks and days immediately preceding the election. Political activity and discussion of political issues may occur at any time of the year. But the period immediately before an election is the distinctive time in which people do most of their information gathering, thinking, and arguing about how they are going to vote, and it is the time in which they are most attentive to election-related messages. Indeed, this is often a period in which other political activity drops off as people and organizations interested in politics focus their energies on the election.

For present purposes, it matters little whether one views the election as a context that is exceptional for First Amendment purposes or simply as a distinctive context that, like so many other contexts, must be governed by its own set of First Amendment principles (as

Frederick Schauer and Richard Pildes argue in Chapter Three). It is enough to say that elections have numerous special characteristics that First Amendment analysis must take into account.

ELECTION REGULATION AND CONSTITUTIONAL LINE-DRAWING

Elections require mechanisms for achieving a democratic collective result. There must be rules for determining eligibility to participate, setting the electoral agenda, sequencing the comparison of electoral alternatives, and focusing electoral deliberation. In a polity characterized by a multiplicity of voters who, with varying degrees of intensity, hold conflicting views across a wide range of issues, there is no one right mechanism for calculating collective preferences. Nor are there universal principles on which all agree. Different electoral rules and procedures will give different weights to different conflicting yet legitimate substantive values, such as political stability and responsiveness to change, majority rule and minority representation. The rules for electoral choice will inevitably affect electoral outcomes. They will also be, at least in part, the product of political judgments. More important for present purposes, the rules often constrain election-related political activity—who can run for office, who can vote for whom, who can nominate whom—and run head on into associational and free speech rights.

The Supreme Court's jurisprudence in this area reflects a dilemma: Democracy needs rules but the notion of democracy does not itself determine what those rules will be. The commitment to decision making by means of elections does not itself determine how elections should be run. The strict scrutiny that courts apply when reviewing governmental efforts to regulate political speech and association—with its insistence that the infringement be justified by indisputable governmental interests and that it be carefully tailored to maximize liberty—is in tension with the basic indeterminacy concerning what principles should govern the electoral process. Given the multiple conflicting values at stake, it would be difficult to show that any particular rule, including rules that regulate election-related political expression, is strictly necessary for democratic decision making. Perhaps as a result, strict judicial scrutiny of laws regulating elections is not always invoked and, even when invoked, it is not always applied.

The Court has often deferred to legislatures to determine the substantive values a polity may seek to advance through its election rules. For example, the avoidance of "factionalism" and the narrowing of choice in order to produce a majority (rather than a plurality) winner have repeatedly been treated as legitimate electoral goals. When a state asserts these and other similar interests, the Court has often accepted the claims uncritically, relaxing the burden on the state to prove that a restriction on election-related political activity is necessary to advance such an election-related interest and discarding the narrow tailoring requirement. As the Court stated in *Munro v. Socialist Workers Party,* "we have never required a State to make a particularized showing of the existence" of the factors—such as voter confusion, ballot overcrowding, or frivolous candidacies—that have been held to justify restrictions on the listing of candidates on the ballot.[28] Similarly, in *Timmons v. Twin Cities Area New Party,*[29] the Court found that a state could bar one party from nominating the candidate of another party without providing "empirical verification of the weightiness of the State's asserted justification" of avoiding voter confusion and preventing party splintering.

Despite the fundamental rights at stake, the Court has often expressed a preference for contextualized approaches and balancing tests rather than per se rules. The doctrine governing ballot access restrictions on third parties and independents, for example, "provides no litmus-paper test for separating those restrictions that are valid from those that are invidious. . . . Decision in this context, as in others, is very much a 'matter of degree.' "[30] In *Timmons* the Court observed that "no bright line separates permissible election-related regulation from unconstitutional infringements on First Amendment freedoms."

To be sure, state discretion is not unlimited and even fuzzy lines can have bite. The Court has been especially concerned to protect the equal right to vote in the face of other asserted state interests. States may not limit the electorate, dilute the representation of minority groups, unduly constrain electoral competition, or exclude new parties or independents who demonstrate some substantial support.[31] Still, what is striking about the jurisprudence of elections is the Court's willingness to let legislatures determine some of the substantive values that election rules may advance and, at times, to defer to legislatures in balancing individual rights against the need to organize collective decision making.

The Court's deference may sometimes go too far. Certainly, the Court's willingness to sustain state laws that bolster the two major parties has been cogently criticized for "entrenching the duopoly"[32] and permitting "partisan lockups of the democratic process."[33] Nevertheless, although the Court's particular decisions may be wrong, it correctly recognizes that election rules vindicate collective interests as well as individual rights. This insight should affect not only the substance of constitutional doctrine but the nature of constitutional line-drawing as well. The absence of clear, incontestable principles for organizing elections means that governments must have more discretion in structuring elections than in regulating other political activity.

LOCATING THE ELECTION/POLITICS LINE

Election-related activities are different from other forms of political activity, and necessarily more subject to regulation. What are the implications of the distinctive nature of elections for where and how the election/politics line is to be drawn?

One possibility is that given the dangers inherent in governmental regulation of the political process, an "election" ought to be defined very narrowly, and treated as an unusual and highly insulated exception to the general rule that political activity is protected from regulation. The Supreme Court has frequently taken this approach, implying that the domain of elections ought to be tightly focused on the casting and counting of ballots itself.

Certainly, balloting is at the heart of the electoral process. The Court has been most zealous in defense of individual election-related rights when a state law would interfere with the right of an otherwise qualified citizen to cast a ballot. On the other hand, it has been most deferential to those state laws restricting the inclusion of candidates' names on ballots. In *Burson v. Freeman*,[34] the Court extended the notion of the ballot to include the place and time of balloting but stressed the close connection between casting a ballot and the place of balloting. The law in *Burson* banned electioneering within one hundred feet of a polling place. It was a "content-based" prohibition on speech, meaning that the law singled out certain messages for regulation, a step that the Court typically reviews most skeptically. Yet the restriction on political activity was not subject to strict scrutiny.

Instead, the Court applied the more relaxed standard that it applies to ballot access restrictions, and deferred to the state "as recognized administrator of elections."

The ballot is surely the fulcrum of an election, but it is not the election *tout court*. Elections entail the casting and counting of ballots, but for the election to serve as a mechanism of collective choice there must be considerable election-related activity before balloting can occur. Candidates test the waters, seek support, sound their themes, and announce their candidacies for nomination. Over time, some candidates drop away, others gather strength. As the number of candidates is winnowed down to a relative handful and Election Day approaches, voters can focus on the finalists. During the election campaign, candidates, parties, interest groups, and interested individuals undertake efforts to persuade the voters how to cast their ballots. The campaign period enables citizen-voters to inform themselves about the candidates and ballot propositions and decide how they will vote—which is formalized by the casting of the Election Day ballot. The election campaign is thus a central part of the process of structured choice and democratic deliberation that constitutes an election. A fair opportunity for all participants in the electoral process to present arguments to the voters is critical to the legitimacy of the election as a mechanism of collective decision making.

The Court has often defined an election broadly to include pre-Election Day activities or has deferred to congressional regulation that regulates pre-Election Day activities as part of the electoral process. In *Terry v. Adams*,[35] for example, the Court treated the White Primary—the private political activity that preceded the general election and informally but effectively supplanted that election—as a part of the election in order to protect the equal right to vote. The Court has indicated that Congress can treat party nomination procedures as part of an election,[36] and that Congress can use the pre-election campaign season to define the obligations of broadcasters.[37] The Court has also indicated that the rules that translate Election Day results into the structure of government are part of the election. The one person, one vote doctrine, the minority vote dilution doctrine, and the judicial review of partisan gerrymandering all grow out of the right to vote even though none of these doctrines concern Election Day activities. Due to the nexus between voting and representation, legislative apportionment has become part of the domain of elections.[38]

To be sure, the ballot nicely symbolizes the mix of individual and collective concerns at stake in the regulation of elections. Indeed, as the Court noted in *Burson,* the state-created ballot is itself an artifact of the state's involvement in the electoral process. The state-created ballot promotes the integrity of elections by safeguarding voter choice from private interference. Yet by requiring voters to use an official, state-controlled ballot, states have displaced the role of parties, candidates, and individual voters in preparing ballots and in framing the choices available to the electorate. The questions concerning which candidates and parties can be listed on ballots, whether states can limit the ability of parties to endorse the candidates of other parties, and whether states must count write-in ballots arise solely because of the state's displacement of privately provided ballots with the state's ballot. The state-created ballot, like many voting rules, simultaneously constrains and advances collective choice. But the ballot is not all there is to an election and the election certainly includes campaign activity that precedes the casting of ballots.

With the election not limited to the act of balloting, there is no obvious definition of when an election begins or ends. Drawing the election/politics line requires a contextualized assessment of the relationship between the law or practice at issue and the role of the election as a mechanism for the creation of a democratically accountable government. Like some of the rules internal to the law of elections, the scope of the law of elections is more a matter of degree than of bright lines. Certainly, the closer a practice is to casting a ballot, the easier it is to treat as part of the election. But the real test is how closely connected the activity is to the values and concerns central to elections— values like political equality, openness to participation, informed deliberation, structured choice—rather than to the ballot itself.

CAMPAIGN FINANCE REGULATION

What are the implications of the jurisprudence of elections for the regulation of campaign finance? Some of the basic concerns of election law—openness to participation, informed choice, political equality, and the impact of the election on representative governance—are implicated by campaign finance regulation. The centerpiece of the

Buckley doctrine—"exacting scrutiny" of limitations on campaign money—grows out of the role the campaign plays in enabling an election to be a mechanism for democratic choice. Candidates and others with an interest in the outcome of an election need to be able to communicate their views to the voters. More important, the legitimacy of decision making by election turns on the ability of voters to receive the information they need to cast informed votes. Money is not speech, but in a large and heterogeneous society, money can play an important role in disseminating election-related information to the voters. *Buckley* expressly linked up protection of election expenditures to the broad protection the First Amendment generally affords political speech and association. Yet strict scrutiny of limitations on campaign activity is also consistent with the notion that there is a distinctive jurisprudence of elections under which an opportunity for wide-open campaigning is essential to the legitimacy and the effectiveness of the election as a mechanism for collective choice.

By the same token, the Court's validation of some forms of campaign finance regulation represents a departure from the general rules respecting political speech and suggests a concern for the distinctive role that elections play in our political system. *Buckley*'s approval of contribution limits must be attributable to the view that such limits advance the central purpose of an election—the selection of the officials who will constitute a government. To be sure, one strand of *Buckley* and subsequent campaign finance cases denigrated contributions as a lower order of indirect speech—"speech by proxy."[39] But this never seemed persuasive, given both the need for contributions to fund expenditures and the role of contributions in political association. Rather, it is the other strand of the analysis that must have moved the Court to approve of contribution limits, despite their impact on political speech and association—the concern that campaign finance rules affect the behavior of government. Large private contributions raise the danger that officeholders will be too attentive to the interests of donors and prospective donors and insufficiently concerned about the public interest. Campaign contributions may be limited, according to *Buckley,* not because they are not political speech but because "political quid pro quo's from current and potential office holders" to donors and potential donors threaten the "integrity of our system of representative democracy."

Similarly, the collective nature of electoral choice, as well as the connection between elections and office holding, may play a role in the Court's willingness to sustain rules requiring donors to disclose their identities in the electoral context. Despite their potential for infringing on privacy of association and belief, disclosure requirements can be an important source of voter information. As *Buckley* put it:

> Disclosure provides the electorate with information "as to where political campaign money comes from and how it is spent by the candidate" in order to aid the voters in evaluating those who seek . . . office. It allows voters to place each candidate in the political spectrum more precisely than is often possible solely on the basis of party labels and campaign speeches. The sources of a candidate's financial support also alert the voter to the interests to which a candidate is most likely to be responsive and thus facilitate predictions of future performance in office.

It is uncertain whether the benefits of increased information would offset the chilling effect of disclosure in an ordinary political speech context. The Court has certainly suggested otherwise.[40] But in the electoral setting, voter choice is not just a matter of personal information and belief. Instead, citizens as voters are under a political obligation to make choices, choices that inevitably bind the polity as a whole and set the course of government for the next political term. There is a collective interest in increasing the amount of relevant information available to the voters in the hope of improving the quality of collective decision making.

Buckley even upheld FECA's provisions requiring people who make independent expenditures to disclose their identities, going so far as to impose the same requirement on people who contribute to organizations that then make independent expenditures. The Court upheld these rules although it had already concluded that independent spending presented no danger of corruption and even though there was a distinct possibility that such disclosure might chill the groups and their supporters. The Court's rationale was that such disclosure "increases the fund of information concerning those who support candidates." This "informational interest" in the sources of independent spending can be as strong as the interest in the sources of candidates' funds because disclosure by independent committees "helps voters to define more of the candidates' constituencies."

The Court's deference to Congress's judgment concerning the specific dollar limitations on contributions and the thresholds for reporting and disclosure resembles the Court's deference to political judgments concerning line-drawing in other areas of election regulation. In upholding FECA's limits on donations and the Act's low reporting and record-keeping thresholds, *Buckley* stated "we cannot require Congress to establish that it has chosen the highest reasonable threshold." That "line" was "best left . . . to congressional discretion." It was upheld because it was not "wholly without rationality"—a standard even more relaxed than that used in reviewing ballot access rules in the cases mentioned earlier. The Court has also deferred to congressional judgments that certain campaign finance restrictions are constitutionally appropriate not because of their direct effects in preventing corruption or informing voters but because of their indirect benefits in preventing evasion or circumvention of the regulations that directly address the prevention of corruption and the provision of election-related information.[41]

To be sure, a central concern of election law is equality of participation. Equality concerns play out differently in the campaign finance context than in other areas of election law, such as the right to vote or to be a candidate. In those areas, a concern for political equality has been used to strike down laws restricting participation— or, put another way, the political equality argument is a force for increased participation. But in the campaign finance setting, equality is asserted as a justification for spending restrictions that would limit participation. Such egalitarian restriction may be justified, but it is certainly in tension with the goals of wide-open political participation and electoral communication. So long as the law allows all participants to spend as much as they can muster, it is simply unclear how far the notion of political equality sustains limits on the election-related uses of unequal private resources.

This uncertainty about the meaning of equality is reflected in campaign finance doctrine. As we have seen, *Buckley* announced that "the concept that government may restrict the speech of some elements of our society in order to enhance the relative voice of others is wholly foreign to the First Amendment," and proceeded to invalidate FECA's limits on expenditures by candidates and independent spenders. Yet, as Ronald Dworkin points out, this ruling is in tension with *Austin*,[42] where the Court upheld federal and state restrictions on expenditures by business corporations on the theory that the financial resources these organizations can deploy for political purposes "have little or no correlation to the public's support for [their] ideas." Prohibiting corporations from using treasury funds to finance campaign expenditures "ensures that expenditures reflect actual public support for the political ideas espoused by corporations," the Court observed. To be sure, the Court linked these restrictions to the assertedly "unique state-conferred" advantages that enable corporations to "amass large treasuries" and resolutely opposed the imposition of limits on expenditures by other campaign participants, such as wealthy individuals, where there may be a similar gap between the funds available for election-related activity and the extent of public support for the positions espoused by the spenders.

The Court's decisions validating restrictions on corporate activities suggest that the place of equality in campaign finance law is not fully resolved. But the campaign finance cases do reflect the other central election law concerns with the function of an election in creating an effective, politically accountable government. Reporting and disclosure requirements and contribution restrictions have been held to advance that function by increasing the prospects for informed choice, reducing the danger that the campaign process will make elective officials too attentive to the private interests of their financial backers, and addressing the particular perils posed by corporate and union political participation.

The scope of constitutionally permissible campaign finance regulation is determined not just by the substantive values of campaign finance law but also by the definition of which finance practices are considered to be a part of the campaign. The current use of "express advocacy" to determine which contributions and expenditures are campaign-related is an open invitation to circumvention. The legal definition of election-related speech needs to be redrawn in light of the principles that underlie election regulation. Reconsidering express advocacy is also necessary to vindicate the more basic principle that if an activity may be subject to regulation then it ought to be subject to effective regulation.

IV. EXPRESS ADVOCACY RECONSIDERED

The definition of election-related speech should reflect the concerns that justify campaign finance regulation. Under *Buckley,* these include providing voters with information concerning those who are spending money to influence the outcome of an election, curtailing the potential effects of large contributions on officeholders, and restricting the ability of corporations and unions to convert treasury funds into election war chests. At bottom, all three concerns reflect the central purpose of elections—the aggregation of popular preferences into a government.

Disclosure affects voter choice in a setting where voters' choices ultimately bind other voters by producing a government for the entire polity. Contribution limits look to the effect of campaign finance practices on the government that emerges from the election. Limits on corporate and union war chests are intended to prevent corporate and union treasury funds from "distorting" election results by making them less representative of popular sentiment. All three justifications for regulation, then, grow out of the connections among campaign finance practices, electoral decision making, election results, and the role of elections in creating and shaping government. The definition of election-related speech subject to disclosure or limitation should take these concerns into account.

The definition of election-related speech must also be consistent with the First Amendment values that led the Court to adopt the express advocacy test in the first place. Certainly, the definition should avoid vagueness. Vague standards chill speech that could not be constitutionally proscribed, can lead to an unnecessary and excessive reduction in political activity, and vest unwarranted discretion in administrators and courts. Vague standards force speakers to divert precious funds from communicating political messages to retaining lawyers and litigating cases. Clarity ought to be a goal of election regulation, even apart from the First Amendment. To be effective, election regulation ought to proceed in "real time," that is, in the heat of the political campaign. It would be far better if mandatory disclosures were made—and contribution limits and corporate spending prohibitions observed—during the election than if these rules were honored only by the imposition of fines and penalties years after the election. Clear rules facilitate compliance and enforcement as well as avoid chilling effects.

Similarly, the test should not include an intrusive evaluation of the speaker's intent. A test that depended for example on a judgment of whether the speaker intended to influence the election would introduce many of the same pitfalls as vagueness. While it may be fair to assume that speakers know what they intend to achieve, no speaker can be confident of what intent some governmental entity might attribute to a communication. So a test based upon intent carries some of the same dangers of chilling, litigiousness, and delayed enforcement as a vague standard. Plus, as noted earlier, it introduces an additional danger of governmental inquiries into the inner political motives of an individual or into the internal communications of an organization.

Finally, the test should be drawn in a way that focuses as narrowly as possible on speech that is related to elections, without sweeping into the regulatory realm too much political speech that is unrelated to elections. To use the legal jargon, the definition should not be *overbroad*. A test, for example, that treated as election-related any ad that mentioned the name of a candidate, no matter when that ad was aired, would be fatally overbroad, for it would restrict all sorts of political speech—discussion of the McCain-Feingold Bill or the Hyde Amendment, for example—that has nothing to do with elections. That is not to say that a law defining election-related speech would be invalid just because one could imagine an ad that is neither intended to nor likely to affect voting decisions yet still technically falls within the definition. Rather, the First Amendment requires only that the law be drawn in a way that minimizes the likelihood that that would happen.

To be sure, *Buckley*'s express advocacy standard satisfies each of these criteria. But the bright-line test it establishes is grounded entirely on the content of the ad—the presence of words expressly advocating the election or defeat of a clearly identified candidate. There are other ways to avoid vagueness, mind-probing, and overbreadth without limiting the inquiry exclusively to the script of an ad.

One of the most salient features that *Buckley*'s express advocacy test ignores is the context of the communication. As even Judge Hornby, one of the most zealous defenders of a narrow definition of express advocacy, has acknowledged, "it is a commonplace that the meaning of words is not fixed, but depends heavily on context as well as the shared assumptions of speaker and listener."[43] The meaning of content is shaped by context, and the impact of a communication will be affected by its context. Context and content together are necessary to assess whether a communication is election-related. So when we try to frame a test that more accurately maps the line between elections and politics, we must take context into account. But to avoid vagueness and frame a test that is easy to apply, the test should incorporate only those features of the context that are easy to measure, are obvious to the speakers, and determine whether the communication is likely to affect the outcome of an election.

What does it mean to say that a communication is election-related? Consistent with the avoidance of vagueness and of unnecessary restrictions on non-election-related behavior, a legislature should be permitted to define as election-related any communications that refer to the participants in the election, occur during the election, and have characteristics that make them reasonably likely to have some impact on the outcome of the election. "Reasonably likely" means possibility not probability. It can never be certain before an election what activities will have an effect on the result. On the other hand, it does not include practices or activities that are likely to have little effect. Nor does the notion of possible effect on the result refer to the outcome of a particular election—one election may be a foregone conclusion that would not be affected by any political activity, while another election may be so tight that truly trivial activities could have an effect. Rather, the focus should be on a class of similar elections. If there is some reasonable likelihood that a communication could affect the outcome of a class of elections then a legislature should be permitted to treat it as election-related.

Whether a communication should be treated as election-related for purposes of campaign finance regulation (including disclosure rules, contribution limits, and rules governing the use of corporate and union treasury funds) should turn primarily on three criteria: content, timing, and the amount of money involved. Obviously, if a communication includes the magic words of express advocacy, it ought to be regulated as election-related regardless of when it airs or how much it costs. But beyond that, a legislature should be permitted to broaden the definition of election-related so long as it sensitively defines these three criteria in a way that permits effective regulation, avoids vagueness, and protects non-election-related speech.

Specifically, it should be constitutional to adopt a definition that regulates as election-related any communication that (1) refers to a clearly identified candidate; (2) is made within a defined period of time before an election, probably no more than four weeks before a general election or two weeks before a primary; and (3) involves a sufficiently large expenditure—at least 1 percent and possibly as much as 5 percent of the average expenditure of the winning candidate for the office in question in the two preceding elections. In addition, there need to be specific rules for two regularly recurring situations: advertising by major political parties, and issuance of voter guides by organizations interested in political issues. Given the nature of our parties, major party advertising that refers to a clearly identified candidate ought to be treated as election-related no matter when it occurs. Expenditures for voter guides should be treated as part of an organization's internal communications and exempt from regulation regardless of their references to candidates, timing, or cost, to the extent that the voter guide is distributed to the organization's membership or to regular recipients of the organization's publications. Additional expenditures to distribute the voter guide to a wider public should be treated as election-related to the extent that they satisfy the three elements of reference to a candidate, timing, and amount.

Such a standard would be clear and focused on speech that has potential to influence an election. It would place a minimal burden on issue-oriented organizations. It targets the sophisticated political participants best able to accommodate their actions to legal requirements. It is unlikely to chill any nonelectoral speech, and it respects the associational autonomy of politically active groups. It is surely underinclusive, particularly in its temporal definition of the electoral campaign and its exclusion of voter guides distributed within an organization, but that represents a necessary accommodation to First Amendment values. In any event, this test would come a lot closer to accurately mapping the election/politics distinction and vindicating the purposes of election regulation than does the existing definition of express advocacy.

CONTENT: CLEARLY IDENTIFIED CANDIDATE

This component of the test corresponds to one element of the existing express advocacy doctrine. Some reference to a clearly identified candidate is necessary to mark election-related communication off from other forms of political speech.[44] If no reference to a candidate were required, the test would be far too open-ended and would easily encompass pure discussions of political issues. A clear reference to a candidate—either naming the candidate or using the candidate's likeness—is thus a necessary condition for regulation even if it is not sufficient to distinguish electoral from other political speech. Some reference to a candidate is also required to put speakers and broadcasters on notice that their messages are subject to regulation. Finally, despite the increasing sophistication of campaign advertising, it seems unlikely that a message that makes no reference at all to a clearly identified candidate will have a significant impact on an election. (A possible exception to this general statement might be a message that includes a reference to a *group* of candidates—such as "Republicans" or "House Democrats." Given the central role of parties in elections, it might be permissible to treat references to candidates by party affiliation as tantamount to express references to those candidates by name.)

Virtually all of the blatant uses of issue advocacy to avoid campaign finance regulation in the 1996 election involved use of a candidate's name or likeness. As the Annenberg study found, hardly any so-called issue advocacy advertising actually discussed issues without mentioning candidates. Conversely, a group or individual interested in communicating views to the public on a political issue could avoid regulation simply by avoiding reference to a candidate. There is no vagueness and no need to analyze the intent of the speaker.

Should a communication explicitly call for the election or defeat of a clearly identified candidate then there would be no problem regulating it, as *Buckley* currently provides that such a statement is express advocacy. Conversely, not all communications that refer to a candidate ought to be treated as election-related. As we have already seen, a candidate's name may be mentioned in passing as part of a shorthand reference to pending legislation or a political program, such as the McCain-Feingold Bill or the Clinton health care plan. An organization may use a candidate's name to underscore what the organization stands for and to build membership and institutional support, as when liberal organizations attack Newt Gingrich or Jesse Helms and conservative organizations attack Bill Clinton or Ted Kennedy.[45] These are all political messages that ought to be free from government regulation.

Reference to a candidate is thus a necessary but not a sufficient condition for a finding of election-relatedness. On the other hand, the requirement of express advocacy—a clear exhortation to vote for or against a candidate—is so easy to evade that many plainly election-related statements concerning candidates will be exempt from coverage.

Following *Furgatch,* some campaign finance reforms would continue to focus primarily on the content of the speech but would permit greater interpretation of that content "with limited reference to external events such as proximity to the election." Thus, the FEC has by regulation defined express advocacy to include communications that:

> When taken as a whole and with limited reference to external events such as proximity to the election could only be interpreted by a reasonable person as containing advocacy of the election or defeat of one or more clearly identified candidate(s) because—
>
> (1) The electoral portion of the communication is unmistakable, unambiguous, and suggestive of only one meaning; and
>
> (2) Reasonable minds could not differ as to whether it encourages actions to elect or defeat one or more clearly identified candidate(s) or encourage some other kind of action.[46]

The House of Representatives used similar language in one of several alternative definitions of express advocacy in the Shays-Meehan Bipartisan Campaign Reform Act of 1999, which passed the House in September 1999. This provision of Shays-Meehan would regulate as election-related any communication that advocates the election or defeat of a candidate by "expressing unmistakable and unambiguous support for or opposition to one or more clearly identified candidates when taken as a whole and with limited reference to external events, such as proximity to an election."[47]

This more context-sensitive definition of express advocacy could very well constitute the most accurate measure of election-related speech, but it would be difficult to apply during the heat of an election, is open to considerable variation in interpretation, and relies so heavily on adjectives like "unmistakable" and "unambiguous" that it signals the means of its evasion. With the Fourth Circuit in *Christian Action Network* finding that the anti-Clinton ad at issue in that case could reasonably be interpreted as an anti-gay ad and not an anti-

Clinton ad, it should be easy for political advertisers to inject just enough ambiguity to avoid coverage. In any event the definition's openness to interpretation makes it susceptible to attack as unconstitutionally vague, an attack that has already twice succeeded against the FEC's regulation.[48]

TIMING: ELECTION-PERIOD SPEECH AS PRESUMPTIVELY ELECTION-RELATED

Both the FEC regulation and the provision of the Shays-Meehan bill would take "proximity to an election" into account in determining whether a communication is election-related. This approach appreciates that for many television watchers and radio listeners the meaning of a political message that features a candidate (without an exhortation to vote) and some issue discussion might depend upon proximity in time to the election. Unfortunately, proximity to an election is too hazy and uncertain a concept to be the basis of an enforceable definition. Rather than make proximity a factor of uncertain meaning or weight in the assessment of whether a communication is election-related, the definition of election-related communications should be tied to a precise time period.

As previously noted, elections have a distinctive timing. Discussion of political issues may go on without resolution, but election-related activity is focused on persuading voters to make a choice among contending candidates shortly before a precise date on which they have a political obligation to choose. Although election-related activity long precedes the actual moment of voting, the pace and sequence of election-oriented messages are focused on influencing voters' Election Day decisions. It is thus entirely appropriate for the timing of a message to be a factor in the determination of whether a message is election-related.

Communications that refer to a clearly identified candidate or group of candidates and that are published, broadcast, or otherwise disseminated in the period immediately before an election ought to be presumed to be election-related. First, this is the high point of the election campaign, the period in which the voters are most likely to be considering their Election Day decisions. Information and arguments concerning candidates presented in the period shortly before an election raise the reasonable possibility of having an impact on the election.

Second, it is unlikely that communications referring to candidates that are disseminated in this period are intended to have any impact on political activity other than the election itself, even if the communications refer to issues or ideas as well as candidates. Typically, in the days and weeks before Election Day, politics becomes increasingly focused on the election. Legislative bodies whose members are up for election generally go out of session. Executive branch officials who are up for election devote themselves to their campaigns. In this period political activity involving clearly identified candidates is likely to be election-related activity. As a result, presuming that election-eve, candidate-identifying speech is regulable election-related speech will place little burden on other political speech.

Third, the timing of the message does affect its meaning. An election-eve message that combines references to candidates and to issues is far more likely to affect voter thinking about the election than about political issues in general precisely because the message is mailed, published, or broadcast on the eve of the election. Judge Hornby recoiled from the FEC's reference to proximity to the election as a factor in determining whether a communication is express advocacy, complaining that under the FEC's approach "what is issue advocacy a year before the election may become express advocacy on the eve of the election and the speaker must continually re-evaluate his or her words as the election approaches." But, in fact, the import and impact of a communication will vary with proximity to an election. A broadcast denunciation of President Clinton's health care policies will mean one thing and can have one effect when those policies are being debated by Congress more than a year before the election and will have another meaning and a different effect a few weeks before an election, when Congress is in recess, and the president and members of Congress are campaigning for reelection. Indeed, the 1998 Annenberg Center study demonstrated that issue ads aired in the immediate pre-election period differ from ads broadcast at other times of year. The study, which examined 423 ads, found that issue ads released in the immediate pre-election period were far more likely to refer to candidates or officeholders by name, far less likely to discuss legislation, and far more likely to be attack ads than those aired in the preceding twenty months. In 1997–98, only 35 percent of the ads released before September 1, 1998, mentioned a candidate; but 80 percent of the ads aired after that date named a candidate.[49] Conversely, 81 percent of issue ads aired before September 1 mentioned pending legislation, while only 21.6 percent of ads disseminated after September 1 mentioned pending legislation.[50] Just one-third of issue ads released before September 1 were attack ads, but a little over half of the issue ads in the two months before Election Day were attack ads.[51]

If regulation is to be based upon the timing of the message, the legislature must define the election period. The real vice in the FEC's definition of express advocacy was not the inclusion of a reference to the timing of the message but its failure to prescribe precisely what constituted temporal proximity to an election. There must be a bright-line definition that makes it clear to speakers, regulators, and courts whether the speech falls within the pre-election period. The harder question is, of course, what the temporal scope of the pre-election period should be. That decision should be based on an assessment of political science data concerning when voters focus on and make decisions concerning their election choices as well as on empirical data concerning the slowdown in other political activity that occurs as political actors focus their energies and attention on the upcoming election. Ideally, the pre-election period would begin when the rising line of voter attention to the election crosses the falling line of other political activity on the graph of political life. This point may well be different from one jurisdiction to the next.

Of course, that graph does not exist, and any actual determination of the pre-election period is inherently arbitrary. There are currently numerous proposals for some time-based definition of election-related speech. One group of political scientists has proposed that corporations, unions, trade associations, and issue groups be required to report expenditures with respect to an identifiable federal candidate within six months of an election.[52] This, however, is far too broad a definition. In a jurisdiction with both a primary and a general election, it could turn more than a year in every two-year election cycle into the pre-election period.

A Brookings Institution–American Enterprise Institute task force has proposed that all paid communications that use a federal candidate's name or likeness within ninety days of a primary or general election should be considered election-related and subject to regulation.[53] The proponents note that ninety days before an election is the same period in which members of the House of Representatives are barred from using the congressional frank for mass mailings to their districts.[54] This period is also too long for regulating issue advocacy by nonincumbents. The congressional frank, one of the many advantages an incumbent enjoys, represents the use of public resources, and it is likely that material sent by a member of Congress is going to be part of that member's reelection drive. Communications by independent organizations do not involve public resources, are not necessarily pro-incumbent, and may in fact be aimed at affecting public opinion and legislative deliberations concerning a political issue. A ninety-day period—reaching back from early November to early August for the general election, and from a June primary back to March— simply defines too much of the political year as part of the election campaign.

The Shays-Meehan Bill—in addition to the quoted provision— would treat as express advocacy a communication with respect to a clearly identified candidate "in a paid advertisement that is broadcast" on television or radio within sixty days of an election in a state in which the candidate is running. Sixty days is certainly more reasonable than ninety days, and it is consistent with the Annenberg Center findings, which show a sharp shift in content from the discussion of legislation to the discussion of candidates sixty days before the election. But a sixty-day rule would convert four months of an election year into the period in which communications referring to candidates are presumptively election-related, including the month of September, which will often be a period in which Congress is seeking to resolve pending matters prior to adjournment.[55] There is also no reason to have a special time-based definition of express advocacy limited to broadcasting since issue advocacy campaigns can make intensive use of mass mailings and telephone banks as well as broadcast advertising.[56]

My armchair analysis suggests that the period ought to be no more than four weeks before a general election and two weeks before a primary. The general election period ought to be longer because the general election tends to dominate the rest of politics more than a primary does. The legislature is more likely to be out of session— and elected officials are more likely to be out on the hustings rather than involved in governance—for a longer period of time before the general election than before the primary. Public attention is also more likely to be focused on the general election, and to focus on it earlier, than on the primary. As a result messages that mix candidate and issue references may be more likely to affect electoral choice rather than political views for a longer period before a general election than before a primary. Unfortunately, the 1998 Annenberg Center study did not compare issue ads broadcast in September 1998 with those broadcast in October 1998 to determine if the frequency of references to pending legislation and to candidates changed between sixty days and thirty days before the 1998 congressional elections.

Four weeks seems to be about the outer limit of the pre-election period in terms of both the attention of the voters and the extent of the diversion of political actors from other political activity.[57] A longer period would raise a greater danger of regulation of the discussion of political issues and of messages that affect political debate generally rather than electoral choice. It is really only in the month before a general election that other political activity drops off sharply, that political debate is focused primarily on the upcoming election, and that the public's interest begins to turn to the election. Indeed, this is the period in which most issue advocacy advertising appears to occur.

Even four weeks may be too long. In 1998, a Congress tangled up in impeachment and budget issues remained in session until two weeks before Election Day. Even as the general election loomed, political debate did not shift entirely from pending legislative action to the election itself. There is some temptation to tie the onset of the election eve period to the adjournment of Congress, provided that it is thirty days or less before the election, but that could create uncertainty and would give the incumbent Congress too much power to manipulate the starting point of the election-eve period. If the party in power believed that it would be the primary beneficiary of issue advocacy advertising it could avoid formal recess or adjournment altogether in order to limit disclosure and facilitate the use of corporate or union funds in the election.

Like the number of petition signatures needed to place a candidate on the ballot or, more pertinently, the number of feet from the polling place in which a state may bar electioneering, this seems like the "matter of degree" for which the courts ought to give federal and state regulators a little leeway. Given the difficulty of proving that a communication affects readers or viewers, it would be inappropriate to require "empirical verification" or a "particularized showing" that there is some abrupt rise in the impact of communications at five or ten or twenty days before an election. Just as there are no magic words, there are no magic days. But it is reasonably likely that election-eve communications that mention clearly identified candidates are more likely to affect readers', viewers', or listeners' views about their electoral choices than their views about political issues unanchored to candidates. Regulating such communications is not likely to interfere with a robust issues debate because most political debate on the eve of the election is about the election itself rather than about issues per se. A bright-line test is constitutionally necessary even though no particular bright line is likely to be empirically compelling. Applying the approach taken in *Munro* and *Burson* to legislative line-drawing in election regulation, any line thirty days or less before the election ought to be constitutionally acceptable.[58]

AMOUNT OF MONEY: RAISING THE THRESHOLD FOR REGULATION

Consistent with the notion that the definition of election-related activity should focus on communications that have a reasonable likelihood of affecting electoral outcomes, only substantial expenditures referring to candidates and occurring within the defined pre-election period should be treated as election-related. The threshold ought to be at least 1 percent of the average expenditure of the successful candidate for the office in question over the last two or three elections, and possibly higher, up to 5 percent. If the average expenditure for successful candidates for the House of Representatives over 1992, 1994, and 1996 was around $600,000, that 1 percent test would make the dollar threshold $6,000; the 5 percent test would place the threshold at $30,000. For the presidential general election, the figure would be 1 percent of the limit on the major party candidates receiving public funding. In 1996, the public grant was about $60 million, so the threshold for determining whether an expenditure concerning a presidential candidate in the general election is election-related would be around $600,000. (Given that many expenditures might be targeted on one or a small number of states, it might be appropriate to develop state spending thresholds under the national threshold for presidential elections.)

These thresholds are significantly higher than FECA's current thresholds for reporting by independent committees engaged in express advocacy, and are generally higher than the thresholds used by the states to trigger reporting requirements.[59]

Employing a higher monetary threshold in the definition of election-related expenditures serves three purposes: first, treating all advertising that mentions a clearly identified candidate for federal office in a defined pre-election period as election-related is likely to subject to regulation some communications that discuss issues or focus on public affairs apart from the upcoming election. To be sure, the express reference to a candidate means that the advertisement is likely to have an impact on the listener's or viewer's decision about that candidate, but in some cases the combination of issue discussion and the avoidance of an express call for the election or defeat of a candidate might create some ambiguity as to whether the advertisement will have an impact on the election. In other words, a precise thirty-day rule overcomes the problem of vagueness at the price of raising the specter of overbreadth, that is, of regulating speech that is not clearly election-related. One way to mitigate the overbreadth concern is to focus on political communications that are more likely to have an effect on voter decision making and to exempt from regulation communications that are unlikely to have much consequence. One way to do that is to employ a higher monetary threshold. I do not mean to argue that a specific monetary threshold is constitutionally mandated. But with the higher monetary threshold it becomes more likely that the standard of election-relatedness—which also requires specific reference to a candidate and either *Buckley*'s express advocacy test or a precise pre-election period—will optimally balance the competing constitutional concerns of vindicating the norms of election regulation and minimizing the burden on general political speech.

FECA sets very low reporting and disclosure thresholds.[60] With major party candidates spending well in excess of $500,000 in contested congressional elections, it is unlikely that expenditures of $1,000 will have any perceptible impact on electoral outcomes. Nor is it likely that voter decision making would be enhanced if the sources of a few hundred dollars are required to be disclosed. If the purpose of the definition of election-related is to vindicate the underlying concerns of campaign finance regulation—to provide voters with information concerning the identities of those who support or oppose particular candidates, to deter the potential for corruption, to reduce the role of political war chests uncorrelated with the extent of public support for the political positions taken—these concerns are simply not affected by such small sums. Knowing about them provides the voters with little in the way of useful information. These amounts are unlikely to trigger quid pro quo obligations to the individuals or organizations who provide them. Nor are they likely to raise the potential for undue influence on electoral outcomes.

Only the larger sums of money represented by thresholds represented by 1 percent to 5 percent of average spending for the office in question present any realistic possibility of actually affecting the election. Consistent with the principles of justifying the definition of election-related speech in terms of the possibility of an impact on the election while minimizing the regulatory burden on general political speech, the threshold for the definition of election-related speech should be increased. This is, strictly speaking, a pragmatic argument, not a constitutional one. Yet in the campaign finance reform area pragmatic and constitutional concerns are, and ought to be, intertwined. Campaign finance regulations do place some burdens on political speech; these burdens are justified only to the extent that they advance the goals of campaign finance regulation. A definition of election-relatedness that is difficult for campaign participants to comply with or for regulators to enforce raises the unwelcome prospect of burdens without benefits and ultimately mocks the constitutional values underlying campaign finance regulation. A more enforceable definition is a more constitutional one to the extent that it means that the restrictions on political communication resulting from regulation are vindicated by the more certain disclosure of information, more complete compliance with limits on corporate or union expenditures, and, more generally, more effective attainment of the norms justifying the restrictions.

Second, cases like *McIntyre v. Ohio Elections Commission* reflect considerable judicial discomfort with governmental regulation of grassroots political activity. Justice Stevens's opinion for the Court dwelt on the "personally crafted" nature of Ms. McIntyre's leaflet, and Justice Ginsburg's concurrence spoke of the "individual leafleteer who, within her local community, spoke her mind." Not only is there less public benefit in regulating small spenders, but there may be a greater burden on political expression and personal autonomy if the regulation includes individuals or grassroots groups whose small expenditures are more likely to reflect deeply held personal views.

Third, focusing regulation on communications involving larger sums of money enhances the prospects for compliance and enforcement. A higher threshold targets only the major electoral players, that is, those participants in political spending who are best able to understand the law and comply with its requirements. Entities that spend larger sums of money are simply less likely to stumble across the election/politics line and are more capable of carefully separating their electoral from their other political efforts. Thus a higher threshold minimizes the regulation of nonelectoral speech. By the same token, in limiting the scope of regulation, a higher threshold enables regulators to husband their resources and target their efforts on assuring compliance by the major actors. This also increases the possibility of compliance within the election campaign itself.[61]

As with the definition of the pre-election period, there is no magic to the 1 percent threshold, and no clear justification for 1 percent as opposed to 2 percent, 3 percent, 5 percent, or 10 percent. As with the other questions of election law line-drawing, these ought to be "matters of degree" with appropriate deference to political decision-makers. The critical point is that a definition more carefully focused on larger expenditures, determined relative to the actual levels of spending by candidates, both does a better job of achieving the goals of campaign finance regulation and is more respectful of First Amendment interests.

SPECIFIC RULES

The proposed definition of election-related communications is intended to balance the protection of general political speech from government regulation against the interest in effective enforcement of campaign finance laws that are consistent with, indeed, supportive of, the basic role of elections in creating a structure of democratic self-governance. The definition expands *Buckley*'s coverage of election-related speech beyond the easily evaded express advocacy standard to include clear references to a candidate during the election campaign that involve the expenditure of a threshold sum of money, but it uses a relatively short pre-election period and a high expenditure threshold to protect issue-oriented individuals and groups and grassroots organizations engaged in true issue advocacy from the toils of the election laws. For some identifiable groups or activities, however, the balance of interests may tip in favor of a different—a wider or a narrower—definition of election-related communication. The two special cases that come to mind are political parties and voter guides issued by advocacy groups.

Issue Advocacy by the Major Political Parties. The Annenberg study found that the major parties accounted for more than half the issue advocacy expenditures in 1996 and for more than 70 percent of issue advocacy expenditures in the two months before Election Day 1998.[62] Political party advocacy presents a much stronger case for regulation, while raising fewer of the concerns that would demand a narrower definition of election-related activities. Unlike many ideological advocacy groups, the major political parties receive corporate and union funds in their soft money accounts. Indeed, major party issue advocacy provides an important conduit for corporate and union participation in elections. The two major parties are also powerful organizations. Between them, they control the overwhelming majority of federal and state offices. Unlike the case for small, independent, or grassroots organizations, the reporting and disclosure of contributions to and expenditures by the parties is unlikely to have a chilling effect on the parties, their supporters, or the vendors from whom they buy services. In addition, with their staffs of skilled campaign professionals, the major political parties are in the best position to conform their activities to legal requirements. And as they are already subject to considerable regulation, the reporting and disclosure of additional campaign activities would not create significant new administrative burdens for them.

Most important, the raison d'être of the two major political parties is to fight and win elections.[63] They make communications concerning issues primarily to advance the prospects of their candidates for elective office. Given the electoral focus of the major parties, such party communications concerning issues are presumptively election-related.

The First Amendment should tolerate a much broader definition of election-related activities when it comes to the major political parties. It would be perfectly constitutional to expand the election-period limitation or to lower the monetary threshold. Indeed, given the connections between parties and candidates, I would suggest that as a constitutional matter when considering major party advertising that refers to a clearly identified candidate for federal office both the temporal and monetary elements of the general definition of election-relatedness may be dispensed with. As a practical matter, however, some monetary threshold would be desirable to focus enforcement efforts on more substantial activities; similarly, the determination of whether a person referred to in an advertisement is a candidate for federal office is likely to have a significant temporal element.

Such an approach is not barred by *Colorado Republican Federal Campaign Committee v. FEC.*[64] That decision held that a party's spending is not inherently coordinated with the spending of its candidate for purposes of the FECA provision limiting "coordinated spending." But in finding that parties may be able to engage in "independent spending," the Court did not consider whether, once an election is under way, parties can engage in issue advocacy in addition to independent spending. Party independent spending, like other forms of independent spending, is subject to reporting and disclosure requirements and contribution limitations and prohibitions; these are the very regulations that would be avoided if a communication is defined as issue advocacy. *Colorado Republican* establishes that a major party can support its candidates in a manner independent of the candidate's campaign, but that is in no way inconsistent with a determination that a party's expenditures concerning a clearly identified candidate are part of the election that the candidate is contesting.

The institutional commitment of parties to candidate-related activities and the lack of danger that expanded regulation would interfere with communications solely concerning issues support a broader definition that treats party advertising concerning clearly identified candidates as election-related speech, subject to disclosure requirements and limits on the size and sources of contributions. Disclosure is unlikely to chill contributions to the major parties. Moreover, the greater public interest in information concerning the financial support for the two major parties that together dominate our political system, combined with the increased reliance of the major parties on funding from sources—corporations and unions—that are specially restricted, militates in favor of a broader definition for election-relatedness for major party spending.

Voter Guides. One of the most frequent causes of legal conflict under the existing express advocacy/issue advocacy distinction is the treatment of so-called voter guides, that is, compilations of how a candidate has voted or the positions a candidate has taken with respect to issues of interest to the organization publishing the guide.[65] These guides also frequently include some characterization of how a candidate's votes or issue positions stack up against the organization's own positions. Voter guides present a particularly thorny problem because they are the rare form of issue advocacy that actually provides information concerning issues, yet they can—and are surely intended to—affect how people will vote in an election. The FEC has tried to regulate corporate and labor organization voter guides that are distributed to the general public. The FEC standard turns in part on the presence or absence of "an electioneering message" or whether the guide "score[s] or rate[s] the candidates' responses in such a way as to convey an electioneering message."[66]

Classifying voter guides according to the content of their messages— much like the attempt to develop an entirely content-based measure of issue advocacy generally—is unlikely to pass constitutional muster. The concept of "electioneering" is inherently vague and creates uncertainties for both the publishers of voting guides and enforcement agencies. Would a voter guide that combines a statement of a candidate's votes or positions on certain issues with a statement of the sponsoring organization's positions on the same issues be engaged in "electioneering"? What about a guide that underscores the names of candidates who generally support the organization's positions or the name of the candidate in each pair of opposing candidates whose positions come closer to those of the issuing organization?

Rather than attempt to distinguish electioneering from nonelectioneering materials, I would draw a different line. I would distinguish between voting record information distributed internally—to an organization's officers, members, affiliates, or the regular recipients of publications and other mailings of the organization—and externally, that is, to the general public. Communications within an organization concerning the organization's positions on political issues implicate the core of freedom of association. The officers, members, and other persons who have voluntarily chosen to affiliate with an organization have a distinct interest—different from and greater than that of the general public—in learning the organization's views concerning candidates. Conversely, there is little benefit in terms of the accepted goals of campaign regulation to treating such communications as regulable speech. There is only a limited informational gain from applying disclosure requirements to the expenditure of funds for internal dissemination of voter guides since officers, members, and regular recipients of organization publications presumably already know quite a bit about the organization and its views on issues. Nor does communication among persons who have a common affiliation raise the same concern about the projection of an organization's war chest into the electoral arena—which is the principal rationale supporting restrictions on corporate and union electoral activity. Indeed, FECA's restrictions on corporations and unions do not apply to such internal communications.[67] If the internal communication of a voter guide is not coordinated with a candidate, it could not be treated as a contribution and regulation could not be justified in terms of the goals that support contribution limitations.

The distribution of a voter guide to the general public is a very different story.[68] The associational interest is diminished and the danger of the projection of economic power into the political arena is strengthened where there is no preexisting connection between the organization and the persons who receive the message. Given the lack of such a connection between sponsor and audience, and the increasingly cryptic names of many of the organizations participating in election campaigns, disclosure of the source of funds for the organization distributing a voter guide can be critical to the voters' appraisal of the information provided. As long as the organization disseminating the voter guide operates at arm's length from the candidates, its activities would be treated as an independent expenditure, not a contribution. The principal burden on a sponsor who crossed the monetary threshold for regulation would be reporting and disclosure. There would be no limit on expenditures for the dissemination of an independently prepared and distributed voter guide or on contributions that finance such a guide.

Thus expenditures that cross the monetary threshold within the pre-election period for distribution of a voter guide to the general public should be regulable as election-related communications. That would mean the sources of funds would have to be disclosed, and corporations and unions would be completely barred from using treasury funds for financing such activity. But expenditures for the internal dissemination of such a guide—even if the expenditures cross the monetary threshold and the distribution occurs within the election-eve period—should be constitutionally protected from regulation.

THE DEFINITION OF ELECTION-RELATED SPEECH AND THE SCOPE OF CAMPAIGN FINANCE REGULATION

I noted at the outset of this chapter that the definition of election-related speech and the scope of campaign regulation are separate questions. Certainly, the determination of what forms of campaign finance regulation are constitutionally permissible does not determine what kinds of activities fall into the category of campaign activities. Yet although the two questions are logically distinct they may be, in practice, connected.

It may be easier, as a practical matter, to justify an expansion of the category of election-related speech when the consequences would be minimally burdensome: requiring reporting and disclosure by organizations spending relatively large sums of money; requiring corporations and unions to finance these communications from their PACs rather than from treasury funds (and under Supreme Court precedent many ideological groups that have taken the corporate form, such as right-to-life organizations, would be exempt from this requirement); forcing parties to reclassify certain activities as independent expenditures rather than issue advocacy with attendant disclosure requirements but no expenditure limitations. Not only would the proposed redefinition of election-related speech address some of the blatant evasion that makes a mockery of the entire campaign finance enterprise, but the principal consequences—increased information and more effective enforcement of the constitutionally valid limitations on corporate and union campaign activities—are also consistent with the broader values of the First Amendment.

Conversely, if the Constitution were amended or interpreted to permit greater regulation of election-related speech, particularly if it permitted the imposition of expenditure limits on candidates and independent spending, as some chapters in this book support, the question of the definition of election-related speech could become more difficult. An expansion of the goals and techniques of campaign finance regulations would surely reflect a reconsideration of the place of equality of participation in the definition of a fair and democratic process. If the Constitution were held to permit regulations that equalize the opportunity to influence election outcomes by limiting candidate, party, and especially independent committee spending, then the determination of what spending is considered to be election-related would become even more important than it is under the current regime. The logic of giving greater attention to the distinctive features of, and the particular mix of collective and individual rights concerns implicated by, an election in the constitutional definition of election-relatedness would remain. But the impact on political speech of simultaneously expanding both the definition of an election and the permissible regulation of election-related communications would lead to a much greater intrusion on political speech than either step by itself. A broader definition of election-relatedness, as I have called for in this chapter, could thus, paradoxically, prove an obstacle to an expansion of the constitutionally permissible forms and purposes of campaign finance regulation, including the imposition of spending limits. Alternatively, if spending limits were constitutionally permissible, the courts might be even more wary of expanding the definition of what constitutes campaign spending.

Thus, any effort to expand campaign finance regulation to include spending limits must take seriously the conceptual and practical difficulties of drawing the election/politics line. In theory, the question of what constitutes an election is unrelated to how election finance practices may be regulated, but the stakes would be much higher, and the burdens on political activity greater, in a post-*Buckley* regime that permits spending limits.

V. CONCLUSION

Some distinction between election-related spending and other political spending is essential for any campaign finance regime, whether a minimally regulatory regime focused purely on disclosure or a more ambitious effort to limit contributions or expenditures. The distinction *Buckley v. Valeo* draws between express advocacy and issue advocacy fails to correspond to the actual distinctions between elections and the rest of politics. Instead, it has become an open invitation to evasion of campaign finance regulation. A better definition of election-related speech would incorporate both the legitimate governmental interest in designing a fair and legitimate process for collective selection of a democratic government and the First Amendment interest in protecting non-election-related speech. It would provide a clear line, although the actual location of that line would necessarily reflect political judgments about the relative importance of a number of conflicting values rather than an extrapolation from incontestable principles. Such a line ought to look to the timing of the communication and the amount of money spent on it, as well as to the express words of the message. The identity of the speaker (whether it is a major political party) and the nature of communication (whether it is an internal communication from an organization to its members) are relevant as well. The resulting definition would be both more effective in practice and more accurate in theory in mapping the elusive but essential election/politics line.

I should address, briefly, three of the many criticisms that I anticipate will be leveled at this proposal. These correspond to the types of arguments that Albert O. Hirschman flagged in *The Rhetoric of Reaction:* futility, perversity, and jeopardy.[69] First, it may be that this approach, like so many campaign finance reforms, will prove futile. In the twenty-five years since Watergate sparked the amendments to the Federal Election Campaign Act that produced our current regulatory regime, politicians and organizations seeking to influence electoral politics have repeatedly demonstrated their ability to frustrate legislative efforts to restrict the flow of campaign dollars. The rise of such institutions as independent committees, bundling, soft money, and issue advocacy demonstrates the capacity of electoral actors to frustrate reform.

One argument, then, is that a redefinition of election-related spending, whatever its appeal in theory, is, like other forms of campaign finance reform, doomed to failure. This is quite possibly true. Certainly, a quarter-century of campaign finance reform has done little to constrain the role of money in politics. Yet the futility thesis fails to acknowledge that some reforms—public funding, individual contribution limits—have had consequences. The very need for politicians and political organizations to invent new campaign finance techniques is a backhanded testimonial to the effectiveness of some rules in curtailing or eliminating some practices. Moreover, some reforms—such as public funding of congressional elections—were never attempted, while others were hamstrung from the outset by judicial interpretation. Central components of the current campaign finance regime—such as the narrow express advocacy definition of election-related spending—have operated to curtail the effectiveness of regulation. It will not be clear if the redefinition of election-related is futile unless it is tried.

The argument for the futility of reform may really be an argument about its perversity. Campaign finance reform has repeatedly demonstrated the law of unanticipated consequences. Restrictions on individual donations to candidates contributed directly to the rise of political action committees and to the emergence of bundling, much as the limits incident to the public funding of presidential candidates stimulated the rise of independent committees, soft money, and issue advocacy. Campaign reform rules in some sense "work" in that they limit the activities they directly address, but they may also lead to new practices that not only permit the circumvention of the rules but also increase the role of special interest groups, political intermediaries, and other financial power brokers, to the detriment of our democratic system.

Again, this may very well be a valid criticism, providing a useful caution about the need to think through the possible consequences of reform. How will those now engaged in issue advocacy react if they are restrained from doing so? Certainly, they are likely to engage in more issue spending earlier in the political cycle—probably in the weeks before the one-month election-eve period, and possibly even earlier than that. Expanding the definition of regulable election-related speech may also lead to a shift in spending from elections to political advocacy outside the electoral context—what might be called actual issue advocacy, in contrast to the so-called issue advocacy that is really election-related speech. We could see more ads like the "Harry & Louise" campaign that marked the battle over the Clinton health plan.

Would the costs of these developments offset, if not outweigh, the gains from expanding the definition of election-related speech? Displacing issue advocacy to the earlier weeks of the campaign does raise the danger that issue ads could set the tone of the campaign before it gets under way. Of course, nothing now prevents parties and special interest organizations from focusing their advocacy on the opening phases of an electoral cycle if it is in their self-interest. If the proposed definition of election-related speech would force parties and committees that would rather hold their fire until the final weeks of the campaign—because they think the most effective use of funds is to take to the airwaves later—to air their ads earlier, then regulation could make issue advocacy less effective. More issue advocacy in the earlier weeks of a campaign may offset the benefits of regulating it in later weeks, but the result could still be an overall reduction in the impact of issue advocacy. Certainly, it would be more feasible for candidates targeted by issue ads to attempt a rejoinder and for the news media to explore the content of the allegations in and the sources of the funds behind issue ads if the ads were to appear earlier in a campaign rather than in the final weeks. By increasing the information available to the voters concerning campaign finances, this could increase the quality of electoral decision making.

As for the possibility that the regulation of so-called issue ads might stimulate greater actual issue advocacy, with political groups devoting more resources to mass media campaigns aimed at affecting legislative deliberations rather than election outcomes, it is hard to tell if society would be worse off. Again, there is currently no constraint on such activity, and, as the Harry & Louise ads suggest, true issue advocacy may be growing even though so-called issue advocacy focused on electoral campaigns is unrestrained. Moreover, such campaigns may be less harmful to democratic decision making than campaigns targeted at elections. Actual issue campaigns would be aimed at affecting the climate of public opinion in which public officials act, but not at the selection of public officials and the makeup of the government. The effects of these campaigns may be more limited and uncertain. They may affect public opinion without affecting public officials, and even if they affect public action on some issues, there will be many other public issues that have not been targeted by issue campaigns. Still, some recognition of the hydraulic nature of political money, and some acknowledgment of the fact that private wealth blocked from so-called issue advocacy is likely to show up somewhere else in the political process is necessary to temper any expectations concerning the practical benefits of expanding the definition of election-related speech to encompass so-called issue advocacy.

Finally, my argument for broader election-related spending regulation relies on Supreme Court election law decisions, particularly the ballot access cases that have upheld state laws that limit the ability of minor parties and independents to get on the ballot. These cases have been criticized for their valorization of the two-party system, their willingness to allow the major parties to insulate themselves from challenges from third parties and independents, and their failure to subject restrictions on voters' choices and political associations to the strict judicial scrutiny appropriate when fundamental rights are at stake. Certainly, the Court's assertion of the virtues of the two-party system in justifying limits on minor parties and independents raises important concerns about the ability of incumbents to use election regulations to fortify themselves against challengers. Viewing the issue advocacy problem through the prism of the ballot access cases thus arguably entrenches these cases and the protections they provide the political status quo in constitutional law, and may be said to jeopardize the value of open and unfettered political competition.

The ballot access cases do raise questions about the degree of appropriate judicial deference to rules about the electoral process that have been adopted by incumbents. Still, it is far from clear that extending the approach of the ballot access cases, particularly the assumption that election regulation involves the balancing of individual rights and the collective concern in organizing the electoral process, would be harmful. First, the ballot access cases seem pretty well entrenched already. Indeed, over time, the Court appears to have become increasingly deferential to state policies in this area. These cases may be mistaken, but it is not clear that applying their reasoning to campaign finance regulation does any new harm. As long as these cases are established constitutional law, we might want to see how they can be useful in analyzing the issues posed by governmental regulation of campaign spending.

Second, and more important, the ballot access cases do get at something significant in thinking about elections. These cases usefully underscore the role of the election as a mechanism for collective choice, and the need to review state regulations of the electoral process not only from the perspective of individual rights but also in terms of their impact on the role of the election in producing a government. The particular lines the Court has drawn may reflect an undue suspicion of third parties and independents, unwarranted hostility to write-in ballots, and an excessive acceptance of political incumbents' tributes to the two-party system. But the basic idea that elections must be regulated if they are to perform their function of providing a mechanism for collective decision making, and that election regulation involves the reconciliation of conflicting individual and collective concerns, is not only right but an appropriate basis for thinking about the regulation of election-related spending.

5

SOFT LANDINGS

Burt Neuborne

What would happen to the First Amendment if *Buckley v. Valeo* were overruled? *Buckley*'s defenders maintain that the decision, which holds that uncontrolled campaign spending is fully protected by the First Amendment, is compelled by constitutional principle. Ignore First Amendment principle, they warn, and free speech protection will be significantly weakened.

If the price of doing away with *Buckley* were a significant erosion of constitutional protection for free speech, I would argue that we should learn to live with the decision and its consequences, just as we've learned to live with the foolish, harmful, even hateful speech that is the inevitable by-product of principled protection for robust free speech. But if *Buckley*'s passing would cause hardly a ripple in the First Amendment pond, the truly devastating effect on American democracy caused by our current inability to limit runaway campaign spending argues powerfully for its overthrow.[1] In effect, *Buckley*'s defenders tell us that we must choose between principled constitutional free speech protection and a vibrant democracy. But I believe that they pose a false dichotomy. In fact, we can enjoy both robust protection of free speech and a democracy that is not dominated by the super-rich.

I. THE FREE SPEECH PRINCIPLE

The crucial First Amendment principle on which *Buckley* is said to rest is the constitutional right to speak vigorously on political issues free from government interference. Robust free speech protection—especially for political speech—is, I heartily agree, a principle worth defending. In a free society, speech about politics should be the business of autonomous individuals, not governments. That is the essence of what Ronald Dworkin calls the "democratic wager." To decide whether reversing *Buckley* would jeopardize the robust protection of political speech, I propose to look closely at the free speech principle as it is recognized and enforced by the Supreme Court, and ask whether reversing *Buckley* would threaten its continued existence. To illustrate the operation of the free speech principle, I will invoke the two most celebrated free speech controversies in recent years—the Nazis in Skokie and flag burning.

In *Collin v. Smith*,[2] a ragtag group of Nazis sought to spread their message of hate by marching in full Nazi regalia through the streets of Skokie, Illinois, a Chicago suburb with a large Jewish population that included many Holocaust survivors. If ever political speech posed an appealing case for suppression, it was the Nazis' march in Skokie. The Nazis had targeted Skokie solely because of its large Jewish population. The content of their message was, figuratively if not literally, unspeakably vile, propagating a vision of racial and religious bigotry that mocks a tolerant democratic society. Their message was overwhelmingly unwelcome, offensive to almost all hearers; painful, even frightening, to many Holocaust survivors. Their mode of speech, a procession through the public streets displaying Nazi symbols, caused significant physical dislocation, forced the expenditure of significant community resources, and was overtly confrontational. And yet our commitment to free speech about politics is so intense that Skokie was an easy legal case, whatever its emotional difficulty. Virtually every judge who considered the case agreed that the power to decide whether to speak, what to say, and how and where to say it rested with the Nazi speakers, not the state or the reluctant audience.

Similarly, in *Texas v. Johnson*[3] and *United States v. Eichman*,[4] opponents of American policy and culture sought to express their intense revulsion by publicly burning American flags in violation of statutes designed to shield the flag from desecration. The legal arguments in favor of banning flag burning were not trivial. In both flag burning cases, they persuaded four justices of the Supreme Court, including Justice Stevens. In the past, they had even persuaded First Amendment stalwarts like Chief Justice Warren, Justice Black,[5] and, quite possibly, Justice Douglas. In support of banning flag burning, the government argued that virtually every culture adopts symbols that help unify its members by providing emotional rallying points. Flag burners, argued the government, undermine one of the nation's most important symbolic rallying points, while causing intense distress to onlookers for whom the flag has deep meaning.[6] Moreover, unlike the Nazi march in Skokie where the effort to censor was driven by the hateful content of the Nazis' message, a universally applicable effort to protect the national symbol is not designed to suppress the speaker's message. Frustrated flag burners would remain perfectly free to express their hatred of American policy and culture by holding a rally, delivering vituperative speeches, and displaying provocative banners on the very site where they wished to burn a flag.

Once again, though, despite the power of the government's arguments and the emotional baggage associated with the flag, flag burning turns out to be an easy case for the free speech principle. The five justices who formed the majority in the flag burning cases recognized that a ban on flag burning is inherently biased against critics of American policy, since supporters would hardly be likely to choose burning the flag as a means of expressing pro-American views. Most important, they recognized that judgments about how Americans express themselves on political issues should be made by autonomous individuals, not government regulators, even when the political expression is in dreadful taste, potentially corrosive of national unity, and deeply offensive to many unwilling hearers.

II. Is Campaign Spending Really a Form of Autonomous Speech?

Buckley's defenders argue, with surface plausibility, that if Nazis and flag burners are free to make their own political decisions about what to say and how to say it, surely political candidates and campaign donors should be free to spend unlimited amounts on infinitely more desirable electoral speech. But the effort to embed unlimited campaign spending within the free speech principle is too facile. In fact, when one compares *Buckley* to celebrated examples of the free speech principle at work, like flag burning and Nazi ranting, it becomes clear that overruling *Buckley* would not threaten—indeed it might well strengthen—the protection of autonomous political speech that is at the core of the First Amendment.

The heart of the free speech principle that emerges from *Skokie* and the flag burning cases is respect for the inherent dignity of an autonomous speaker. Once an individual (even a foolish or hateful individual) makes an autonomous decision to speak, the free speech principle trumps most countervailing regulatory values, like offensiveness, annoyance, anger, inconvenience, modest expense, even mild fear. Only genuinely "compelling" governmental interests, like preventing an imminent threat to national security or an imminent outbreak of violence, can overcome the strong presumptive tilt toward free expression required by the free speech principle.

Overruling *Buckley* simply would not threaten such a free speech principle. The *Buckley* Court believed that it was defending the freedom of candidates and contributors to make autonomous judgments about whether and how intensely to talk about politics. But twenty-three years of experience with *Buckley* demonstrates that the Court got the first two aspects of the free speech analysis empirically wrong. At some point, uncontrolled, massive political spending stops being pure speech and becomes an exercise in power. Moreover, many—perhaps most—participants in an uncontrolled campaign spending process are simply not autonomous speakers.

One of the most controversial aspects of the *Buckley* opinion is its insistence that campaign spending must be treated for First Amendment purposes as though it were pure speech. Since, argues the *Buckley* Court, the spending of campaign money is intended to generate campaign speech, efforts to regulate campaign spending must be treated as if they were efforts to regulate campaign speech itself. As an abstract matter, the Court's application of the First Amendment to spending that ultimately culminates in speech seems dubious. Merely because the act of spending money ultimately leads to speech does not make it speech, as Frederick Schauer and Richard Pildes so aptly demonstrate in Chapter Three. For example, if I own a newspaper, the wages I pay to my reporters are intended, ultimately, to generate speech. But the act of paying those wages is a form of conduct subject to government regulation and taxation, even though the wages make possible the publication of my newspaper. From a First Amendment perspective, why should spending money on political campaigns be different from spending money on reporters' wages?

The issue is more complicated, though, because, on the facts of *Buckley*, the Court's insistence on collapsing campaign spending and campaign speaking into a single First Amendment activity made sense. The spending limits imposed by the congressional legislation before the *Buckley* Court were absurdly low. Congressional general election campaigns were capped at $70,000, far less than the amount needed to mount a serious campaign in most congressional districts. Senate general election campaigns were similarly capped at 12 cents per voter, a grossly inadequate sum. Independent spending in support of a candidate was capped at $1,000, less than the amount needed to take out a quarter-page ad in the *New York Times*. Confronted with such draconian restrictions on the ability to spend money to generate electoral speech, the *Buckley* Court quite correctly treated the extremely low spending restrictions as *de facto* limits on political speech. Returning to my hypothetical newspaper, if the government tells me that I may hire only one reporter and must pay no more than the minimum wage, it would be fair to treat that restriction as an unreasonable limit on my ability to publish the news. But merely because we subject to strict First Amendment review draconian spending restrictions that make it impossible to speak at all, that does not mean that all spending restrictions, even extremely generous ones, must be tested by identical First Amendment standards.

At some point, a restriction on massive spending ceases to be a speech restriction and becomes more like a regulation of behavior— behavior involving the power to amplify and repeat a message in order to dominate discourse. If the Court were to view massive campaign spending as a combination of speech and conduct designed to

amplify and repeat the speech, regulation of the amplification component would not threaten the free speech principle any more than
existing law permitting regulation of sound trucks,[7] applying antitrust
principles to newspapers to prevent market domination,[8] and requiring cable broadcasters to carry channels they would prefer to reject.[9]
If the Nazis wanted to march in Skokie all day, every day, using bull-
horns and dominating opposing voices, limits on the massive repetition of the Nazi message would not be governed by the same rules
that assured the group a fair opportunity to be heard at all. In short,
modifying *Buckley* to permit regulation of extremely high levels of
campaign spending as a species of conduct would pose no real risk to
the free speech principle at work in *Skokie* or the flag burning cases.

The *Buckley* decision also badly misread the relationship between
autonomy and campaign speech. The *Buckley* Court characterized
candidates and donors as free-standing, autonomous individuals,
making their own decisions about how to advance their political ends.
How better to reinforce such free-standing autonomy than to eliminate government interference? The *Buckley* opinion's most colorful
metaphor analogizes a candidate to the driver of a car, with campaign money as gasoline. It should, reasoned the *Buckley* Court, be up
to the driver, not the government, to decide how far to drive the car.
But the metaphor of a single driver taking a drive in the country does
not accurately describe the reality of a contested political campaign.
For one thing, an election campaign is not a drive in the country, but
a race between two or more contestants. If money really is gasoline,
how can you have a fair race when only one car has enough fuel?
And when that fuel must be obtained from interested suppliers, who
is it that really decides where the car ultimately goes?

In fact, a candidate's decisions about campaign spending are not
made in an autonomous vacuum, but as a series of reciprocal
responses to the spending of opponents. The more apt analogy, therefore, is not to an autonomous speaker deciding how much to say,
but to participants in a superpower arms race. As our own recent
past demonstrates, at some point in the arms race both participants
wish to stop because further spending is harmful to themselves, but
neither can afford to act unilaterally. Both are trapped in a mutually
destructive spiral having nothing to do with autonomy or free will. As
uncontrollable campaign spending spirals higher and higher, it impris-
ons candidates and officials involuntarily in a never-ending search

for funds, deflecting their time and attention from substance,[10] and rendering them more and more vulnerable to subtle and not-so-subtle pressures by self-interested donors. But no one can stop the destructive upward spiral, because unilateral disarmament may be disastrous. (Even the 1998 victory of Senator Russell Feingold, who voluntarily capped his campaign spending and forswore millions in support from the Democratic Party, confirms the point, for the self-imposed limits cost him a double-digit lead and almost cost him the election.) In fact, the political autonomy that *Buckley* sought to enhance turns out to be a classic prisoners' dilemma in which candidates and officials are trapped in an involuntary, indeed deeply distasteful, fundraising spiral. And they can't escape because they fear that if they unilaterally stop spending they will be outgunned by their opponents.

The classic solution to such an arms race is collective action imposing a ceiling that is fair to both participants. But *Buckley* prevents the setting of such a ceiling.

The ceiling that was before the Court in *Buckley* was unfair to challengers because it was too low to permit a serious effort to unseat an incumbent. It was also unfair to voters because it robbed them of a chance to hear a full-fledged debate on the issues. Accordingly, I believe the *Buckley* Court was right in striking it down. But generous ceilings, set high enough to permit challengers to make a strong case and to assure full ventilation of campaign issues, would be far closer to the true wishes of campaign participants than the current laissez-faire process that promises autonomy but delivers the destructive coercion of a prisoner's dilemma.

Nor is the contribution side of the picture much prettier. The *Buckley* Court assumed that contributors were autonomous individuals making up their minds about how intensely to support or oppose a particular candidate because they agree or disagree with that candidate's politics. But reality is a far cry from the Court's romantic vision of autonomous contributors. In fact, a subtle undercurrent of bribery and extortion runs through the campaign contribution process, at least when very significant sums are involved. Large campaign contributors rarely make donations for altruistic purposes. They expect something in return. Sometimes, the expected return is completely innocent—the victory of an ideological soul mate who can be counted upon to advance the contributor's ideas and interests.

But often, the return involves more specific obligations. At a minimum, large contributors expect preferred access to candidates and officials. All too often, they expect privileged treatment when policy gets made. Nor do contributors always act freely. Often, a large campaign contribution is an insurance premium designed to position the contributor on the right side of an official with significant power. Powerful officials encourage interested donors to make campaign contributions with just a whiff of extortion. Even when the initial contribution was completely innocent, no official desperate for campaign funds can ignore the fact that future contributions may well depend on behavior that pleases a large contributor.

The *Buckley* Court recognized the potential for involuntary behavior latent in large contributions by upholding a $1,000 contribution ceiling for gifts to a single candidate in an election, and a $25,000 ceiling on all contributions toward federal elections. During the early years of the *Buckley* regime, the contribution ceilings limited the potential for extortion and bribery latent in the process. But with the rise of unlimited soft money contributions to political parties, and the emergence of so-called issue advertisements as thinly veiled campaign weapons—phenomena that Frank Sorauf documents in detail in Chapter One—the system of contribution limits upheld in *Buckley* has imploded. The potential for bribery and extortion under a veneer of political participation is now a reality. Corporate executives complain bitterly of being required to make large contributions. Candidates and officials complain bitterly of feeling that they have lost control of their decision-making processes. In fact, the idealized *Buckley* vision of autonomous individuals making huge campaign contributions freely because of political principle is simply a romantic illusion.

If the current Court were to acknowledge that most campaign spending at very high levels is not truly autonomous, but is involuntarily driven in an ascending spiral by reciprocal fears about the spending of opponents and the power of incumbents, the imposition of a reasonable ceiling designed to free candidates from an arms race mentality—and contributors from a shadow world of undue influence—should be viewed as an enhancement of and not a threat to genuinely autonomous decisions about campaign spending. Rather than eroding a free speech principle founded on respect for autonomy, reversing *Buckley* to permit generous ceilings on campaign spending, and to reestablish effective ceilings on campaign contributions, would actually enhance it.

III. Do "Compelling" Governmental Interests Justify Limits on Campaign Spending?

Even if the Court were to continue to assume that spending and speech are legally indistinguishable even at very high levels, and even if it continues to insist that campaign spending at very high levels is truly autonomous, an alternative route to overturning *Buckley* exists that would leave free speech doctrine intact. Pursuant to settled free speech doctrine, autonomous political speech can be regulated only to advance a compelling governmental interest that cannot be advanced by less drastic means. In *Buckley*, the Court recognized that avoidance of the appearance or reality of corruption was a compelling interest that justified reasonable limits on the size and source of campaign contributions. If the Court were to recognize additional compelling interests in regulating massive campaign spending, reasonable restrictions on campaign spending could be upheld with no change at all in First Amendment doctrine.

Contemporary First Amendment doctrine requires two closely connected fundamental judgments on the quality and imminence of any alleged justification for censorship. Ordinary justifications must be distinguished from so-called *compelling* justifications; and the imminence of the harm underlying the compelling need for regulation must be gauged. Once again, the *Skokie* and flag burning cases provide excellent examples of free speech doctrine in action. In both sets of cases, legitimate reasons for regulating speech were present. In the *Skokie* case, an unwelcome message was being foisted on an audience that had every reason to be deeply disturbed, even terrified, by the explicit expression of Nazi hatred for Jews. In the flag burning cases, a cherished national symbol was treated with contempt, causing deep pain and resentment. In both cases, however, the Court carefully distinguished between two levels of justification for regulating speech.

On the one hand are reasons like annoyance, anger, and generalized anxiety that may be legitimate but are nevertheless insufficient to overcome the presumption in favor of free expression. On the other hand are more serious harms, like fear caused by face-to-face threats or the likelihood of imminent violence, which would justify regulation. While claims were made in both sets of cases that the more serious types of harms were, in fact, present, the Court insisted on a showing of greater imminence. The mere possibility of a harm serious enough to generate a compelling need for censorship was not sufficient.

In *Buckley* itself, the Court recognized that avoiding the reality or appearance of corruption inherent in large campaign contributions was a compelling interest that justified a ceiling on the size of campaign contributions. In the twenty-three years since the *Buckley* decision, at least three additional compelling interests have emerged that justify limits on uncontrolled campaign spending. First, the spectacle of uncontrolled campaign spending has eroded fath in democracy, plunging the nation into a free fall in electoral participation. Recognition that a compelling interest exists in restoring faith in the democratic process that can be advanced by placing a generous ceiling on campaign spending would be completely consistent with existing First Amendment doctrine. In the 1998 congressional elections, the turnout fell to 37 percent of the eligible electorate, the lowest level of national electoral participation in the nation's history. Participation in the 1996 presidential elections fell to 48 percent, the lowest rate of participation since 1824. Participation in local elections is even lower. The justices in *Buckley* could not have known that uncontrolled campaign spending would take such a terrible toll on the public's trust in democracy. While an appropriate factual showing would be necessary to demonstrate the link between unlimited campaign spending and loss of faith in democracy, all indicia of public perception and behavior indicate the immense price we pay in public trust for an electoral process that appears to be bought and paid for by the highest bidders.

Where sufficiently compelling interests exist, current free speech doctrine permits narrow efforts to limit speech. For example, if outsiders attempted to burn an American flag at a veteran's funeral, the need to respect the grief of the mourners would, in my opinion, be deemed a compelling interest justifying regulation. Similarly, if Nazis targeted a particular family for face-to-face threats and vituperation, a sufficient interest would justify limiting the speech. Given the threat that uncontrolled campaign spending poses to democracy, the identical analytical process justifies the setting of generous limits on campaign spending.

The government asserted a second compelling interest in *Buckley,* an interest in preserving political equality. While the Court acknowledged the importance of enhancing political equality, holding that it would justify a program of campaign subsidies, the *Buckley* Court found that enhancing political equality was not sufficiently compelling to justify limiting campaign spending. Twenty-three years of experience with *Buckley* strongly suggests that the Court's ambivalent approach to the interest in enhancing political equality as a justification for regulating campaign financing was quite wrong. In fact, the failure to acknowledge the compelling need to limit campaign spending in order to restore a modicum of political equality to American democracy may well have been *Buckley*'s gravest mistake.

The history of American democracy is a halting journey toward political equality. When Thomas Jefferson became the first presidential candidate to oust an incumbent, only white men of property were deemed worthy of participation in the democratic process. Impediments to political equality have been removed one by one until, as a formal matter, all voters now wield equal political power. In reality, though, uncontrolled campaign spending reintroduces the massive inequality of the early nineteenth century. Under a regime of uncontrolled campaign spending, the richest 2 percent of the population exercises massively disproportionate political power. They decide which candidates can run for office. They decide which issues make their way onto the national agenda. They decide who wins closely contested elections.

The *Buckley* Court recognized the threat to equal political power created by a laissez-faire approach to campaign spending. But the only response the Court was prepared to condone was the use of voluntary campaign subsidies. As a policy matter, campaign subsidies provide an opportunity to enhance political equality without restricting speech. But the subsidy route has its own difficulties, including cost, allocational criteria, and the difficulty of persuading incumbents to subsidize candidates to run against them. Subsidy is not, however, the only way to enhance political equality. Existing First Amendment doctrine permits the setting of generous ceilings on campaign spending in order to enhance political equality.

As I have argued,[11] in a wide variety of settings where speech takes place within a "bounded" institutional context, we routinely approve (and even require) regulations designed to limit the speech opportunities of particularly powerful players so as to advance the optimal performance of the institution.[12] For example, the rules of civil and criminal procedure (to say nothing of the Due Process Clause) require that counsel be given roughly equivalent opportunities to speak to the court. We would never openly countenance a market mechanism that allocated oral argument time on the basis of a litigant's ability to pay. In the institutionally bounded setting of a litigation, we accept significant equality-driven speech restraints because we understand that the institution's proper functioning demands it. Similarly, in a classroom, we routinely ration the speaking time of various participants. No serious educator would tolerate ground rules that allowed the wealthiest students to dominate classroom discussion, or to write longer, more elaborate examinations simply because they could afford to do so. In the institutionally bounded setting of a classroom, we understand that equality-driven speech constraints are necessary to permit the educational enterprise to function optimally. Yet a third example of speech constraints in an institutionally bounded setting is the near universal resort to rules of parliamentary procedure such as Robert's Rules of Order to structure discussion in deliberative settings ranging from corporate boards to national legislatures. No one would hold a serious deliberative meeting that allocated speaking time on the basis of wealth because we know that if only the wealthy get to speak, speech cannot perform its instrumental role within the institutional context.

We already view elections, as opposed to election campaigns, as bounded institutions, with First Amendment activity subject to extensive instrumental regulation to assure the proper operation of the electoral process. By the beginning of the twentieth century, the institution of "the election" had been separated from the idea of "the campaign," had been assigned a discrete instrumental role, and had been subjected to rules that infringed on speech significantly but were designed to assure the efficient performance of its assigned role.

Three recent cases demonstrate the Supreme Court's treatment of an election as a bounded institution with a narrow instrumental role justifying highly restrictive speech rules. In *Burdick v. Takushi*,[13] the Court upheld Hawaii's absolute ban on write-in votes, observing that an election was designed to choose a winner, not to provide a forum for expression. Similarly, in *Timmons v. Twin Cities Area New Party*,[14] the Court upheld a ban on fusion candidacies, the practice of two political parties nominating the same candidate. The ban did not stop a voter from supporting the candidate of choice, even though it was on the "wrong" party line. In so holding the Court rejected the argument that voters had a First Amendment right to use the ballot to send a message to the candidate about the nature of their support. Indeed, *Timmons* explicitly justifies significant limitations on First Amendment electoral activity in aid of stable electoral results. Finally, in *Burson v. Freeman*,[15] the Supreme Court upheld a ban on core political speech on Election Day within a hundred feet of the polls as reasonably necessary to preserve the orderly administration of the election. For good or ill, therefore, the Supreme Court has severed the "election" from the "campaign" and upheld very significant restrictions on First Amendment activity in the name of the efficient operation of an election as a bounded institution.

The Court has even made tentative steps toward viewing the election campaign, as opposed to the election itself, as a bounded institution. As Richard Briffault describes in great detail in Chapter Four, in *Buckley*, the Court sought to distinguish "issue advocacy" from so-called "express advocacy of the election or defeat of a specific candidate" in order to impose contribution limits and disclosure requirements on election campaign speech, while freeing speech about issues from any restrictions. And, in *Austin v. Michigan Chamber of Commerce*,[16] the Court upheld restrictions on campaign spending by corporations in order to shield the election campaign from distortions caused by disproportionate exercises of wealth. In each case, the Court's willingness to ban big money was justified by a desire to protect the election campaign—viewed as a bounded institution—from the distorting effects of great wealth, even though the speech was otherwise clearly protected. If we already regulate institutionally bounded speech in aid of the proper functioning of the institution, and if we already recognize elections as bounded institutions, and if we have already upheld significant regulation of campaign speech to prevent powerful speakers from distorting the campaign process, why can't we make the narrow jump remaining? Why can't we acknowledge that *Buckley* was wrong, and that generous content-neutral limits on campaign spending designed to level the electoral playing field between the extremely rich and everyone else do not violate the First Amendment?

Yet a third compelling interest exists justifying limits on campaign spending. The interest in avoiding corruption recognized in *Buckley* can be seen as broader than merely preventing bribery and extortion. Corruption prevents the democratic process from working. If an official's vote can be bought, the assumptions that underlie representative government go out the window. Not surprisingly, the Supreme Court has recognized that prevention of the appearance or reality of corruption is a compelling interest that justifies regulation of campaign contributions, despite the restriction on political autonomy.

The Court has never been very clear on what it meant when it used the term *corruption*. At one extreme, of course, such a quid pro quo arrangement violates extortion and bribery laws by linking a specific official act to the payment of money. At the other extreme, however, there is nothing wrong with giving money to candidates because you are confident that they will vote in a particular way on an issue that you feel strongly about. Thus it is not corrupt to give money to a pro-choice candidate because you expect that candidate to vote against efforts to restrict abortion. Similarly, it is not corrupt to give money to a candidate whose speeches and past acts indicate a preference for voting a particular way on issues that affect your business. It is corrupt, however, to buy a candidate's vote with a specific bribe, whether or not the quid pro quo is explicitly spelled out.

The dividing line appears to permit contributions based on predictions of official behavior, but forbids contributions designed to affect official behavior. The difficulty, of course, is that an initial contribution given as a prediction will not be repeated unless the official's behavior in office remains consistent with the prediction—and both the donor and the official know it.

It is thus critically important, in cataloging the values at issue in the campaign finance debate, to refine the meaning of *corruption*. The Supreme Court appears to think that the term has a broader reach than simply an exchange of money in return for performing, or failing to perform, a specific official act. One possible extension beyond classic bribery and extortion is to treat as corrupt the use of money to influence legislators by making them more likely to respond to large donors than to the needs of ordinary citizens, perhaps by giving the donors preferred access. The phenomenon of large donors making contributions to both candidates is often explained as a way of assuring access to whoever is elected.

The next possible extension of the idea of corruption is to apply it to financial arrangements that might cause an official to tailor behavior in office to the wishes of large donors in order to assure a continuing flow of contributions, even though nothing is ever said about any quid pro quo obligation. What is at stake in such a situation is not corruption in the narrow sense but the erosion of the capacity of a public official to make independent judgments free from financial pressures. A political system that subordinates the independence and free will of its officials to the need to raise money may be said to be corrupt in the structural sense.

An even broader idea of corruption would include financial arrangements that put pressure on officials to compromise their independence by taking a political position, not because they believe in it, but because it has financial consequences for them. Under such a conception of corruption, not a word need be exchanged about a link between money and official action, as long as the financing system rewards officials for behaving one way and punishes them for acting another.

At this point, what is really at stake is the political autonomy of a public official. How much independence should an elected official have from the wishes of the constituency? That difficult question poses fundamental questions about the nature of representation in a democracy. Should a representative function as a conduit for constituents' desires? Or should a representative exercise independent judgment, subject only to periodic correction at the polls? If you believe in the conduit theory of representation, using money as a way to keep your representative in line isn't corruption at all. It's just an excellent way to monitor the performance of your legislative agent. But such a conduit theory runs up against the enduring question of why only rich people get to monitor their legislative agents. Thus even under a conduit theory the use of money to monitor is corrupt. On the other hand, if you embrace Edmund Burke's theory of representation that calls upon officials to exercise independent judgment, financial pressure that interferes with the ability to exercise such judgment may also be called corrupt.

Finally, the broadest idea of corruption is linked, not to the reality of corruption, but to its mere appearance. The Supreme Court has already announced that campaign contributions can be limited to prevent the mere appearance of a quid pro quo arrangement between a large donor and a public official. The unanswered question is whether the appearance rationale applies to more expansive definitions of corruption. For example, can campaign spending be regulated because it creates an appearance that legislators are no longer exercising independent judgment, but are being unduly swayed by fundraising considerations? At that point, preventing the appearance of corruption merges into the value of enhancing confidence and respect for the democratic process. While it is possible to package a "confidence and respect" argument as a broad corruption argument (indeed, it may be strategically valuable to do so in order to benefit from the Supreme Court's endorsement of prevention of corruption as a compelling interest), it is a good idea to keep the two arguments analytically distinct, if only to prevent misunderstanding.

In the campaign finance context, therefore, preventing corruption has at least three possible meanings: (1) preventing bribery and other forms of crude quid pro quo financial arrangements, (2) enhancing a representative's ability to exercise independent judgment on the issues free from considerations of financial self-interest, and (3) enhancing respect and confidence in the democratic process by removing even the appearance that legislators are acting in their own financial self-interest. Each qualifies as a compelling interest justifying restrictions on uncontrolled campaign spending.

IV. CONCLUSION

Whether one approaches the issue by rethinking the relationship between speech and money at extremely high levels of spending; the degree to which uncontrolled campaign spending is genuinely autonomous; or the existence of compelling interests in reestablishing faith in democracy, enhancing political equality, and reinforcing the proper operation of the democratic process, overturning *Buckley* would not dilute existing First Amendment theory. Indeed, the values that underlie existing free speech doctrine would be advanced, not endangered, by the placement of generous ceilings on campaign spending.

NOTES

INTRODUCTION

1. Editorial, "Time to Rethink *Buckley v. Valeo*," *New York Times*, November 12, 1998, p. A28, col. 1; Burt Neuborne, "Court's Decision Has Been Disastrous for Democracy," *St. Louis Post Dispatch*, February 18, 1997, p. 7B.

2. Diane E. Brown, "Time to Change Campaign Funding," *Chicago Tribune*, April 1, 1998, 26; David Orr, "Close Loot Loophole," *Chicago Tribune*, April 6, 1997, p. 16.

3. J. Skelly Wright, *Money and the Pollution of Politics: Is the First Amendment an Obstacle to Political Equality?* 82 Colum. L. Rev. 609 (1982).

4. Robert V. Keeley, "Two of the Worst Supreme Court Decisions," *Charleston (W. Va.) Sunday Gazette-Mail*, October 5, 1997, p. 10B.

5. Elizabeth Drew, "Let's Force Politicians to Reform Campaign Finance," *Salt Lake Tribune*, November 10, 1996, p. AA12.

6. Joseph Lieberman, *The Politics of Money and the Road to Self-Destruction*, 16 Yale L. & Pol'y Rev. 425, 442 (1998).

7. Frank J. Sorauf, *Politics, Experience, and the First Amendment: The Case of American Campaign Finance*, 94 Colum. L. Rev. 1348, 1349 (1994).

8. Keeley, "Two of the Worst Supreme Court Decisions."

9. Ronald Dworkin, "The Curse of American Politics," *New York Review of Books*, October 17, 1996, p. 19.

10. Scott Turow, "The High Court's Twenty-Year-Old Mistake," *New York Times*, October 12, 1997, Section 4, p. 15, col. 1; *see also* Martin Dyckman, "Brady Ruling Ends One of Court's Worst Weeks," *St. Petersburg Times*, June 29, 1997, 3D (*Buckley* "has done more to undermine American democracy than anything since the Dred Scott case"); Martin Dyckman, "Real Political Scandal About Money, Not Sex," *Raleigh (N.C.) News & Observer*, March 22, 1998, A29 (*"Buckley* was the worst decision since Dredd [sic] Scott").

11. *Buckley v. Valeo*, 424 U.S. 1 (1976) *(per curiam)*.

12. Joseph A. Califano, Jr., "Run for Money," *Washington Post*, May 7, 1998, p. A23 (comparing *Buckley* to *Plessy*).

13. Editorial, "Time to Rethink *Buckley v. Valeo.*"

14. Dyckman, "Real Political Scandal About Money, Not Sex."

15. Martin Schram, "High Court Needs Reality Check on Campaign Finance," *Houston Chronicle*, November 23, 1998, p. A23.

16. Turow, "The High Court's Twenty-Year-Old Mistake."

17. Keeley, "Two of the Worst Supreme Court Decisions."

18. Burt Neuborne, *The Supreme Court and Free Speech: Love and a Question*, 42 St. Louis U. L.J. 789, 795 (1998).

19. *See* E. Joshua Rosenkranz, *Buckley Stops Here* (New York: Twentieth Century Fund, 1998).

20. *National Black Police Ass'n v. D.C. Board of Elections*, 924 F. Supp. 270 (D.D.C. 1996), *appeal dismissed*, 108 F.3d 346 (D.C. Cir. 1997); *Wilkinson v. Jones*, 876 F. Supp. 916 (W.D. Ky. 1995); *Day v. Hayes*, 863 F. Supp. 940 (D. Minn.), *aff'd in relevant part sub nom. Day v. Holahan*, 34 F.3d 1356 (8th Cir. 1994), *cert. denied*, 513 U.S. 1127 (1995); *Carver v. Nixon*, 72 F.3d 633 (8th Cir. 1995), *cert. denied*, 518 U.S. 1033 (1996); *Russell v. Burris*, 146 F.3d 563 (8th Cir. 1998), *cert. denied*, 119 S. Ct. 510 (1998), 119 S. Ct. 1040 (1990); *California Prolife Council PAC v. Scully*, 989 F. Supp. 1282 (E.D. Cal.), *aff'd in part and rev'd in part*, 164 F.3d 1189 (9th Cir. 1999).

21. *Shrink Missouri Government PAC v. Maupin*, 71 F.3d 1422, 1427 (8th Cir. 1995), *cert. denied*, 518 U.S. 1033 (1996).

22. *Vannatta v. Keisling*, 899 F. Supp. 488, 496 (D. Or. 1995), *aff'd*, 151 F.3d 1215 (9th Cir. 1998), *cert. denied*, 119 S. Ct. 870 (1999).

23. *FEC v. Christian Action Network*, 110 F.3d 1049 (4th Cir. 1997).

24. Each of the quotes in the passage is drawn from a letter of Joel Gora of the ACLU to Sen. Mitch McConnell, page 2 (February 20, 1997).

25. *Colorado Republican Federal Campaign Committee v. FEC*, 518 U.S. 604 (1996).

26. *Shrink Missouri Government PAC v. Adams*, 161 F.3d 519 (8th Cir. 1998), *cert. granted sub nom. Nixon v. Shrink Missouri Government PAC*, 119 S. Ct. 901 (1999).

CHAPTER 1

1. October 25, 1982.

2. Kay L. Schlozman and John T. Tierney, in *Organized Interests and American Democracy* (New York: Harper & Row, 1986) (reporting that 40% of all the interest groups with Washington offices were founded after 1960).

3. For Senate incumbents the reelection percentages in 1976, 1978, and 1980 ranged from 55% to 64%, but from 1982 through 1988 they were all above 75% and some climbed above 90%.

4. Under FECA party committees are limited, just as PACs are, to contributions of $5,000 per candidate per election. In addition they may spend up to a designated limit "on behalf of candidates"; those limits are the same for all House candidates, but differ for Senate candidates according to the voting age population of their states. These "on behalf of" expenditures are also commonly called "coordinated expenditures," indicating that, unlike independent spending, the parties may make them in cooperation with the candidates. The limits on them are indexed.

5. *Colorado Republican Federal Campaign Committee v. FEC*, 518 U.S. 604 (1996).

6. *See* Trevor Potter, Introduction to Chapter 7, in Anthony Corrado, Thomas Mann, Daniel Ortiz, Trevor Potter, and Frank Sorauf, *Campaign Finance Reform: A Sourcebook* (Washington: Brookings, 1997), p. 227. Potter's entire introduction to the chapter is a succinct summary of the legal and judicial history of issue advocacy through mid-1997.

7. *FEC v. Massachusetts Citizens for Life, Inc.*, 479 U.S. 238 (1986).

8. *FEC v. Christian Action Network*, 894 F. Supp. 946 (W.D. Va. 1995), *aff'd mem.*, 92 F.3d 1178 (4th Cir. 1996).

9. I have relied on Anthony Corrado's introduction to Chapter 6 of Corrado, Mann, Ortiz, Potter, and Sorauf, *Campaign Finance Reform*, pp. 167–77, for much of this and the following paragraphs.

10. *See* Jill Abramson and Leslie Wayne, "Nonprofit Groups Were Partner to Both Parties in Last Election," *New York Times*, October 24, 1997, p. A1.

11. On the campaign finance of the first half of the century, see Louise Overacker, *Money in Elections* (New York: Macmillan, 1932) and Alexander Heard, *The Costs of Democracy* (Chapel Hill: University of North Carolina Press, 1960).

12. *See* Steven E. Frantzich, *Political Parties in the Technological Age* (New York: Longman, 1989).

13. The 1978 data are reported as transfers from out-of state. Some of them may be from committees in other states, but I think it fair to assume that most or all came from the national party committees.

14. *Colorado Republican Federal Campaign Committee v. FEC*, 518 U.S. 604 (1996).

15. These data are from the party committees' FEC reports. The hard money data are for all party committees—national, state, and local committees—raising hard (that is, federal) dollars and are limited to those hard dollars. The data for soft money are limited to the three national committees of each of the parties, their national committees and their campaign committees in the House and Senate.

16. Amicus Brief of Committee for Party Renewal, *Colorado Republican Federal Campaign Committee v. FEC*, 518 U.S. 604 (1996).

17. Herbert Alexander (ed.), *Campaign Money* (New York: Free Press, 1976), p. 1.

18. *Developments in the Law: Elections*, 88 Harv. L. Rev. 1111–1339, 1254, especially section V, subsection B on "Campaign Finance" (April 1975).

19. *See also* Ruth S. Jones, "State Public Financing and the State Parties," in Michael Malbin (ed.), *Parties, Interest Groups, and Campaign Finance Laws* (Washington: American Enterprise Institute, 1980), pp. 283–303.

20. Alexander, *Campaign Money*, (listing the total as thirty-one states).

21. *See New State Ice Co. v. Liebmann*, 285 U.S. 262, 311 (1932) (Brandeis, J., dissenting).

22. *See Developments in the Law: Elections*, 88 Harv. L. Rev. 111-1339, 1255–1256 (April 1975).

23. So "few" in fact that the *Harvard Law Review* survey cited earlier did not count or report their frequency in 1975.

24. Malbin, *Campaign Finance Laws*, p. 84.

25. Michael J. Malbin and Thomas L. Gais, *The Day After Reform: Sobering Campaign Finance Lessons from the American States* (Albany: Rockefeller Institute Press, 1998), pp. 174–175.

26. A total of twenty-three permit initiatives and a total of twenty-three permit referenda. Because the two universes coincide almost perfectly, a total of twenty-five permits one or the other or both. *Book of the States*, vol. 31 (Lexington, Ky.: Council of State Governments, 1996–97), p. 209 (Table 5.15).

27. *See First National Bank of Boston v. Bellotti*, 435 U.S. 765 (1978); *Citizens Against Rent Control v. City of Berkeley*, 454 U.S. 290 (1981).

28. "Direct Legislation in the American States," in David Butler and Austin Ranney, *Referendums Around the World* (Washington: AEI Press, 1994), Chapter 7, p. 232.

29. Todd S. Purdum, "Ballot Initiatives Flourishing as Way to Bypass Politicians," *New York Times* (March 31, 1998), p. A–1 (citing the data of John M. Allswang, a professor of history at California State University at Los Angeles).

30. Betty H. Zisk, *Money, Media, and the Grassroots: State Ballot Issues and the Electoral Process* (Thousand Oaks, Calif.: Sage, 1987), pp. 93–95 and 198–199.

31. Corey Cook, *Campaign Finance Reform* (Sacramento: California Research Bureau, California State Library, 1994), p. 19.

32. Herbert E. Alexander and Lori Cox NyBlom, *Campaign Reform on the Ballot: 1972–1994* (Los Angeles: Citizens' Research Foundation, 1996), Tables 1, 2, and 4.

33. *See, e.g., Carver v. Nixon*, 72 F.3d 633 (8th Cir. 1995), *cert. denied*, 518 U.S. 1033 (1996).

34. Data come from Herbert E. Alexander, Eugene R. Goss, and Jeffrey A. Schwartz, *Public Financing of State Elections* (Los Angeles: Citizens' Research Foundation, 1992), pp. 4–6 and 15.

35. Malbin and Gais, *The Day After Reform*, pp. 106–107. Note that the data report only limits on direct party contributions to candidates, not spending, even if coordinated.

36. The data for forty of the states come from Council on Governmental Ethics Laws (COGEL), *Blue Book,* 9th ed. (Lexington, Ky.: Council of State Governments, 1993), pp. 77-85, Table 14; the data on the remaining ten are from *Campaign Finance Law* 94.

37. Anthony Gierzynski and David A. Breaux, "The Financing Role of Parties," Chapter 10 in Joel A. Thompson and Gary F. Moncrief, *Campaign Finance in State Legislative Elections* (Washington: Congressional Quarterly, 1998), p. 189.

38. Malbin and Gais, *The Day After Reform,* Chapter 6.

39. Diana Dwyre and Jeffrey M. Stonecash, "Where's the Party? Changing State Party Organizations," *American Politics Quarterly,* 20 (July 1992), pp. 334–336. The calculations of the ratios between party legislative campaign committee and candidate spending are mine. One other note: It is not clear whether or not the "on behalf of spending" reported includes more general party spending (such as capital expenditures, generic party advertising).

40. Kent D. Redfield, *Cash Clout: Political Money in Illinois Legislative Elections* (Springfield: University of Illinois at Springfield, 1995). Malbin and Gais report that Redfield's analysis of 1994 data raised the percentage above 50; *see* p. 157. For data on the growth of LCCs in the 1980s, see Anthony Gierzynski, *Legislative Party Campaign Committees in the American States* (Lexington: University Press of Kentucky, 1992).

41. *See* Dwyre and Stonecash, "Where's the Party?"

42. Richard A. Clucas, "Legislative Leadership and Campaign Support in California," *Legislative Studies Quarterly* 17 (May 1992), pp. 265–284.

43. Daniel M. Shea, *Transforming Democracy: Legislative Campaign Committees and Political Parties* (Albany: State University of New York Press, 1995), especially Chapters 5 and 7.

44. Malbin and Gais, *The Day After Reform,* pp. 14–19.

45. *Day v. Holahan,* 34 F.3d 1356 (8th Cir. 1994), *cert. denied,* 513 U.S. 1127 (1995); *Carver v. Nixon,* 72 F.3d 633 (8th Cir. 1995), *cert. denied,* 518 U.S. 1033 (1996); and *Shrink Missouri Government PAC v. Maupin,* 71 F.3d 1422 (8th Cir. 1995), *cert. denied,* 518 U.S. 1033 (1996).

46. *Gard v. Wisconsin State Elections Board,* 156 Wis. 2d 28, 456 N.W.2d 809, *cert. denied,* 498 U.S. 982 (1990).

47. The beginnings of issue advocacy in Wisconsin are treated fully—with recommended legislation—in the 1997 report of the Governor's Blue-Ribbon Commission on Campaign Finance. It is titled only "Report of the Commission."

48. Most of the information and all the quotes come from Tim Weiner, "Courting Donors: The Background," *New York Times,* February 27, 1997, p. B8 (emphasis added).

49. George Hager, "Amid Cries for Reform, Parties and Politicians Pack Coffers," *Congressional Quarterly* (August 9, 1997), p. 1912 (emphasis added).

50. The hard money spending was $132 million for the presidential and $651 million for the congressional general election campaigns. My conservative estimates for the nonregulated expenditures are $135 million for issue ads (including those by state party committees), $25 million for all independent spending, totaling $160 million, or one-fifth of the $783 million spent within the statutory regime of FECA.

51. *Burroughs v. United States,* 290 U.S. 534, 545 (1934).

52. *Buckley v. Valeo,* 519 F.2d 821 (D.C. Cir. 1975).

53. *Buckley v. Valeo,* 424 U.S. 1, 48-49 (1976) (quoting *New York Times v. Sullivan,* 376 U.S. 254, 266 [1964]; *Associated Press v. United States,* 326 U.S. 1, 20 [1945]).

54. I have drawn this quote and much of this whole paragraph from a paper, *Political Party Committees and Coordinated Spending,* that Krasno and I wrote for the Federal Election Commission in the *Colorado Republican* case in defense of FECA's regulation of coordinated spending by party committees in congressional elections.

55. *See, e.g.,* James Bennet, "Quick, Pay for a Campaign Before the Rules Change," *New York Times,* December 8, 1998, p. A24; "A New Year for Campaign Reform," *New York Times,* December 27, 1998, Section 4, p. 8.

Chapter 2

1. I expand on the claim that free speech and democracy are conceptually connected in that way in my 1996 book, *Freedom's Law* (Harvard University Press).

2. For a fuller account of the partnership conception, elaborating the summary comments in this and the following paragraphs, see the introduction to *Freedom's Law*.

3. On this point, and for general observations about equality of influence as a democratic goal, see my article, *What Is Equality? Part 4: Political Equality* in 22 U. of San Francisco L. Rev. xx (1987).

4. In a society of greatly unequal wealth and other resources, some citizens will have much greater opportunity to occupy each of these positions of heightened influence only because they are richer, and that is indeed an insult to citizen equality. But that more general unfairness could not be ended except through a vast redistribution of wealth and what wealth brings. The more specific unfairness that brings influence to the rich only because they can afford large contributions to politicians could be ended or minimized through the simple expedient of expenditure limits.

5. *Austin v. Michigan Chamber of Commerce*, 494 U.S. 652, 679 (1990).

6. I have argued this point at some length elsewhere. See *Freedom's Law*, Chapters 9 and 10.

7. *Lochner v. New York*, 198 U.S. 45 (1905) (striking law that imposed a cap on the number of hours an employer could require a laborer to work).

8. As John Hart Ely argues in *Democracy and Distrust* (Cambridge, Mass.: Harvard University Press, 1981).

9. *Whitney v. California*, 274 U.S. 357, 375 (1927) (Brandeis, J., dissenting).

10. *New York Times Co. v. Sullivan*, 376 U.S. 254 (1964).

11. *New York Times Co. v. United States*, 403 U.S. 713 (1971).

12. *Collin v. Smith*, 578 F.2d 1197 (7th Cir.), *cert. denied*, 439 U.S. 916 (1978).

13. *Texas v. Johnson*, 491 U.S. 397 (1989); *United States v. Eichman*, 496 U.S. 310 (1990).

14. *Colorado Republican Federal Campaign Committee v. FEC*, 518 U.S. 604 (1996) (protecting the right of political parties to spend unlimited amounts of money on electioneering "independent" of their candidates).

15. *Red Lion Broadcasting Co. v. FCC*, 395 U.S. 367 (1969).

16. *Miami Herald Publishing Co. v. Tornillo*, 418 U.S. 241 (1974).

17. *Turner Broadcasting System, Inc. v. FCC,* 512 U.S. 622 (1991) *[Turner I]; Turner Broadcasting System, Inc. v. FCC,* 520 U.S. 180 (1997) *[Turner II]*.

18. *Burson v. Freeman,* 504 U.S. 191 (1992).

19. *Burson v. Freeman,* 504 U.S. at 217 (Stevens, J., dissenting).

20. *Mills v. Alabama,* 384 U.S. 214 (1966).

21. *Austin v. Michigan Chamber of Commerce,* 494 U.S. 652 (1990).

22. *First National Bank of Boston v. Bellotti,* 435 U.S. 765 (1978).

23. *Meet the Press,* Sunday, November 9, 1997.

CHAPTER 3

1. *Arkansas Educational Television Commission v. Forbes,* 523 U.S. 666 (1998).

2. *See, e.g., National Endowment for the Arts v. Finley,* 524 U.S. 569 (1998); *Rosenberger v. Rector of the University of Virginia,* 515 U.S. 819 (1995). *See generally* Susan H. Williams, *Content Discrimination and the First Amendment,* 139 U. Pa. L. Rev. 615 (1991).

3. *See Miami Herald Publishing Co. v. Tornillo,* 418 U.S. 241 (1974).

4. *See* C. Edwin Baker, *Campaign Expenditures and Free Speech,* 33 Harv. Civ. Rts-Civ. Lib. L. Rev. 1 (1998).

5. *See First National Bank of Boston v. Bellotti,* 435 U.S. 765 (1978); *Bolger v. Youngs Drug Products Corp.,* 463 U.S. 60 (1983); *New York Times Co. v. Sullivan,* 376 U.S. 254 (1964); *Ginzburg v. United States,* 383 U.S. 463 (1966).

6. *Compare* Jerome Barron, *Access to the Press: A New First Amendment Right,* 80 Harv. L. Rev. 1641 (1967), and Jerome Barron, *An Emerging First Amendment Right of Access to the Media?,* 37 Geo. Wash. L. Rev. 487 (1969), *with* David Lange, *The Role of the Access Doctrine in the Regulation of the Mass Media: A Critical Review and Assessment,* 52 N.C. L. Rev. 1 (1973); Lucas A. Powe Jr., *Tornillo,* 1987 Sup. Ct. Rev. 345; *Miami Herald Publishing Co. v. Tornillo,* 418 U.S. 241 (1974). *See also* Lee C. Bollinger, *Images of a Free Press* (Chicago: University of Chicago Press, 1991).

7. *See* Alvin I. Goldman and James C. Cox, *Speech, Truth, and the Free Market for Ideas,* 2 Legal Theory 1 (1996).

8. *Compare* Lucas A. Powe Jr., *Scholarship and Markets*, 56 Geo. Wash. L. Rev. 172 (1987), *with* Owen Fiss, *Why the State?* 100 Harv. L. Rev. 781 (1987); Owen Fiss, *Free Speech and Social Structure*, 71 Iowa L. Rev. 1405 (1986).

9. *See* Walter Sinnott-Armstrong, *Moral Dilemmas* (Oxford: Blackwell Publishers, 1988); Frederick Schauer, *A Comment on the Structure of Rights*, 27 Ga. L. Rev. 415 (1993).

10. *See* Richard H. Pildes, *Why Rights Are Not Trumps: Social Meanings, Expressive Harms, and Constitutionalism*, 27 J. Leg. Stud. 725 (1998).

11. *New York Times v. Sullivan*, 376 U.S. 254 (1964).

12. *Watts v. United States*, 394 U.S. 705 (1969); *United States v. Van Imschoot*, 390 F. Supp. 994 (S.D.N.Y. 1974).

13. *Virgil v. Time, Inc.*, 527 F.2d 1122 (9th Cir. 1975), *cert. denied*, 425 U.S. 998 (1976).

14. *FCC v. Pacifica Foundation*, 438 U.S. 726 (1978).

15. *International Society for Krishna Consciousness v. Lee*, 505 U.S. 672 (1992).

16. *Chaplinsky v. New Hampshire*, 315 U.S. 568 (1942).

17. *Brandenburg v. Ohio*, 395 U.S. 444 (1969).

18. *See* Frederick Schauer, *Free Speech: A Philosophical Enquiry*, Chapter 6 (Cambridge: Cambridge University Press, 1982).

19. *See Brown v. Hartlage*, 456 U.S. 45 (1982) (Court holds that campaign promises and statements can be regulated so long as the misstatement meets the stringent standards of *New York Times Co. v. Sullivan*, 376 U.S. 254 [1964], rather than holding that campaign promises and statements are never regulable, except by the voters in casting their ballots).

20. *Brandenburg v. Ohio*, 395 U.S. 444 (1969) (prohibiting government from punishing speech unless it presents a clear and present danger).

21. *New York Times Co. v. Sullivan*, 376 U.S. 254 (1964) (providing First Amendment protection in libel cases).

22. *New York Times Co. v. United States*, 403 U.S. 713 (1971) (prohibiting prior restraints).

23. *Cohen v. California*, 403 U.S. 15 (1971) (protecting offensive words, even if displayed on a jacket in a courtroom).

24. *Texas v. Johnson*, 491 U.S. 397 (1989) (protecting flag burning).

25. *See generally* Frederick Schauer, *Exceptions*, 58 U. Chi. L. Rev. 871 (1991).

26. Lillian BeVier, *Money and Politics: A Perspective on the First Amendment and Campaign Finance Reform,* 73 Cal. L. Rev. 1045 (1985); Daniel Polsby, *Buckley v. Valeo: The Special Nature of Political Speech,* 1976 Sup. Ct. Rev. 1.

27. *See* Gerald Gunther, *Foreword: In Search of Evolving Doctrine on a Changing Court: A Model for a Newer Equal Protection,* 86 Harv. L. Rev. 1 (1972) (noting that strict scrutiny tended to be "fatal in fact").

28. *See* Cass R. Sunstein, *Democracy and the Problem of Free Speech* (New York: Free Press, 1995).

29. *See* Catharine A. MacKinnon, *Only Words* (Cambridge, Mass.: Harvard University Press, 1993); *compare* Ronald Dworkin, *Freedom's Law: The Moral Reading of the American Constitution* (Cambridge, Mass.: Harvard University Press, 1996), pp. 214–243.

30. *See* Larry A. Alexander, *Trouble on Track Two: Incidental Regulations of Speech and Free Speech Theory,* 44 Hastings L.J. 921 (1993).

31. *See San Antonio Independent School District v. Rodriguez,* 411 U.S. 1 (1973).

32. *Compare Mueller v. Allen,* 463 U.S. 388 (1983) (sustaining a system of income tax deductions for private school expenses, even though the overwhelming majority of those expenses were for parochial school expenses that the state could not constitutionally have supported directly).

33. A claim famously challenged in J. Skelly Wright, *Politics and the Constitution: Is Money Speech?* 85 Yale L.J. 1001 (1976). *See also* J. Skelly Wright, *Money and the Pollution of Politics: Is the First Amendment an Obstacle to Political Equality?* 82 Colum. L. Rev. 609 (1982).

34. *See* Frederick Schauer, *Categories and the First Amendment: A Play in Three Acts,* 34 Vand. L. Rev. 265 (1981).

35. *See* Frederick Schauer, *Exceptions,* 58 U. Chi. L. Rev. 871 (1991).

36. *See* Geoffrey R. Stone, *Content Regulation and the First Amendment,* 25 Wm. & Mary L. Rev. 189 (1983). *See also* Marjorie Heins, *Viewpoint Discrimination,* 24 Hastings Const. L. Q. 99 (1996).

37. *Reno v. American Civil Liberties Union,* 521 U.S. 844 (1997); *Denver Area Educational Television Consortium, Inc. v. FCC,* 518 U.S. 727 (1996); *Turner Broadcasting System, Inc. v. FCC,* 520 U.S. 180 (1997). *See generally* Thomas Krattenmaker and Lucas A. Powe Jr., *Regulating Broadcast Programming* (Cambridge, Mass.: MIT Press, 1996).

38. *See* Frederick Schauer, *Principles, Institutions, and the First Amendment*, 112 Harv. L. Rev. 84 (1998). *See also* Frederick Schauer, *Prediction and Particularity*, 78 B.U. L. Rev. 773 (1998).

39. *New York Times Co. v. Sullivan*, 376 U.S. 254 (1964); *City of Ladue v. Gilleo*, 512 U.S. 43 (1994); Daniel Farber, *Free Speech Without Romance*, 105 Harv. L. Rev. 554 (1991); William J. Brennan, *The Supreme Court and the Meiklejohn Interpretation of the First Amendment*, 79 Harv. L. Rev. 1 (1965).

40. *See McIntyre v. Ohio Elections Commission*, 514 U.S. 334 (1995).

41. *Los Angeles City Council v. Taxpayers for Vincent*, 466 U.S. 789 (1984).

42. *Red Lion Broadcasting Co. v. FCC*, 395 U.S. 367 (1969).

43. *Tinker v. Des Moines Independent Community School District*, 393 U.S. 503 (1969).

44. *Pickering v. Board of Education*, 391 U.S. 563 (1968). *See also Connick v. Myers*, 461 U.S. 138 (1983); *Rutan v. Republican Party of Illinois*, 497 U.S. 62 (1990).

45. *See R.A.V. v. City of St. Paul*, 505 U.S. 377 (1992); *Dawson v. Delaware*, 503 U.S. 159 (1992); *National Socialist Party of America v. Village of Skokie*, 432 U.S. 43 (1977) *(per curiam); Collin v. Smith*, 578 F.2d 1197 (7th Cir. 1978), *cert. denied*, 439 U.S. 916 (1978).

46. *Metromedia, Inc. v. San Diego*, 453 U.S. 490 (1981).

47. *Los Angeles City Council v. Taxpayers for Vincent*, 466 U.S. 789 (1984).

48. *City of Ladue v. Gilleo*, 512 U.S. 43 (1994).

49. *Bethel School District No. 403 v. Fraser*, 478 U.S. 675 (1986).

50. *Papish v. Board of Curators of University of Missouri*, 410 U.S. 667 (1973).

51. *Connick v. Myers*, 461 U.S. 138 (1983).

52. *Burson v. Freeman*, 504 U.S. 191 (1992).

53. *E.g., FEC v. Massachusetts Citizens for Life, Inc.*, 479 U.S. 238 (1986).

54. *Pittsburgh Press Co. v. Pittsburgh Commission on Human Relations*, 413 U.S. 376, 402 (1973) (Stewart, J., dissenting).

55. *See* Frederick Schauer, *Slippery Slopes*, 99 Harv. L. Rev. 361 (1985).

56. *See 44 Liquormart v. Rhode Island*, 517 U.S. 484 (1996); *Central Hudson Gas & Electric Co. v. Public Service Commission*, 447 U.S. 557 (1980).

57. *Memoirs of a Woman of Pleasure v. Massachusetts*, 383 U.S. 413 (1966).

58. *See* Frederick Schauer, *The Law of Obscenity* (Washington, D.C.: BNA Books, 1976).

59. *E.g., Austin v. Michigan Chamber of Commerce*, 494 U.S. 652 (1990).

60. *Young v. American Mini Theatres, Inc.*, 427 U.S. 50 (1976).

61. *FCC v. Pacifica Foundation*, 438 U.S. 726 (1978).

62. *National Endowment for the Arts v. Finley*, 524 U.S. 569 (1998).

63. Anthony Amsterdam, *The Void-for-Vagueness Doctrine in the Supreme Court*, 109 U. Pa. L. Rev. 67 (1960); Frederick Schauer, *Fear, Risk, and the First Amendment: Unraveling the "Chilling Effect,"* 58 B.U. L. Rev. 685 (1978).

CHAPTER 4

1. Public Citizen, "Phony 'Issue Ads': The Newest Loophole," http://www.citizen.org/orgs/public_citizen/congress/reform/issue_ads.html. Public Citizen quotes the ad as stating "her nose was not broken." In other sources, the ad states "her nose was broken." *See, e.g.,* Senator Joe Lieberman, "Tax-Exempt Groups Abused Spirit, Letter of Law in '96 Elections, February 9, 1998, http://www.senate.gov/member/ct/lieberman/releases/s020998a/html; "Will Closing a Campaign Finance Loophole Strangle Nonprofit Issue Advocacy?" Newsletter of the National Committee for Responsive Philanthropy, http://www.ncrp.org/articles/rp/campfinref.html. The latter reading makes more sense and I have amended the Public Citizen quotation accordingly.

2. *See* Deborah Beck et al., *Issue Advocacy Advertising During the 1996 Campaign*, 22 (Annenberg Public Policy Center, 1997) (hereinafter "Issue Advocacy Advertising 1996").

3. *See* David Johnson, "Ruling May Hurt Campaign Finance Cases," *New York Times*, October 11, 1998, p. A27 (pretrial ruling in federal prosecution of Yah Lin Trie concerning contributions to the Democratic Party). The statutory ban on campaign contributions by foreign nationals does not apply to aliens admitted to permanent residence in the United States.

4. *Colorado Republican Federal Campaign v. FEC*, 518 U.S. 604, 631 (1996) (Thomas, J., concurring in the judgment and dissenting in

part) (calling for invalidation of restrictions on contributions); *see also* Kathleen Sullivan, *Political Money and Freedom of Speech*, 30 U.C. Davis L. Rev. 663, 688–89 (1997).

5. *FEC v. Massachusetts Citizens for Life, Inc.*, 479 U.S. 238 (1986).

6. *FEC v. Christian Action Network*, 894 F. Supp. 946 (W.D. Va. 1995), *aff'd mem.*, 92 F.3d 1178 (4th Cir. 1996).

7. *FEC v. Christian Action Network*, 110 F.3d 1049 (4th Cir. 1997).

8. *FEC v. Furgatch*, 807 F.2d 857 (9th Cir.), *cert. denied*, 484 U.S. 850 (1987).

9. *See, e.g., Faucher v. FEC*, 928 F.2d 468 (1st Cir.), *cert. denied*, 502 U.S. 820 (1991); *Maine Right to Life Committee, Inc. v. FEC*, 98 F.3d 1 (1st Cir. 1996), *cert. denied*, 118 S. Ct. 52 (1997); *see also Clifton v. FEC*, 114 F.3d 1309 (1st Cir. 1997), *cert. denied*, 522 U.S. 1108 (1998).

10. *See Maine Right to Life Committee, Inc. v. FEC*, 98 F.3d 1 (1st Cir. 1996), *aff'g* 914 F. Supp. 8 (D. Me. 1996); *Right to Life of Dutchess Co., Inc. v. FEC*, 6 F. Supp. 2d 248 (S.D.N.Y. 1998); *see also* 11 C.F.R. § 100.22(b).

11. *See, e.g., Wisconsin Manufacturers & Commerce v. Wisconsin Elections Board*, 978 F. Supp. 1200 (W.D. Wisc. 1997).

12. "Issue Advocacy Advertising 1996."

13. *See* James Dao, "The 1997 Elections: Fund-Raising; Soft Money Finds Its Way into Two Hard-Fought Races," *New York Times*, October 28, 1997, p. B6; Richard L. Berke, "Interest Groups Prepare to Spend on Campaign Spin," *New York Times*, January 11, 1998, Section 1, p. 1.

14. Jeffrey Stanger and Douglas Rivlin, "Issue Advocacy Advertising During the 1997–1998 Election Cycle" (Annenberg Public Policy Center, 1998) (hereinafter, "Issue Advocacy Advertising 1998").

15. "Issue Advocacy Advertising 1996," pp. 9–10 (41% of issue ads were attack ads compared to 24% of presidential candidate ads); "Issue Advocacy Advertising 1998," p. 8 (51.5% of issue ads aired after September 1, 1998, were attack ads while only 23.9% of candidate ads aired in that period were attack ads).

16. "Issue Advocacy Advertising 1998," p. 4.

17. Elizabeth Drew, *Whatever It Takes: The Real Struggle for Political Power in America*, rev. ed. (New York: Penguin Books, 1998), pp. 74-76.

18. Drew, *Whatever It Takes*, pp. 5–6, 22, 24; "Issue Advocacy Advertising 1996," p. 22.

19. "Issue Advocacy Advertising 1996," p. 16; Drew, *Whatever It Takes,* pp. 223.

20. "Issue Advocacy Advertising 1996," pp. 34, 55 (in 1995–96, the Democratic Party spent $44 million and the Republican Party $34 million, or together $78 million out of the estimated total of $135–$150 million of issue advocacy expenditures).

21. See Michael J. Malbin and Thomas L. Gais, *The Day After Reform: Sobering Campaign Finance Lessons from the American States* (Albany: Rockefeller Institute Press, 1998), p. 91.

22. *Wesberry v. Sanders,* 376 U.S. 1, 17 (1964).

23. *Reynolds v. Sims,* 377 U.S. 533, 561–62 (1964).

24. *See, e.g., Williams v. Rhodes,* 393 U.S. 23 (1969).

25. *Bullock v. Carter,* 405 U.S. 134, 140–41 (1972).

26. *Burdick v. Takushi,* 504 U.S. 428, 441 (1992).

27. *Timmons v. Twin Cities Area New Party,* 520 U.S. 351 (1997).

28. *Munro v. Socialist Workers Party,* 479 U.S. 189, 194–95 (1986).

29. *Timmons v. Twin Cities Area New Party,* 520 U.S. 351 (1997).

30. *Storer v. Brown,* 415 U.S. 724, 730 (1974).

31. *See Williams v. Rhodes,* 393 U.S. 23 (1969).

32. Richard L. Hasen, *Entrenching the Duopoly: Why the Supreme Court Should Not Allow the States to Protect the Democrats and Republicans from Political Competition,* 1997 Sup. Ct. Rev. 331.

33. Samuel Issacharoff and Richard H. Pildes, *Politics as Markets: Partisan Lockups of the Democratic Process,* 50 Stan. L. Rev. 643 (1998).

34. *Burson v. Freeman,* 504 U.S. 191 (1992).

35. *Terry v. Adams,* 345 U.S. 461 (1953).

36. *See, e.g., Morse v. Republican Party of Virginia,* 517 U.S. 186 (1996).

37. *CBS, Inc. v. FCC,* 453 U.S. 367 (1981).

38. *See, e.g., Allen v. State Board of Elections,* 393 U.S. 544 (1969); Pamela Karlan, *The Rights to Vote: Some Pessimism About Formalism,* 71 Tex. L. Rev. 1705, 1712–16 (1993).

39. *California Medical Ass'n v. FEC,* 453 U.S. 182, 196 (1981) (plurality opinion).

40. *McIntyre v. Ohio Elections Commission,* 514 U.S. 334 (1995).

41. *California Medical Ass'n v. FEC,* 453 U.S. at 197–98, 201.

42. *Austin v. Michigan Chamber of Commerce,* 494 U.S. 652 (1990).

43. *Maine Right to Life Committee, Inc. v. FEC,* 914 F. Supp. at 12.

44. This is based on an analysis of the rules governing elections for public office. Consideration of the election/politics distinction in the content of ballot proposition campaigns is beyond the scope of this book.

45. *See, e.g., FEC v. Survival Education Fund, Inc.,* 65 F.3d 285 (2d Cir. 1995); *FEC v. National Organization for Women,* 713 F. Supp. 428 (D.D.C. 1989).

46. 11 C.F.R. § 100.22(b).

47. Shays-Meehan Bipartisan Campaign Reform Act of 1999, H.R. 417, § 201(b) (amending 2 U.S.C. § 431).

48. *Maine Right to Life Committee, Inc. v. FEC,* 98 F.3d 1 (1st Cir. 1996), *aff'g* 914 F. Supp. 8 (D. Me. 1996); *Right to Life of Dutchess Co., Inc. v. FEC,* 6 F. Supp. 2d 248 (S.D.N.Y. 1998). *But see* Michael D. Leffel, *Note: A More Sensible Approach to Regulating Independent Expenditures: Defending the Constitutionality of the FEC's New Express Advocacy Standard,* 95 Mich. L. Rev. 686, 708–710 (1995) (arguing that the FEC regulation is not unconstitutionally vague).

49. "Issue Advocacy Advertising 1998," p. 4.

50. "Issue Advocacy Advertising 1998," p. 4.

51. "Issue Advocacy Advertising 1998," p. 7.

52. Citizens' Research Foundation, "New Realities, New Thinking: Report of the Task Force on Campaign Finance Reform," p. 12, http://www.usc.edu/dept/CRF/DATA/newrnewt.html (May 27, 1997).

53. "New Campaign Finance Reform Proposals for the 105th Congress," http://www.brook.edu/GS/NEWCFR/reform.html (Issued December 17, 1996; revised May 7, 1997).

54. "New Campaign Finance Reform Proposals for the 105th Congress"; *see* 39 U.S.C. §3210(a)(6)(A).

55. *Cf. West Virginians for Life, Inc. v. Smith,* 960 F. Supp. 1036 (S.D. W. Va. 1996) (invalidating West Virginia law providing that voter guides distributed within sixty days of an election is presumed to be election-related for purposes of state law requiring reporting and disclosure of election expenditures).

56. *See* "Issue Advocacy Advertising 1996"; *see also* Drew, *Whatever It Takes,* p. 223 (Americans for Tax Reform used Republican National Committee's $4.6 million to mail 17 million pieces of literature and make 4 million telephone calls).

57. *Cf. Planned Parenthood Affiliates of Michigan, Inc. v. Miller,* 21 F. Supp. 2d 740 (E.D. Mich. 1998) (enjoining enforcement of Michigan regulation prohibiting a corporation from using a candidate's name or

likeness on a communication made within forty-five days of an election unless the corporation uses separate, segregated funds for the communication; forty-five day period was tied to the absentee voting time period).

58. *But cf.* Allison Rittenhouse Hayward, *Stalking the Elusive Express Advocacy Standard,* 10 J.L. & Pol. 51 (1993) (calling for a five-day election-eve standard for the definition of express advocacy).

59. *See, e.g., Brownsburg Area Patrons Affecting Change v. Baldwin,* 137 F.3d 503 (7th Cir. 1998) (challenge to Indiana law requiring reports of expenditures greater than $100); *Vermont Right to Life Committee, Inc. v. Sorrell,* 19 F. Supp. 2d 204 (D. Vt. 1998) (Vermont law with $500 trigger for reporting election expenditures); *Virginia Society for Human Life, Inc. v. Caldwell,* 256 Va. 151, 500 S.E.2d 814 (1998) (Virginia law with $100 threshold for reporting).

60. *See* 2 U.S.C. § 434(b)(3)(A) (contributions over $200 to political committee must be reported); 2 U.S.C. § 434(c)(1), (2) (independent expenditures over $200 must be reported).

61. On the difficulties of enforcing disclosure requirement and the importance of factoring enforcement concerns into the substance of regulation, see Malbin and Gais, *The Day After Reform,* pp. 33–50.

62. Political party issue ads were particularly likely to consist of attacks on a candidate. The 1998 Annenberg study found that 23.9% of ads aired by candidates in the last two months of an election were attack ads, and that 32.0% of the ads aired by non-party issue organizations in that period were attack ads, but that 59.5% of party issue ads in the preelection period were attack ads. "Issue Advocacy Advertising 1998," p. 8.

63. *See, e.g.,* John H. Aldrich, *Why Parties? The Origin and Transformation of Political Parties in America* (Chicago: University of Chicago Press, 1995).

64. *Colorado Republican Federal Campaign Committee v. FEC,* 518 U.S. 604 (1996).

65. *See, e.g., Faucher v. FEC,* 928 F.2d 468 (1st Cir.), *cert. denied,* 502 U.S. 820 (1991); *Clifton v. FEC,* 114 F.3d 1309 (1st Cir. 1997); *West Virginians for Life, Inc. v. Smith,* 960 F. Supp. 1036 (S.D. W. Va. 1996); *North Carolina Right to Life, Inc. v. Bartlett,* 3 F. Supp. 2d 675 (E.D.N.C. 1998), *aff'd in part and rev'd in part,* 168 F.3d 705 (4th Cir. 1999); *see also MCFL,* 479 U.S. 238 (1986) ("Special Edition" of organization newsletter contained voter guide).

66. 11 C.F.R. § 114.4(c)(5)(D), (E).

67. *See* 2 U.S.C. § 441b(b)(2)(A).

68. *Compare United States v. UAW,* 352 U.S. 567 (1957) (reversing dismissal of indictment brought against labor union under predecessor to FECA for paying for television broadcasts aimed at the general electorate and endorsing candidates) *with United States v. CIO,* 335 U.S. 106 (1948) (affirming dismissal of indictment against labor union brought under predecessor to FECA for spending money to distribute to union members a union newspaper containing union endorsements of political candidates). *See also* C. Edwin Baker, *Campaign Expenditures and Free Speech,* 33 Harv. Civ. Rts-Civ. Lib. L. Rev. 1, 49 & n.173 (1998) (drawing similar distinction).

69. Albert O. Hirschman, *The Rhetoric of Reaction: Perversity, Futility, Jeopardy* (Cambridge, Mass.: Harvard University Press, 1991).

CHAPTER 5

1. I have attempted to chronicle the corrosive effect of *Buckley*'s insistence on uncontrolled campaign spending on American democracy, ranging from massive cynicism that translates into precipitous declines in voter turnout to garden variety corruption to the evolution of a political caste system that vests the extremely wealthy with disproportionate power to set the American political agenda. *See* Burt Neuborne, *Buckley's Analytical Flaws,* 6 J. L. & Pol'y 111 (1998); Burt Neuborne, *One Dollar— One Vote: A Preface to Debating Campaign Finance Reform,* 37 Washburn L.J. 1 (1997); Burt Neuborne, *The Supreme Court and Free Speech: Love and a Question,* 42 St. Louis U. L.J. 789 (1998); Burt Neuborne, *Toward a Democracy-Centered Reading of the First Amendment,* Northwestern L. Rev. (forthcoming 1999); Burt Neuborne, *Is Money Different?* 77 Tex. L. Rev. 1609 (1999).

2. *Collin v. Smith,* 578 F.2d 1197 (7th Cir.), *cert. denied,* 439 U.S. 916 (1978).

3. *Texas v. Johnson,* 491 U.S. 397 (1989).

4. *United States v. Eichman,* 496 U.S. 310 (1990).

5. *Street v. New York,* 394 U.S. 576, 605 (1969) (Warren, C.J., dissenting); *id.* at 610 (Black, J., dissenting).

6. *Texas v. Johnson*, 491 U.S. 397, 421 (1989) (Rehnquist, C.J., dissenting) (a heartfelt opinion bearing witness to the pain caused by flag burning).

7. *See Kovacs v. Cooper*, 336 U.S. 77 (1949).

8. *See Associated Press v. United States*, 326 U.S. 1 (1945); *Lorain Journal Co. v. United States*, 342 U.S. 143 (1951).

9. *See Turner Broadcasting System, Inc. v. FCC*, 512 U.S. 622 (1994).

10. *See Vincent Blasi, Free Speech and the Widening Gyre of Fund-Raising: Why Campaign Spending Limits May Not Violate the First Amendment After All*, 94 Colum. L. Rev. 1281 (1994).

11. Neuborne, *The Supreme Court and Free Speech*.

12. In Chapter Three, Frederick Schauer and Richard Pildes describe the increasingly context-specific rules governing speech in different settings. For more detail, see Robert Post, *Constitutional Domains* (Cambridge, Mass.: Harvard University Press, 1995); Steven H. Shiffrin, *The First Amendment, Democracy, and Romance* (Cambridge, Mass.: Harvard University Press, 1990); Richard H. Fallon Jr., *Sexual Harassment, Context Neutrality, and the First Amendment Dog That Didn't Bark*, 1994 Sup. Ct. Rev. 1; Richard Pildes, *Avoiding Balancing: The Role of Exclusionary Reasons in Constitutional Law*, 45 Hastings Const. L.Q. 711 (1994).

13. *Burdick v. Takushi*, 504 U.S. 428 (1992); *see* David L. Perlmut and Joseph P. Verdon, Note, *Protecting the American Tradition of Write-In Voting After Burdick v. Takushi*, 9 J.L. & Pol'y 185 (1992).

14. *Timmons v. Twin Cities Area New Party*, 520 U.S. 351 (1997).

15. *Burson v. Freeman*, 504 U.S. 191 (1992).

16. *Austin v. Michigan Chamber of Commerce*, 494 U.S. 652 (1990).

INDEX

About the Editor

E. Joshua Rosenkranz is the founding executive director of the Brennan Center for Justice at New York University School of Law. Mr. Rosenkranz has written and litigated extensively about ballot access and campaign finance reform. He authored *Voter Choice 1996: A Fifty-State Survey of Ballot Access Rules* (1996) and Buckley *Stops Here: Loosening the Judicial Stranglehold on Campaign Finance Reform* (Twentieth Century Fund Press, 1998) and is the coauthor (with Richard Winger) of the forthcoming *What Choice Do We Have?* He is also the editor (with Bernard Schwartz) of *Reason and Passion: Justice Brennan's Enduring Influence* (Norton, 1997). His articles on campaign finance have appeared in a wide range of publications, including the *New York Times,* the *Boston Review,* the *Chicago Tribune,* and the *Nation.*

Mr. Rosenkranz clerked for Justice William J. Brennan Jr. on the Supreme Court of the United States in the 1987–88 term. He also clerked for Hon. Antonin Scalia and Hon. Stephen F. Williams on the United States Court of Appeals for the District of Columbia Circuit.

Before joining the Brennan Center, Mr. Rosenkranz founded, and for eight years ran, New York City's acclaimed Office of the Appellate Defender. In that capacity, Mr. Rosenkranz personally argued over a hundred appeals and was the attorney of record for some fifteen hundred more. In 1996, *American Lawyer Magazine* named Mr. Rosenkranz (then thirty-four) one of the top forty-five public interest lawyers under forty-five.

ABOUT THE AUTHORS

RICHARD BRIFFAULT: Professor Briffault is Joseph P. Chamberlain Professor of Legislation, director of the Legislative Drafting Research Fund, and vice-dean of Columbia Law School. He is the author of *Balancing Acts: The Reality Behind State Balanced Budget Requirements,* as well as numerous law review articles concerning state and local government law and the legal regulation of politics. Before joining the Columbia faculty, he was assistant counsel to Governor Hugh L. Carey of New York. Professor Briffault was a consultant to New York State's Temporary Commission on Constitutional Revision, the New York City Charter Revision Commission, and the New York City Council Districting Commission, and he was a member of the New York City Real Property Tax Reform Commission.

RONALD DWORKIN: Professor Dworkin is a professor of jurisprudence at Oxford and has been a fellow at University College since 1969 and, in a joint appointment since 1975, a professor of law at New York University School of Law. A fellow of the British Academy and a member of the American Academy of Arts and Sciences, Professor Dworkin has written numerous articles in philosophical and legal journals. He has also written on legal and political subjects in the *New York Review of Books.* His many books include *Taking Rights Seriously, A Matter of Principle, Law's Empire, Philosophical Issues in Senile Dementia, A Bill of Rights for Britain, Life's Dominion,* and *Freedom's Law.* Several of these books have been translated into the major European languages, Japanese, and Chinese.

BURT NEUBORNE: Professor Neuborne is John Norton Pomeroy Professor of Law at New York University School of Law, where he has taught since 1974, and legal director of the Brennan Center for Justice. As national legal director of the American Civil Liberties Union (1982–86) and assistant legal director (1972–74), Professor Neuborne litigated cases influencing the law on such diverse topics as political contributions, commercial and corporate speech, academic freedom, the Vietnam War, CIA mail opening, immigration, and federal jurisdiction. One of the nation's leading constitutional lawyers, he has authored or coauthored four books, including *The Rights of Candidates and Voters* and two volumes of *Political and Civil Rights in the United States.*

RICHARD H. PILDES: A leading lecturer and author on race and the United States political system, Professor Pildes is a professor of law at the University of Michigan Law School, where he teaches Constitutional law, history of American legal thought, legislation, and the law of democracy, a course on voting rights and political participation. Professor Pildes is coauthor of the casebook, *The Law of Democracy,* and numerous articles on issues of democracy and constitutional law.

FREDERICK SCHAUER: Professor Schauer is academic dean and Frank Stanton Professor of the First Amendment at the John F. Kennedy School of Government at Harvard University. Formerly chair of the Association of American Law Schools Section on Constitutional Law, he is vice-president of the American Society for Political and Legal Philosophy and a founding coeditor of the journal *Legal Theory.* He has written extensively about legal and philosophical issues. He is the author of *The Law of Obscenity, Free Speech: A Philosophical Enquiry,* and *Playing By the Rules: A Philosophical Examination of Rule-Based Decision-Making in Law and in Life,* and is coauthor of *The Philosophy of Law: Classic and Contemporary Readings With Commentary* and *The First Amendment: A Reader.*

FRANK J. SORAUF: Regents' Professor Emeritus at the University of Minnesota, Professor Sorauf has taught political science for almost forty-five years. Professor Sorauf has received several honors from the American Political Science Association, including the Atherton

Prize for the best original scholarly manuscript in political science; the 1993 Fenno Prize for the best book on legislatures or legislative politics, by the section on legislatures of the APSA; and the Career Award, for a "lifetime of professional and scholarly contribution to the field" presented by the section on political organizations and parties. Professor Sorauf has published numerous articles and books on American politics and campaign finance reform, the most recent being a chapter titled "Political Parties and the New World of Campaign Finance" in *The Parties Respond* (3rd edition).